1990

Reel Politics

Reel Politics

American Political Movies from
Birth of a Nation to *Platoon*

Terry Christensen

Basil Blackwell

Library of Congress Cataloging in Publication Data
Christensen, Terry
Reel politics: American political movies from Birth of a nation
to Platoon/Terry Christensen.
p.   cm.
Bibliography: p.
Includes index.
ISBN 0–631–15844–8
1. Moving-pictures — Political aspects — United States.   2. Politics
in motion pictures.   3. Moving-pictures — United States — History.
I. Title.
PN1995.9.P6C48   1987
791.43′09′09358–dc19

British Library Cataloguing in Publication Data
Christensen, Terry
Reel politics: American political movies
from Birth of a nation to Platoon.
1. Politics in motion pictures
2. Moving-pictures — United States — History
I. Title
791.43′09′09358   PN1995.9.P6
ISBN 0–631–15844–8

Typeset in 10 on 11½pt Sabon
By Columns of Reading, England
Printed in the USA

All film stills are reproduced with the kind permission of the Film Stills Library,
Museum of Modern Art, New York

Contents

Contents

Contents

Preface

Reel Politics is about two of America's favorite subjects, movies and politics. It's about movies most of us have seen or at least heard about, from *The Birth of a Nation* and *Mr. Smith Goes to Washington* to *All the President's Men* and *Platoon*. The movies featured in this book were made not to educate but to entertain, and many of them do just that. But they also have something to say about politics and politicans.

Because they're "only movies," many of us don't take their politics seriously, yet they tell us a great deal about America and American attitudes about politics, especially when these movies are considered as a group – or genre. They also influence us, and at least a few have mobilized us.

My own interest in both movies and politics goes back to Holton, Kansas, where my grandmother, Mabel McFadden, took me to my first public meeting at the Jackson County Court House and my Great Aunt Ikey took me to my first movie at the Arcada Theatre. Since then a lot of other people have helped me pursue these interests.

Fauneil Rinn, a colleague at San Jose State University, first suggested that I teach a class on political movies. She teamed me up with Jim Zuur, a filmmaker and exhibitor, and the two of them never stopped encouraging me to make a book out of our shared interests.

A sabbatical from San Jose State University supported much of the work on *Reel Politics*, and the Department of Political Science assisted in many other ways as well, especially under the chairmanships of Roy Young and Larry Gerston. Linda Chromik, Judyth Schallenberger, and Wendy Greer helped out with typing before the miracle of word-processing. Many friends and colleagues at the university provided clippings and opinions.

The British Film Institute and National Film Theatre were essential resources in London, and Phillip Bergson generously shared his access to films and filmmakers there. Thanks are also due to Terry Geeskin of the Film Stills Library at the Museum of Modern Art, New York.

Frances Goldin, Peter Dougherty, and Sheila Dallas nursed the book along, and the critiques of Allan Johnson, Stanley Solomon, and Sidney Wise made it better than it otherwise might have been, as did the sharp editing of Donna Ryan.

Katherine Bishop, dreamed the title – literally.

And Ray Allen came along to a lot of movies he didn't really want to see, and provided not only moral support but also much insight.

Foreword

Messages Are Not Only for Western Union

"Messages are for Western Union," movie mogul Samuel Goldwyn pontificated, and his words became Hollywood dogma. Those who live by the Goldwyn rule insist that American audiences expect to be entertained, not educated or harangued, when they go to the movies. Films with messages, they say, are box office poison, and therefore anathema to an industry that exists to make profits as well as art. Besides, these filmmakers point out, when they do make movies with political messages, they are attacked by critics, boycotted by minority groups, and threatened by politicians. Film scholars lament the dearth of American movies about political and social issues, often blaming the film industry's profit orientation. Audience expectations of entertainment are not innate, they assert, but have been inculcated by filmmakers because they are safe and profitable. Indeed, the expectation of entertainment defines the art form most of us think of as "movies."

Yet many movies with messages about politics and social problems have been made and have often been treated as prestige projects. Goldwyn himself sent a few messages. His first film company was publicly committed to "a foundation of intelligence and refinement,"[1] and his productions include many films that went far beyond mindless entertainment, from *Stella Dallas* to *Porgy and Bess*. And it was Goldwyn, after all, who produced Lillian Hellman's *The Little Foxes*, a bone-chilling tale of capitalist greed, and *The Best Years of our Lives*, a poignant story of the aftermath of war. He was also responsible for *The North Star*, one of Hollywood's most blatantly pro-Russian films. Apparently Goldwyn was not so much opposed to messages as ambivalent about them.

So is the rest of the film industry. Directors from D. W. Griffith and King Vidor in the early days to Sidney Lumet and Oliver Stone today, along with some studios, producers, writers, and stars, have defied the Goldwyn rule frequently and flagrantly. At least a few movies with political messages are made every year, and some periods like the 1930s and the late 1970s, have seen higher rates of production. Such movies generally get more than their fair share of recognition: witness the success of *Platoon* in 1986. Hollywood likes to congratulate itself by giving an occasional Academy Award nomination and sometimes even the Oscar itself, to a film that at least pretends to have a message. Critics may give political films a rough ride, but they pay attention to them, and they regard them as "important works." And, contrary to conventional wisdom, audiences do not ignore political films. Although message movies hardly ever rank as blockbusters, many have actually turned a handsome profit.

In short, Goldwyn got it wrong. Movies can, and often do, send messages, but it matters greatly what the message is, how it is presented, and who delivers it.

What Makes a Movie "Political"?

All movies, even those intended as pure entertainment, send messages about politics and society. "Esther Williams made the most political movies ever because she showed a way of life that never was or could be," observed director Costa-Gavras.[2] Similarly, film scholar James Monaco labeled American cinema "protopolitical" because of its concern "with basic ideals of community, family, and relationships. It's a cinema of domestic or sexual politics, if you like, and its aim in general is to try to describe ... the present lineaments of the social contract."[3] Many critics accept this broad definition of politics in American films, noting the consensus orientation of these movies and the way in which they fortify the status quo by making us all want to be part of it. Their happy endings, individualistic solutions, faith in heroes and heroines, and emphasis on competition (usually focusing on winners) are, broadly speaking, political

This extended notion of what constitutes a political message is so widely accepted that even some extremely lightweight movies have been declared political. The message of many musicals, for example, is that if you believe in yourself and work hard, you can overcome all obstacles from witches to loneliness to poverty.[4] Westerns become "political" in this broad sense by changing their themes over the years to reflect social change. The lone stranger riding in to save the town just because it's the right thing to do, for example, signifies belief in a competitive free market, according to Will Wright, while the professional gun-for-hire who is willing to save the town for a price represents the emergence of a planned economy. In both kinds of films, the people rely on heroes to save them without fully surrendering their own sovereignty. Wright referred to this as "an aristocratic tendency with a democratic bias."[5] This may be stretching things a bit, but whether intended or not, most movies say something about class, race, sex, and other social arrangements that have to do with power and thus with politics.

Most movies, in other words, send political or protopolitical messages that we don't even notice, but some films are political in a way that all of us readily perceive: they focus on politicians, elections, government, and the political process. These are the true political films, the message movies that Goldwyn warned against. The tradition of the political film, narrowly defined, began even before *The Birth of a Nation* and is still going strong in the 1980s. Some political movies are comedies, others are thrillers, many are melodramas, and a few are biographies. Many, like *All Quiet on the Western Front* and *Platoon* deal with the issues of war and peace, while others, like *Gentleman's Agreement, I Was a Fugitive from a Chain Gang*, and *Brubaker* confront social problems such as discrimination, the need for prison reform, and the moral responsibility of the press in a free society. More contentious issue movies like *Norma Rae* and *The China Syndrome* are more obviously political. Most of these films criticize specific aspects of the political process, but a few go even further, offering a broad critique of the entire political and social system. All of these movies have as their core a political message that any viewer can perceive; their themes are not hidden beneath a coating of sexual intrigue or couched in the life-style of Esther Williams.

There are enough films in this overtly political category to constitute a genre, although they are not commonly acknowledged as such. In film criticism, a genre is usually defined as a category or group of films about the same subject or marked by the same style – musicals, for example, or western, gangster, war, science fiction, or horror movies. Films in the same genre tend to look alike and observe certain conventions, although there are exceptions to both rules. Critics often group movies into genres for the purpose of comparison and discussion; audiences, sometimes unknowingly, do the same thing.

Why haven't political films been widely recognized as a genre? Perhaps because these motion pictures lack internal consistency. Although many movies center on politics or social problems, the forms of these pictures vary wildly, from comedy to melodrama. Political movies also share fewer conventions and look less alike than do, say, westerns or horror movies. And perhaps a part of the reluctance to recognize a political film genre rises from the old fear that Sam Goldwyn spoke of: the fear that the very word "political" will scare moviegoers away. The makers of *The Right Stuff* and *The Killing Fields*, for example, bent over backwards insisting that their movies were adventures and denying their political content for that very reason. Such fears, with the collusion of critics, may continue to hinder the recognition of political films as a genre.

And yet they are just that. In addition to their substantial number, they have certain characteristics and images in common, such as the way politicians are portrayed. They also share values and assumptions. But whether or not political films are designated as a genre, critics, film lovers, and audiences perceive them as such, although they often allow for variation within the genre by combining descriptions, as in "political comedy" or "political thriller." Some people are undoubtedly turned off by the "political" label, just as others avoid horror movies or musicals, but the unpopularity of political films has been exaggerated: they may not be blockbusters, but they're not box office poison either.

Political Movies and Political Influence

Movies about politics are more than entertainment. They can illuminate our society and political system. They can increase our understanding of government and politics. They can also help shape the way we think and feel about politics and political participation. Some films try very hard to persuade, advocating policy positions on current issues. A few political films, like *The Birth of a Nation* and *The China Syndrome* have had a direct impact on politics.

Every film that deals even peripherally with politics contributes to our political socialization – that is, our familiarity with the political system and our understanding of the part we play in it. Through this process we are taught our society's political ideas and values as well as its accepted political behavior, such as voting and deference to elected officials. The most important agents of political socialization are the family, peer groups, friends and schools, but in a mobile, atomized, fragmented society like the United States, where families break down and friends and peer groups change, the media gain power as socializing agents.

All of the mass media contribute to this political socialization, but movies are the least studied, except perhaps in terms of sexism and racism. The other political messages of films may have received less attention because their impact is impossible to measure or because political films are seldom blockbusters. But political socialization is a cumulative process, to which many forces contribute, and movies are part of that process – teaching, reinforcing, sometimes even challenging.

Film heroes and heroines become our role models. They can teach us that we can't fight city hall, or that we can, and under what conditions.

Movies may be a particularly powerful medium of political socialization because of the way we see them. We go voluntarily, often for social reasons, with a positive, receptive attitude. We expect to be entertained, so our guard is down. We do not go to learn, yet any teacher will tell you that the first problem in teaching is getting the student's attention, and that's what movies are designed to do. The social aspects of moviegoing also enhance their influence. Most of us go to the movies with someone else, and afterward we talk about the film. Perhaps this talk is mostly about acting and action, but sometimes content is mentioned. "Well, maybe nuclear power isn't such a hot idea after all," we say, or "I don't think all politicians are really *that* bad." Any talk at all extends the socializing power of movies, strengthening their message or hardening people's rejection of it. The communal nature of moviegoing also intensifies the experience. When a film holds an audience in rapt attention, when they laugh or cry or boo or applaud, we know something is happening, and the movie's effect is more powerful. The process begins even before we go to the movie because the larger audience helps us choose which film to see. Ads, critics, conversations, friends, the particular people whose opinions about movies we respect – all encourage us to see a film and alert us to its significance. *Gandhi*, for example, was an improbable success. Americans got the idea that this biography of a foreign pacifist, was a "significant" film, a "must see," and they did, often applauding at the end.

Movies are also one of the few things to which we give our exclusive attention. Turn around and look at the rest of the audience sometime. They sit in the dark, eyes riveted to the screen, totally attentive to the unfolding story letting waves of sound and image pour over them. The power of movies is further enhanced by their appeal to emotion rather than intellect through non-verbal elements such as close-ups and music. This emotional manipulation makes movies more effective socializers, giving them a power beyond words. Over half of today's filmgoers are under age twenty-one, and the power of movies may be even greater for them, because they're more impressionable than older filmgoers. That should make us very nervous about the crude political messages of some popular films of the eighties, like *Rambo* and *Invasion U.S.A.*

Other media, especially television, may be more pervasive – and invasive – but movies are a formidable force for the gentle inculcation of ideas and for persuasion. They remain the most talked about and reviewed medium. Their power is even greater because we regard them as mere entertainment and are sometimes unconscious of their influence on us. Only when political films cross the line from entertainment into direct persuasion and propaganda do we begin to resist, and even then we may be unconsciously influenced.

Political films can also help us understand the forces we fear, putting them in perspective and thereby helping us cope with them. Political movies deal with war, corruption, racism, assassination, or the danger of a nuclear accident, providing either catharsis or reassurance. "Entertainment is not a full-scale flight from our problems," Michael Wood writes, "not a means of forgetting them, but rather a rearrangement of our problems into shapes which tame them."[6] Movies are also historical artifacts that help us understand the past and how people then thought about politics. And films may even give voice to a society's subconscious fears and desires. German film theorist Siegfried Kracauer asserted that "the films of a nation reflect its mentality in a more direct way than other artistic media [because they] address themselves and appeal to the anonymous multitude [and] satisfy ... mass desires."[7] Some theorists, known as structuralists because they search for the underlying structures of societies in their myths and stories, see movies as our modern myths, symbolically expressing our deep subconscious. Structuralists tend to focus on horror movies and the like, but explicitly political films also express the wishes, needs, and fears of a nation, reflecting the longing for a strong leader or expressing concern about a war or a new group of immigrants. In so doing, they may arouse us or set our minds at rest.

Movies influence our taste in fashions, hairstyles, music, dance, and cars. A single appearance by Clark Gable without an undershirt in *It Happened One Night* is said to have devastated the men's underwear business. More than forty years later, *Annie Hall* set a trend in women's fashions. In the same way, political movies can shape the way we think and talk about politics, or they can help to define, clarify, and entrench issues or attitudes. President Reagan, for example, often relied on catch phrases from movies in order to make his point. He quoted Knute Rockne ("Win one for the Gipper"), Dirty Harry ("Go ahead – make my day"), Obe Wan Kanobe ("The force is with us"), and Rambo ("We get to win this time"), along with other movie characters.

Besides contributing to the way we think and talk about politics, political moviemakers sometimes make a conscious attempt to influence political issues and even to provoke action. *Country*, *The River*, and *Places in the Heart*, for example, tried to build sympathy for the plight of today's farmers. Similarly, *The China Syndrome* and *Silkwood* were conscious warnings about the dangers of nuclear energy. Throughout the eighties, political filmmakers debated American involvement in Central America and Vietnam. Films like these consciously seek to persuade. Others do so unintentionally. Twenty-eight people are alleged to have died playing Russian roulette after seeing *The Deer Hunter*, and

John Hinckley, Jr., is supposed to have gotten the idea of shooting President Reagan from *Taxi Driver*.[8]

Filmmakers, however, argue that the influence works both ways. "Mass entertainment," one analyst insisted, "cannot depart too far from the tastes and beliefs of the masses."[9] Moviemakers bear their audiences in mind as they create their products. They are constantly aware that audiences seek entertainment, not offense, so it is safer to make movies that reinforce people's biases rather than try to change them. The content of a film may thus be at least to some extent a reflection of what its audience already believes. "Our condition," observes the fictitious movie producer in F. Scott Fitzgerald's novel, *The Last Tycoon*, "is that we have to take people's own favorite folklore and dress it up and give it back to them."[10]

Political films, then, may reflect rather than shape the nation's politics because that is the safest way to draw an audience. When political movies attempt to convert us they risk being rejected as propaganda if they come on too strong or not making their point at all if they are subtle.

Even the most tendentious American political movies usually opt to persuade gently, however, perhaps by introducing us to issues about which they think we are uninformed, like nuclear energy in 1979. Or they try to communicate to us how it feels to be discriminated against, or they evoke our sympathy by using stars in sensitive roles. Sidney Poitier probably did more than we know to increase white tolerance of blacks in the 1960s while Jack Lemmon gave credibility to middle America's doubts about nuclear power and about U.S. involvement in the Chilean counterrevolution. Costa-Gavras, perhaps the most ambitious and successful maker of political films, says that films don't make big changes anyway, "but they can make people feel a little, discuss a little."[11]

Messages Political Movies Send

Americans in general do not trust politicians. In fact, politics as a profession ranks well below medicine, law, engineering, teaching, dentistry, and the ministry. A Gallup poll found that almost two-thirds of those surveyed regarded politics as a corrupt "rat race." Clergymen, pharmacists, doctors, dentists, and professors rated at the top for honesty and ethics. Politicians were close to the bottom with Realtors and union leaders. Only advertising people and car salesmen ranked lower.

People get their ideas about politicians from experience, the news media, and the process of political socialization. Movies play a part in this by creating or reflecting attitudes about politicians, and as we will see, the cinematic portrait of politics and politicians is almost wholly negative. Politicians are often the villains in movies. They are frequently corrupt, greedy, self-serving, and ruthlessly ambitious. Conversely, real politicians of the past, like Abraham Lincoln and Franklin D. Roosevelt, are treated with such reverence that they become boring and unbelievable. Neither depiction is accurate, of course, but both reinforce the popular view of politicians as either murderous crooks or heroic saviors.

Senators Gary Hart and William S. Cohen have condemned the cardboard clichés of corrupt politics and conniving politicians and charged that film and television producers are naive about how Washington really works and are dangerously misleading their viewers.[12] Television commentator Andy Rooney responded that the public "understands that the crooked politician is a standard dramatic cliché that is no more typical of the average politician than the winding marble staircase in a home shown on television is typical of a staircase in an American home."[13] Hart and Cohen suggest that movies and TV shape our view of politicians, while Rooney insists that we know the difference between fact and fiction. Like others who feel maligned by the media, the senators may be laying too much blame on the movies, but Rooney is probably letting filmmakers off the hook too easily. Movies really do shape, reflect, and reinforce our opinions, even though we often dismiss them as silly – "It's only a movie."

Movies, as we noted earlier, also tell us about the political system and how it works, or whether it works – that is, whether it can solve our problems. Usually, they tell us that bad people can mess up the system and good ones can set it right. On the whole, these movies reinforce the status quo, telling us that all is well in America and that any little problems can be worked out, usually with the help of a heroic leader. They seldom point out fundamental defects in the system, and they rarely suggest that social problems can be solved by collective or communal action. They simplify the complex problems of a complex society and solve them quickly and easily so we can have a happy ending. Some critics see a conspiracy in this, but most agree that it is unconscious and to some extent executed in collusion with audiences that are more willing to have their opinions reinforced than challenged. Selective perception enables us to ignore even movies that question our biases. Hollywood's ubiquitous happy endings further mute such challenges by suggesting that problems can be easily solved. The results are what film scholars call "dramas of reassurance," movies that support commonly held ideas and tell us that everything is fine.

Political movies send messages about other important aspects of public life, too. Their images of politics, politicians and the political system influence participation in politics, for example. If politics is corrupt or if heroes and heroines always come to the rescue, perhaps there is no need to fight city hall. If the movie version of politics makes those of us who are not stars irrelevant, perhaps we need not participate. Power is another frequent subject of movies, almost always treated negatively, usually by falling back on the old maxim that power corrupts. Only a handful of totally selfless, god-like leaders like Hollywood's favorite president, Abraham Lincoln, manage to exercise power and still come across virtuously.

Most American political movies avoid, ignore, or denigrate political ideology, yet ideology is essential if we are to understand politics. Ideologies help us make sense of the world around us. They help us decide whether we're satisfied with the status quo or willing to change it. All of us have some sort of ideology, but many Americans pretend they have none, and so do most of our movies. No wonder the political motives of most film characters are personal ambition and greed. The rare ideologues in American political movies are one-dimensional and often silly, thus caricaturing ideology itself. As a consequence, American movies lack a rich variety of perspectives on society; they tend to see conflict as a struggle between good and evil or right and wrong. As a people, Americans are pragmatic rather than ideological. They adapt to conditions rather than reacting to them from a fixed point of view. Such ideology as we have is vague and largely unarticulated. Alternatives are seldom expressed, and we have been taught, partly by political movies, that ideology is foolish, impractical, or evil. Indeed, American ideology as exhibited both in political film and in the larger society might be said to be essentially anti-ideological because of its emphasis on pragmatism and consensus. We like to make things work, and we don't like conflict. Both of these orientations lead us to mute ideology. But we also place a high value on individualism, competition, and social equality, all of which are traditional components of an ideology – and all of which are themes that recur in American political films.

Political movies thus send many different messages. They describe us, shape us, and sometimes move us. Although some themes recur, the messages and our reactions to them tend to vary over time, reflecting the historical and political context. This survey therefore treats American political movies chronologically, although we will often return to their common themes.

Movies as a Medium for Political Messages

The medium of film itself shapes and affects the messages of political movies. Because movies are more visual than verbal, they play on feelings more than on reason. The need for the camera to point toward something, usually a person, helps explain the emphasis on individualism. The need for drama encourages a focus on competition, on conflict.

As we examine specific political films in the chapters that follow, we will see how virtually every aspect of the medium of film is used to communicate ideas.

The process starts with the subject and the script. The words or dialogue may be even more important in political films than in other movies. Politics itself is a medium of words, so more is spoken in these films and what is said is given greater weight. If too much is said, however, the movies become static and boring or worse, obvious, broadcasting the message heavy-handedly and thereby subverting it. On the other hand, if they are too subtle we may miss the message altogether. Movies are probably most effective when they let us reach our own conclusions, or at least let us think we have.

Music is also used to convey ideas in a political film. The sound track tells us who the good guys and bad guys are. Patriotic tunes arouse our emotions, and martial music sets the adrenaline flowing, building excitement. When the campaign catches on in *The Candidate*, so does the music. We know something is happening and we are caught up in it. Music can communicate dread, too. Along with lighting effects, camera angles, and editing, chilling music gives *All the President's Men* some of the qualities of a thriller.

Technical and visual aspects of filmmaking also shape messages. Close-ups, for example, tell us whom to pay attention to and usually whom to sympathize with. Long shots show characters in social contexts. When the camera is pointed up toward a person, the low angle makes that character seem powerful, while a high angle with the camera pointed down makes a person weak, a victim. Subjective use of the camera – filming a scene from the character's point of view – makes us identify more closely with that character, whereas an objective camera is more neutral and we're less involved. Editing techniques serve to juxtapose ideas, suggesting relationships that wouldn't otherwise be apparent. All this and much more can be done without words, yet each technique enhances the political message that the dialogue communicates.

Perhaps the element of filmmaking that most transparently shapes the political message is casting. A director may cast a star in a political role in the hope of attracting large audiences, but star casting is also a shortcut to characterization. Stars like Woody Allen (*The Front*) and Robert Redford (*The Candidate* and *All the President's Men*) bring an established persona to a film. We know a lot about them and we like them, so the movie has a hero right from the start. Some stars insist on maintaining a consistent image – "John Wayne don't run away," a producer instructed screenwriter William Goldman – and because the star is an important commercial element of the film, "protecting the star" may shape the script.[14] When directors use actors who are not stars, our reactions are neutralized and we have to be won over. Such casting confounds our hero-orientation, so these movies can convey different, sometimes more complex political ideas, but they may pay a price in box office receipts.

Finally, the collaborative nature of filmmaking should be noted, for more than most other artistic media, moviemaking is a group endeavor. Although the auteur theory singles out the director as the primary "author" of a film, that theory is vigorously disputed. Writers, producers, and stars have also initiated political films, and all of them, along with photographers, composers, editors, and other technicians, have a hand in conveying the film's message.

What follows is a survey of American political films through ninety years of their history. The movies discussed are popular, commercial, and, for the most part, fictional. These are not necessarily the best political films in terms of either art or philosophical content, but they are the ones Americans saw and are therefore surely the most influential. All of them are recognizably political – that is, they are "about" politics as it is normally, if narrowly, defined; the analysis of the politics of horror films and teen movies must be left to others. Likewise, but more regrettably, underground films and documentaries are not discussed here, although these films have influenced small audiences that include the makers of the commercial movies. While the focus is on content, some of the technical and industrial aspects of filmmaking that shape this content will also be considered. And we will bear in mind the historical context of the films and contemporary reactions to them as indicated by reviews, box office returns, and Academy Awards. Critical notices, ticket sales and Oscar nominations do not mean a film is aesthetically or politically good or bad, but they do indicate contemporary acceptance and can help us put the films in perspective.

As we will see, contrary to the Goldwyn rule, movies have been sending political and social messages for as long as they've been around, and these movies provide a unique understanding of American political culture.

NOTES

1. Ephraim Katz, *The Film Encyclopedia* (New York: Perigee, 1979), p. 491.
2. Costa-Gavras, Guardian Lecture, National Film Theatre, London, 16 March 1984.

3. James Monaco, *American Film Now* (New York: Oxford University Press, 1979), p. 287.
4. See, for example, Ethan Mordden, *The Hollywood Musical* (London: David & Charles, 1981).
5. Will Wright, *Sixguns and Society* (Berkeley: University of California Press, 1975), p. 131.
6. Michael Wood, *America in the Movies* (New York: Basic Books, 1975), p. 22.
7. Siegfried Kracauer, *From Caligari to Hitler* (Princeton, N.J.: Princeton University Press, 1974), pp. v., 5.
8. Peter Koper, "Can Movies Kill?" *American Film*, July-August 1982, p. 46.
9. Randall M. Miller, ed., *The Kaleidoscope Lens* (Englewood, N.J.: Ozer, 1980), p. 13.
10. F. Scott Fitzgerald, *The Last Tycoon* (London: Penguin, 1941), p. 128.
11. Guardian Lecture, 16 March 1984.
12. William S. Cohen and Gary Hart, "TV's Treatment of Washington – It's Capital Punishment," *TV Guide*, 24 August 1985.
13. Andy Rooney, "Anything You Say, Senator Ewing," *San Francisco Chronicle*, 29 September 1985.
14. William Goldman, *Adventures in the Screen Trade* (London: Futura, 1983), pp. 128, 197.

1

"First Seeds"

Politics in the Silent Cinema

Because the medium was so new, the moving images of the first films must have been extraordinarily affecting. Their impact was heightened by the excitement of live music, usually a piano banging away or, in the classier establishments, an organ or sometimes even an orchestra. Thanks to the efforts of film historians, who have begun to show silent movies as they were originally seen – with music, appropriate technical equipment, and good prints – many more people are now able to experience the early cinema. Even so, the audience for these revivals is limited because today's moviegoers expect sound and because the melodramatic acting style that was in vogue at the turn of the century, and that was necessary in a medium that used few words, seems ludicrous now.

Unfortunately, audience taste is not the only thing that limits access to the films of the silent era. Many old movies are in museums or private collections, and more have been lost as a result of neglect. But even a cursory study of these early movies reveals a variety of subjects, styles, and perspectives perhaps richer than that of later eras. This diversity was increased by foreign films, then fully accessible to audiences because language was not a barrier.

One- and Two-Reelers

Movies were telling stories, albeit short ones, right from the beginning. Limited to the amount of film that would fit on one reel of a projector, most early films, like Edwin S. Porter's *The Great Train Robbery* (1903), were less than fifteen minutes long. Predominantly comedies

The Birth of a Nation (1915)

and melodramas, enough of the films of this era survive to give us an idea of what the founders of the American film industry thought about politics.

The birth of the medium at the turn of the century coincided with the Progressive Movement, which dominated American politics into the 1920s. It was a time when crusading reformers and muckraking journalists attacked political machines and big economic interests. And filmmakers joined the attack. According to British film historian I. C. Jarvie, these early days of filmmaking rank with 1930–1934 and 1966–1976 as periods when films were most critical of American society.[1]

Films like *The Ex-Convict* (1905), for example, treated crime as a social problem, showing how poverty could drive a decent family man outside the law. Others, such as *The Eviction* (1907), condemned avaricious landlords. Bankers and factory owners were also targets of criticism. Workers, however, enjoyed a rare moment of favor in the film industry. This sympathy – perhaps a predictable bias in an era of reform – was evident in the treatment of labor-management conflict in films like D. W. Griffith's *The Iconoclast* (1910). This attitude changed in the 1920s when labor activism was equated with Bolshevism and the Russian Revolution – and when filmmaking in Hollywood became an industry and started having labor union problems of its own. One moviemaker, however, remained sympathetic with workers, immigrants, and the downtrodden in general as they struggled to withstand the pressures of an urban, industrial society. He was, of course, Charlie Chaplin. Along with other comics like Mack Sennett, he also touched on politics when he vented his antagonism toward bureaucracy and authority. A more explicit treatment of politics, and one that clearly reflected Progressive attitudes, was *The Politicians* (1915), which condemned corrupt machines and bosses. This film and others of its time nourished the popular "corrupt politician" stereotype that would be reiterated throughout the history of American political film.

Attitudes about race and ethnicity were more ambivalent in the silent era. The Progressives were mostly white Anglo-Saxon Protestant middle- or upper-class citizens who felt threatened by the immigrant masses. Their fear show up in movies in which minority characters were lazy, evil men who lusted after white women. Paradoxically, virtually all of the early movie moguls – including Goldwyn, Fox, Mayer, Loew, Zukor, and the Warner brothers – were immigrants themselves and so might have been expected to show some sympathy for their brethren. Some movies did treat minorities sympathetically, if condescendingly,[2] but even though many film producers and investors were Jewish, the depiction of Jews in films was almost always negative. Perhaps the early movie moguls were pandering to their audiences or conspicuously denying their own background.

Filmmakers' attitudes about America were also shaped by their experience as immigrants. For them, the American dream had come true. Hard work and good fortune had made them rich and famous. Naturally, they believed in the dream, and their faith showed up in their movies. But their flag-waving may have served a political purpose, too. Perhaps it proved how American they had become and thus diverted the kind of criticism that might have led to government control of the film industry, something they were nervous about while the anti-immigrant Progressives were the dominant political force.

Their nervousness was not entirely justified, however, because America's political and intellectual elite in those days ignored movies as an art form and as a medium for ideas, condescendingly assuming that motion pictures were just entertainment for the massess – until D. W. Griffith's *The Birth of a Nation*.

History in Lightning

The Birth of a Nation (1915) was unquestionably the most important film of this early era, both artistically and politically. Griffith made many movies before his epic, but like most others at the time, his earlier films were short, and only a few of them – including *The Politician's Love Story* (1909), *The Iconoclast* (1910), and *The Reformers, or the Lost Art of Minding One's Own Business* (1913) – touched on politics. At over three hours, *The Birth of a Nation* was the longest film ever made in America up to that time and the most technically dazzling, with its creative camera movement and angles, close-ups, long shots, panning and tracking, cross-cutting to simultaneously occurring events, montage editing, iris shots, split screen, fade-ins and fade-outs, and thoughtful framing and composition. These techniques had been used before, but never to such great effect and never in such a way as to involve the audience so deeply. Film historian Kevin Brownlow observes that this was the "first feature to be made in the same fluid way as pictures are made today. It was the most widely seen production of the time and it had the strongest influence."[3] *Birth of a Nation* was ambitious in more than length and technique. Its content also gave it impact, a content so substantial and so controversial that the film was among the first to make people take movies seriously, helping to give birth to film criticism. So many people saw *Birth of a Nation* that the film is credited with widening the film audience beyond the working class to include the middle class and intellectuals. Even President Woodrow Wilson saw it and declared that it was "like writing history in lightning."

Griffith developed his script from *The Clansman* by Thomas Dixon, Jr. From this popular play and novel of the Civil War and Reconstruction, Griffith shaped a film with a distinct point of view on the events, politics, and politicians of its period. The story centers on two families, the southern Camerons and the northern Stonemans. Their friendship as the film begins symbolizes a united country, but Griffith's politics soon become apparent: the "first seeds of disunion," one of the titles explains, were planted by the "bringing of the African to this country." Griffith blames the Civil War and its aftermath on blacks and politicians – with the exception of Abraham Lincoln, who is treated reverentially. In a carefully composed scene replicating the signing of the Emancipation Proclamation, Lincoln is seated apart from the other politicians to make the point that he is different, that his only motive is to do good. When the signing is completed, the camera lingers on Lincoln, alone and looking miserable about what he has just done. Later, as the war comes to an end, he argues against those in his cabinet who would be vindictive toward the South. And when he is assassinated in another meticulously reconstructed sequence, the title announces that "our best friend is gone."

Griffith's once-happy families illustrate the consequences of these events when they are divided by a war that Griffith calls "futile and abhorrent." The large and lavish battle sequences, still hauntingly beautiful, surely must have moved audiences enormously. In these scenes, masses of men move through the smoke of firing cannons, falling and dying. The younger sons of the northern and southern families die romantically in each other's arms, reiterating Griffith's point that a hateful war has divided a loving people. Later, the director suggests the devastating effect of Sherman's march through the South with a single, eloquent close-up of a trembling, fatherless family, from which the camera pans to marching troops in the valley below.

As the fighting ends and Reconstruction begins, *The Birth of a Nation* follows Dixon's story more closely, and its view of history grows more and more distorted. The elder brother returns to his impoverished and grieving southern family, which becomes the focus of the film. He is soon followed by Senator Stoneman, a representative of the evil and vindictive forces of Reconstruction, a man who hopes to build a presidential career by reorganizing the South with carpet-baggers, black voters, and black politicians. His only motive is personal ambition, and he is encouraged by his evil and racially embittered mulatto house servant and mistress. We see Stoneman's black puppets in power in a horrific scene of a black state legislature with slovenly, barefoot politicians slouching in their chambers and lustfully eyeing the white women in the galleries. Senator Stoneman's immediate goal is to put his protégé, the mulatto Silas Lynch, in charge of the state, making him "the peer of any white man living." This ambition sours in the end, however, when Lynch takes Stoneman's promise seriously and, acting as the white man's peer, pursues Stoneman's daughter Elsie, played with doll-like sweetness by Lillian Gish.

Meanwhile, another doll-like daughter precipitates a crisis. Flora Cameron (Mae Marsh), the youngest member of the southern family, skips into the woods to fetch water – an indication of how low the family has fallen since the war. Diverted by the antics of a squirrel – shown in cloying close-up – she wanders too far and is spotted by Gus, an evil black man. His eyes bulge with lust as he follows her through the woods; hers bulge with fear when she spots him. She runs, he follows, and she throws herself off a precipice rather than submit to the advances she assumes he is about to make. Needless to say, this upsets her family. Ben, her eldest brother, scratches his chin and head as he takes a solitary walk, wondering what can be done. The carpetbaggers are running the town, and the Old South is falling apart. Then he sees some white children garbed in white sheets frightening black kids, and an idea is born. He forms a fraternity of white men who wreak vengeance as they ride through the night in white costumes "made by women," according to the titles.

The climax comes when a little band of whites is besieged by angry blacks and the Klan rides to the rescue, just as Silas Lynch is about to have his way with Elsie Stoneman. In one of the greatest chase sequences in American movies, Griffith cuts from the galloping Klansmen to Silas and Elsie and then to the cabin. This exciting and emotional sequence ends happily: the Klan arrives in time, everybody is rescued, and Senator Stoneman is chastised for having betrayed not only his people but his own daughter through his alliance with blacks. In Dixon's view, somewhat obscured in the film, this scene marks the birth of a white nation unified by the pain of war. This political awakening, through the Klan, ends in the deportation of blacks to Africa.

The Birth of a Nation was a vivid and dramatic rewriting of history that suited a lot of people at a time when blacks were migrating to the North in great numbers and racism was emerging there. Whether or not Griffith intended to do so, his film promoted the revival of the Ku Klux Klan outside the South. The son of a Confederate officer, he was simply telling the story as southerners saw it. But it was a distorted and exaggerated version. Blacks held majorities briefly in only two state legislatures and never had much genuine power; the real problem for the South was the white carpetbaggers. But Griffith's version of history – a romantic view of an Old South where everything was fine until the North got meddlesome – endured for a long time. Subsequent movies on the subject followed the same line, although with less offensive racism. Yet Griffith's message was regarded so seriously at the time that schoolchildren were taken to his movie to learn history.

Appalling as its message seems now, *The Birth of a Nation* was the blockbuster of its day. Grossing a pre-inflationary $18 million, it was the second biggest box office success of the silent era. Immediately perceived as a classic, it was re-released in 1921, 1922, and 1930. Some 200 million people saw it before 1946.

This movie was politically significant not only because of its content and popularity but also because of the contemporary reaction to it. Latter-day viewers see it as over-the-top racism, often dismissing it too readily for that reason and perhaps assuming that audiences at the time of its original release were oblivious to its bias or approved of it. But objections to *The Birth of a Nation* in 1915 were intense enough to cause President Wilson to retract his initial praise. Many reviewers condemned its racism, including a *New York Times* critic, who called it "inflammatory" and "controversial" even as he praised it as an "impressive new illustration of the scope of the motion picture camera."[4] The National Association for the Advancement of Colored People (NAACP) organized a precedent-setting national boycott of the film, probably the first such effort and one of the most successful. There was a mass demonstration when the film was shown in Boston, and it was banned in three states and several cities.

Griffith claimed to be shocked by these objections, and denied that he was anti-black, although he warned that the NAACP favored interracial marriage. Nevertheless, the widespread criticism of Griffith's black characters – all whom were either evil or stupid and, perhaps even more offensively, all of whom were played by white actors in blackface – forced him to delete some scenes of blacks molesting white women as well as the final scene in which the blacks were deported to Africa. He had already softened the racism of the novel by adding the "good souls," the Camerons' happy and loyal house servants. But these concessions did not silence the protesters, and their continued objections made other filmmakers skittish about including blacks in their movies. Race, racism, and especially intermarriage were forbidden subjects after *The Birth of a Nation*, and except for a few happy servants like the "good souls," blacks disappeared from mainstream movies until the 1940s.

The Birth of a Nation also portrayed women in a manner that now seems objectionable. Griffith's female characters were doll-like possessions of men; they were treated with reverence, but they were objects. Their purity was all-important; death was preferable to defilement. The only constructive task for Griffith's women was making the Klan costumes. The one exception was the lascivious Lydia, Stoneman's mulatto housekeeper and mistress, who used sex to manipulate her man. At a time when women were fighting for the vote, Griffith's attitude was far from progressive, but he probably was no more sexually conservative than most of his audience.

Griffith's portrait of politics and politicians made use of stereotypes and conventions that later became entrenched in the movies. He used, for example, the contrasting stereotypes of the saintly leader (Lincoln) and the evil politician (Stoneman and Lynch), a device that endures in film to this day. He also provided the kind of populist, collective solution that remains popular in today's political films: instead of seeking a leader to help them or working through the regular political process, Griffith's oppressed white southerners banded together, forming a vigilante group, and took the law into their own hands.

Griffith's main concern, however, was rewriting the history of the South and the Civil War, and he was well aware of the power of his medium. He saw film as an educational tool, and he set out to use it as such, an intention that was in itself political. *The Birth of a Nation* was the first important American political film, not only because it reshaped the image of the South but also because it influenced the way Americans thought about politics.

Intolerance (1916), Griffith's next major project, consisted of four interwoven stories on the theme of intolerance set in different historical periods. In the modern story, an evil industrialist pursues a typical Griffith heroine whose sweetheart is involved with a sleazy political machine. When the lustful capitalist falsely accuses the boy to get him out of the way, the girl saves him by appealing to the governor. A good politician and laws that protect the innocent bring to this story a happy ending that stands in contrast to the suffering of persecuted innocents, including Christ on the cross, in the three other tales. Made partly to refute the charges of racism provoked by *The Birth of a Nation*, *Intolerance* condemned persecution and criticized the excesses of capitalism – only to be labeled "communist" itself.[5] But in *Orphans of the Storm* (1921), a movie about the French Revolution, Griffith made it clear that the rule of the masses was not acceptable either. "The tyranny of kings and nobles is hard to bear," read one of the titles, "but the tyranny of the mob under blood-lusting rulers is intolerable."

Griffith went on to make *America* (1924), a Revolutionary War epic, and later returned to his favorite president with a sound movie, *Abraham Lincoln* (1930). His later political films were less successful than *The Birth of a Nation*, although some film scholars regard *Intolerance* as his masterpiece. All of Griffith's movies with political themes – from the one-reelers to *The Birth of a Nation*, *Intolerance*, and beyond – portrayed politics and politicians in much the same way, however. Most were evil and corrupt, motivated by base self-interest.

Although vigilantes saved the day in *The Birth of a Nation*, Griffith rarely trusted the people, either. More often he advised us to rely on good leaders like the governor in *Intolerance*, Danton in *Orphans of the Storm*, and of course Abe Lincoln. All these attitudes would become fixtures in American movies about politics.

The Politics of Censorship

By the end of World War I, Griffith and others had made the movies a more widely accepted art form with an expanding middle- and upper-class audience. The nation's economic and intellectual elite recognized the potential influence of films and became concerned that this influence might be subversive. The fact that the film industry was dominated by immigrants and Jews made this Yankee elite even more nervous, and they soon advocated government inspection of movies. Film scholar Robert Sklar argues that "the struggle over movies was an aspect of the struggle between classes," with the proponents of censorship demanding the suppression of "any idea or image harmful to the moral, social or political health of the state."[6]

By the early 1920s, eight states and ninety cities had established censors, and in 1922 the public outcry over a widely reported Hollywood sex scandal produced demands for national censorship. At this point filmmakers were spurred to take defensive action. They formed the Motion Picture Producers and Distributors Association (MPPDA) and shrewdly chose Will H. Hays, a former postmaster general and political crony of President Warren G. Harding, as its executive. The "Hays Office" was hyped as a self-policing effort by a concerned industry, but it was really a symbolic action intended to ward off government censorship, and it worked, at least for a time.

Initially subservient to its studio masters, the Hays Office attempted to keep a lid on the private immoralities of the stars. But soon Hays grew bolder, producing a list of two hundred "morally dangerous" people, who were banned from movies. He also published an "index" of books and plays deemed unsuitable for the cinema for moral or political reasons. In 1924, the MPPDA recommended that scripts be submitted to the Hays Office for advance clearance, but that request was generally ignored. In 1927, Hays issued a list of "don'ts" and "be carefuls," warning the industry to keep away from subjects including drug addiction, sexual deviance, miscegenation, and nudity. At this point, a rule was decreed that would endure for years: violations of the Ten Commandments, or the Hays amendments to them, were permissible *only if the perpetrators ended unhappily*. In other words,

Hollywood could titillate its audience, but the final message had to be that sinners were punished. Daring filmmakers broke that rule only at their own peril.

Though rarely specifically directed at political films, this censorship must have had a repressive effect on those who considered producing such movies. Or perhaps the cautious motion pictures of the twenties simply reflected a decade of dull, conservative presidents and politics, a time of prosperity and isolationism when the Progressive Movement faded and died. The emergence of the big studios must also have contributed to the caution and conservatism among political film-makers. Like factories, these studios churned out movies feverishly for an ever-expanding audience. Their near-monopolistic control of the industry, extending to distribution and exhibition, discouraged independent-minded filmmakers and led to a greater reliance on traditional plots and genres, with only slight variations. Nevertheless, the sheer volume of films being produced let some political and even less-than-conservative movies slip through.

The Twenties: Corruption and Redemption

Most of the 10,000 or so films that were produced during the twenties were domestic melodramas, westerns, comedies, love stories, costume dramas, or crime movies, but a few straightforward films about politics were made despite the ominous presence of the Hays Office. The American Film Institute (AFI) index for this period lists fewer than 200 feature films with political themes, although this may be a conservative estimate, since the index's definition of politics is a narrow one.[7] At any rate, the film industry's lack of interest in politics – or fear of political subjects – appears to have been well established by this time.

One safe political topic showed up early in the decade in a group of films reflecting paranoia about the revolution in Russia and unioniza-tion at home. Put those two fears together and you have the Bolshevik labor organizers who were the villains in over a dozen movies of the time. In *Dangerous Hours* (1920), for example, Russian agitators infiltrate American industry, but their efforts to foment a strike are foiled by a good American hero.

Another favorite villain was the political boss, a character that may have reflected the continuing popularity of the Progressive Movement's campaign against machines. Scheming politicians, who indulged in seduction, graft, and blackmail showed up in *Manslaughter* (1922), *By Divine Right* (1924), *The Blind Goddess* (1926), *A Boy in the Streets* (1927), *Broken Barriers* (1928), and *Apache Raiders* (1928). In *Wild*

Honey (1922), a political boss scorned by the heroine schemes to flood a river valley but is foiled when she saves her true love as well as the settlers and the valley. In *Contraband* (1925), the town's leading politician is exposed as a gangster leader, and in *The Vanishing American* (1926), decent Indians are cheated by corrupt government agents. However, the politics of these melodramas was usually so peripheral that audiences probably didn't notice it. Those who did contemplate the political messages of these films could only have concluded that politics was directly related to sin and corruption, and that politicians were very bad men indeed.

At least most of them were men. *Her Honor the Governor* (1926), directed by Chet Withey and written by Doris Anderson, had a woman politician as its central character. Although this film's heroine, Adele Fenway, is the governor, the real power in her state is held by a political boss, not an unusual situation at the time. He frames her son for murder after she blocks a water project that is dear to his heart. The governor's son is convicted, and she can't pardon him because she is herself impeached. Finally, the truth comes out and all is well, but the governor caves in, retires from politics, and remarries. The feminism of the movie was undercut completely by this ultimate retreat from politics, but it had already been weakened by scenes that showed the governor dusting her own office and sewing buttons on her son's clothes. *Her Honor the Governor* was not only an object lesson for women, however. The ultimate message was that politics itself was evil, corrupt, and best avoided by honest people.

Other films of the twenties, however, saw politics as redemptive. *What Every Woman Knows* (1921) and *The Battling Mason* (1924) feature formerly sinful men who run for office in order to prove to the women they love that they have reformed. In other movies, heroes and heroines redeem themselves by exposing crooked political bosses and civic corruption, a means of salvation that would reappear in later films like *On the Waterfront* (1954). In *One Glorious Day* (1924), for instance, a meek professor defeats a gang of political scoundrels after he is nominated for mayor. In *That Old Gang of Mine* (1925), a nasty political situation is cleaned up when the opponents reminisce about their common roots, unite, and overcome a still nastier enemy. In *Law and Order* (1928), a boss is transformed into a reformer as a result of the love of a good woman. Another group of movies shows politicians as martyrs, people who are wrongly accused and who are not really evil: *Short Skirts* (1921), *A Woman's Place* (1921), *The Silent Watcher* (1924), *Flattery* (1925), *Stepping Along* (1926), *Tongues of Scandal* (1927) and *The Head Man* (1928). All of these movies focused more on politics than those in which the politician was clearly the villain, and all were relatively positive about the potential value of political activity.

Some even suggested we could fight city hall and win, a message that must have been encouraging to the reformers of the time.

The historical films of the era were even more positive about politics, although today some of these starry-eyed hagiographies of national leaders seem ludicrous. Filmmakers and audiences in the twenties, perhaps inspired by *The Birth of a Nation* and Griffith's other historical epics, were fascinated by the recreation of history. American biopics like *The Dramatic Life of Abraham Lincoln* (1924) and *George Washington* (1924) were popular, though they lacked real insight or lasting interest.

Social Criticism

A few movies of the twenties clearly offered social criticism without focusing specifically on politicians and government. Perhaps the most renowned of these is Erich von Stroheim's *Greed* (1923), based on the novel *McTeague* by Frank Norris. Von Stroheim's original version took ten hours to tell the grim story of California immigrants and their destruction by the capitalist system and their own avarice. Producer Irving Thalberg cut it to three hours, and some film scholars say he ruined the movie. At any rate, audiences rejected *Greed*. "Spectators laughed and laughed heartily at the audacity of the director," reported *The New York Times*.[8] Other films of the twenties, including Charlie Chaplin's popular classic *The Gold Rush* (1925), commented on the evils of avarice, but none so grimly or at such length.

More successful social commentaries were made by King Vidor, one of Hollywood's most prolific directors and one whose perspective was solidly from the left. His anti-war film, *The Big Parade* (1925), was the biggest box office hit of the silent era, topping even the success of *The Birth of a Nation*. It tells the story of a trio of young men who succumb to social pressure and enlist in the army during World War I. They soon learn that war is horrible, and their romantic illusions dissipate. *The Big Parade*'s remarkable battle scenes are reminiscent of those in *The Birth of a Nation*, but they must have been even more striking to those moviegoers who had fought in the war. When the survivor of the trio goes home, he discovers that he has lost his girl to his brother, who stayed behind to manage the family business. Disillusionment with the war is compounded by disillusionment with the attitudes of the people at home, but in the end the young man is happily reunited with the girl he met in France.

The Big Parade was a resolute but not heavy-handed anti-war film. Audiences loved it, partly because it dealt with a war that was still vivid in their memories. The critics also approved. Calling it "a romance with war as the villain," *The New York Times* rated it one of the ten best films of 1925 (their annual ratings were just starting).[9] It might seem surprising today that an anti-war movie would have been so popular in the twenties, but *The Big Parade* was not radical for its time, nor was it the only anti-war film of the era. Disillusionment with World War I was common, and isolationism was the key concept of America's foreign policy.

Vidor followed *The Big Parade* with *The Crowd* in 1928, the story of a young couple struggling for success in order to differentiate themselves from "the crowd." A softer version of *Greed*, this film is a tough commentary on urban alienation and isolation – at least until the couple strike it rich in a happy ending that was added over Vidor's objections. This imposed ending, like the drastic cutting of *Greed*, illustrates the conservatism and the power of the studios in the 1920s.

Sound and the Depression Mark the End of an Era

The silent movies of this early era had provided a healthy variety of political images, although the conservatism of a country presided over by Coolidge, Harding, and Hoover no doubt muted that variety. The lack of political boldness no doubt also reflected the filmmakers' own fear of censorship, and the Hays Office served to institutionalize that caution.

Change came swiftly at the end of the decade, however, as sound came to the movies and the Great Depression descended on the nation. In 1929, nine "audible" films ranked among *The New York Times*'s top 10 movies, yet even in 1930 sound was still enough of a novelty for critics to marvel at the battle noise in *All Quiet on the Western Front*.

Sound had a special impact on political movies because it gave words greater power in relation to images and thus facilitated the expression of more complex stories and ideas, allowing political films to escape from the realm of pure melodrama. For directors like King Vidor and John Ford, who were grounded in the silents and whose work was highly visual, images remained the primary means of communicating political concepts and words continued to be of secondary importance. But for others, like Frank Capra and Michael Curtiz, words were liberating. Sound was in one way a mixed blessing for political films, however. Even today, the Big Speech, pounding in the message with a sledgehammer, often spoils political movies. Film is still a visual medium, and wordiness still defeats it.

While filmmakers were learning to put words and images together,

137, 175

the prosperous twenties came to a precipitous end with the stock market crash of 1929 and the Great Depression. Political change was in the wind, and Hollywood was soon caught up. What followed was one of the most political periods in the history of American movies.

NOTES

1. I. C. Jarvie, *Movies as Social Criticism* (London: Scarecrow, 1978).
2. See Lewis Jacobs, *The Rise of the American Film* (New York: Harcourt Brace, 1939).
3. Kevin Brownlow, *The Parade's Gone By* (Berkeley: University of California Press, 1968), p. 26.
4. *The New York Times*, 4 March 1915.
5. Larry May, *Screening Out the Past* (Chicago: University of Chicago Press, 1980), p. 86.
6. Robert Sklar, *Movie-Made America* (New York: Random House, 1975), pp. 123–24.
7. Kenneth W. Munden, *American Film Institute Subject Index to Films of the 1920s* (New York: Bowker, 1971).
8. *The New York Times*, 5 December 1924.
9. *The New York Times*, 10 January 1926.

2

"The Country Needs a Man"
Political Movies in the Early Thirties

The Depression and the advent of sound marked the beginning of an extraordinary period in the history of American film. By 1930, some 23,000 movie theaters – the most ever in the United States – were screening films for an average of 90 million people a week, a figure surpassed only in the late forties. Hollywood churned out over 500 films a year to meet this demand, an output made possible by the factorylike production methods of the ever-growing studios, which also owned most of the theaters they were servicing. The massive demand for "product" and the huge volume of films produced during the early thirties resulted in a diversity of content and subject matter rarely matched in the history of American movies. The simple need for a large number of movies to meet this demand may account in part for the abundance of political films made in those years. Producers in search of stories may have been more willing to take a chance on message movies.

This was also an intensely political era, with the Great Depression driving the nation to desperation and Franklin Delano Roosevelt riding to the rescue with his New Deal. This turmoil affected the movies. The Depression caused a widespread questioning of traditional values, faith in the rewards for hard work, and the fairness of the American system. This questioning was most apparent in the social-issue films of the early thirties. At first, the movies were cynical and despairing, offering no hope of salvation, but soon they grew optimistic, offering simple solutions that usually involved reliance on a strong leader. Some flirted with fascism, but others promoted FDR's New Deal, and in fact, once the New Deal became entrenched, the output of social criticism and political films almost ceased.

American filmmakers were growing more aware of their power, too, and as the decade progressed, they dealt more directly with politics and

Gabriel over the White House (1933)

politicians. Still, they worried about government regulation of their industry and so pushed self-censorship to its peak. At the same time, a coherent political left was emerging in Hollywood, partly as a result of the organization of unions, a phenomenon much dreaded by the studio bosses and one that laid the foundation for political activity and controversy later in the decade.

Social Cynicism

One of the first big hits of the era was a political movie intended by its producer to be "a great work for peace," bringing "home the wastefulness of war."[1] Over a hundred million people have seen *All Quiet on the Western Front* (1930) by now. The movie was, and still is, a success with audiences and critics alike. The film industry must have liked it, too, because it won Academy Awards for best picture and best direction, marking the beginning of a long tradition of Oscars for message movies.

Taken from Erich Maria Remarque's anti-war novel, the film told the story of a German soldier in World War I. In a way, it resembled the great box office successes of the silent era, *The Big Parade* and *The Birth of a Nation*. *All Quiet on the Western Front*, however, focused not on an American victim of the war, but on a highly sympathetic German soldier (Lew Ayres), whose ghastly experiences were quite similar to those of the central character in *The Big Parade*. *All Quiet* went a little further than the earlier film, when at one point the soldiers speculate on the causes of war, something more easily done with the dialogue of a sound film than with the images and titles of a silent. One young soldier blames national leaders for the war; another says its causes are rooted in pride; a third blames those who profit from war; a fourth says that things just get out of hand. Their debate may seem progressive today, but *All Quiet* was made for a nation immersed in isolationism, so it was consistent with currently popular policy.

In contrast to the high-minded message of *All Quiet on the Western Front*, other films of the time concerned themselves primarily with low-life. Gangster movies, for example, were a dominant genre of the period. Crime and violence dominated the action in movies like *Little Caesar* (1930) and *Public Enemy* (1931), but these films also dealt with class and ethnic conflict and reflected the emerging doubts and questions about how well the American system was working. Could this system save itself from the Depression? the movies asked. Could ethnic minorities and the working class count on the system to save them? The answers provided by the gangster movies weren't very optimistic. About the best you can do, they seemed to say, is to stand up and die honorably, with guns blazing. Of course the gangsters were punished in the end, but they were usually treated with some sympathy and even admiration, and the movies frequently suggested that society had made them what they were.

While the gangster films criticized society somewhat indirectly, comics like Laurel and Hardy, W. C. Fields, Mae West, and the Marx Brothers made fun of it. All were in their primes in the thirties, and all of them challenged traditional values, from morality to authority. The Marx Brothers' *Duck Soup* (1933), directed by Leo McCarey, was their most direct assault on politics, with Groucho as the tin-pot dictator of Fredonia leading his nation into a farcical war.

Like the gunfire of the gangster movies and the fast talk of the comedies, the songs and thudding tap dances of the musicals of the early thirties celebrated sound. Musicals presented, appropriately, an upbeat outlook on life and on the future, but they did not always skirt the problems of the times. *Gold Diggers of 1933*, for example, opens with Ginger Rogers singing "We're in the Money," but her ironic song is interrupted by workmen, who arrive to repossess the sets and costumes for the show she is rehearsing. Despite their eviction, however, Ginger and the rest of the cast get a show together. Their big number is "The Forgotten Man," a Depression dirge about veterans who fought in World War I and farmed the land but who were forgotten in their hour of need.

The Gold Digger movies (1933 and 1935), *Footlight Parade* (1933), *42nd Street* (1933), and other musicals portrayed groups pulling together to overcome adversity, although at least one critic has suggested that directors like the one played by James Cagney in *Footlight Parade* signified dependence on a strong leader like FDR.[2] While the gangster films reflected the despair of the Depression, the musicals incorporated the optimism of the New Deal. Instead of giving up and going out with a blast, like Little Caesar, chorus boys and girls could work hard and become stars. The system would function, dancers could surmount the barriers of class – provided they submitted to the robotic choreography that was so fashionable at that time.

Many of the gangster films and musicals came from Warner Bros., which has been called "the workingman's studio," not only because of the audience they aimed for but also because their films contained more social comment than most other examples of the two popular genres. The head of the studio was Jack Warner, probably the most liberal and political of all the studio bosses, a friend and ally of President Roosevelt and an ardent supporter of the New Deal. Warner helped with FDR's California campaign in 1932 and is said to have been offered a diplomatic appointment as a reward; later, FDR would call on Warner to help with the war effort.

Given the political predilections of Jack Warner, it isn't surprising that his studio was responsible for several message movies during the Depression. *I Am a Fugitive from a Chain Gang* (1932), directed by Mervyn LeRoy (*Little Caesar*), was a pessimistic study of the victimization of an innocent man by the American legal system. Paul Muni plays the fugitive who is driven further and further outside society and is unable, despite his efforts, to overcome the forces against him. Unlike most films of the era, *Chain Gang* made no attempt at a happy ending. The movie was a modest success with audiences and critics and won Academy Awards for best film and best actor (Muni), demonstrating again the willingness of the film industry to honor "serious" movies. More upbeat endings reflecting the nation's longing for what film scholar Andrew Bergman labels "benevolent authorities"[3] were provided by other Warner productions, however. In *Wild Boys of the Road* (1933), directed by William Wellman (*Public Enemy*), a judge saves the juvenile victims of the Depression, while in *Massacre* (1934) the federal government, symbol of the New Deal, steps in to save the good Indians from their exploiters, just as it would save the nation.

Shysters and Saviors

Explicitly political films about government and elected officials nearly became a genre in and of themselves during the early thirties, as a nation dissatisfied with the way it had been governed by Hoover's complacent Republicans searched for new solutions and a new leader. Nevertheless, the political films of the early thirties were cynical about the possibility of improvement. They projected the nation's disillusionment and held out little hope of change for the better. Most presented politicians as crooks and shysters; only later did a few saviors appear.

Several of these movies were comedies, among them *Politics* (1931), in which the formidable Marie Dressler, then Hollywood's top box office draw, plays the housekeeper of a politically ambitious society matron. When the housekeeper criticizes the incumbent mayor, the women of the town draft her rather than the society matron to run against him, going on strike as part of their campaign. By withholding their labor and their favors and revealing that the mayor is a front for local gangsters, they win an election victory for the housekeeper, making *Politics* one of the most upbeat political films of the period. Its mildly feminist politics and the happy ending for its working-class heroine – thanks to the solidarity of her sisters – were unusual for the early thirties. The underlying message was that the people could win.

The Phantom President (1932) combined the musical and comedy genres in a tale about mistaken identity involving a presidential candidate and an entertainer, both played by George M. Cohan, with Claudette Colbert as his love interest. In the film's prologue, portraits of Washington, Jefferson, Lincoln, and Theodore Roosevelt come to life to sing "The Country Needs a Man" to lead it out of the Depression. A gang of political bosses, which includes a woman senator, wants Theodore K. Blair, a banker, but Blair has "no flair" and, as the woman senator keeps mentioning, "no sex appeal." By chance they come across Varney, a look-alike medicine man and minstrel. "Every time the Congress goes in session," Varney sings, "they achieve a gain in the Depression. Maybe some one ought to wave the flag!"

The politicians know that the country needs "a sober man," but the public wants some one with "ginger and pizzazz" who can deliver "a musical comedy presidential campaign," so they persuade the minstrel to take Blair's place temporarily. "I do the act and he takes the bows," Varney says. He easily wins the nomination, singing "The Country Needs a Medicine Man" as his acceptance speech, but as the election approaches, the envious Blair prepares to "remove him to the Arctic Circle." The girl tumbles to the plot and sets Blair up to be removed instead, coaxing a confession out of Varney at the last minute, then seeing that he runs for president under his own name. In the end, the happy newlyweds enjoy the inauguration.

A lightweight comedy, *The Phantom President* mindlessly reiterates popular clichés about politicians. A close-up of a horse's ass fades to a close-up of an orating politician's face. The country is run by bosses and buffoons, and the people are fools, easily seduced by "a musical comedy presidential campaign." But lest the message seem too cynical, *The Phantom President* opts for what was becoming the movie-cliché solution to all problems: a good man.

The Dark Horse (1932), yet another comedy, was a greater popular and critical success with more to say about politics. A naive nobody played by Guy Kibbee, who would become a favorite casting choice for such parts, is nominated for governor and ruthlessly packaged by Warren William and Bette Davis. Among other things, the candidate is coached always to give the same answer to the press: "Yes – and again, no." *Photoplay* called *The Dark Horse* "a grand political satire," adding that "politicians tell us it's the truth as much as satire."[4] One reviewer speculated that it was inspired by President Warren G. Harding.[5] The film still rings true to some extent, possibly because today we are even more aware of the packaging of candidates. But while the message was funny, it was also cynical: Politics was all pretense and manipulation, an unlikely means of salvation.

Washington Masquerade (1932), a melodrama, was a more serious political film. Kansas Senator Jefferson Keane (Lionel Barrymore), "the People's Choice," fights "the Interests" behind a corrupt water project.

Although seduced and diverted by an evil woman they set on him, he redeems himself by testifying against "the Interests" before he dies.

Washington Merry-Go-Round (1932) tells a similar story about Button Gwinnett Brown (Lee Tracy), a descendant of one of the signers of the Declaration of Independence. Elected to Congress with the help of bosses, he resolves to destroy them and righteously preaches the principles of democracy to everyone he runs into in Washington. But he is shocked to discover that the politicians are all there to get something for themselves. Visiting a camp of Bonus Marchers – unemployed veterans of World War I seeking governmental recompense – he tells them to stop begging, go home, and get people to vote for good men. This is not what they want to hear, and they mob him. His colleagues in Congress react similarly. After he disobeys the commands of his boss, a fraudulent recount of ballots leads to his unseating. But he has already discovered "an invisible government" led by the sinister Norton, who deals in bootlegged alcohol and uses American foreign policy and the U.S. Marines to further his own international interests. "I have plans," Norton says. "Italy has her Mussolini, Russia her Stalin. Such a man will come along in America!" After a message-laden moment of meditation in the Lincoln Memorial, Brown rallies the Bonus Marchers around him. Taking the law into their own hands, they force the evil Norton to commit suicide.

The New York Times picked *Washington Merry-Go-Round* as one of the year's best movies, but newspaper magnate William Randolph Hearst was offended because the character of Norton looked like him and perhaps because Norton influenced American foreign policy to his own advantage, as Hearst had been known to do. Ads for films by the movie's producer, Walter Wanger, were banned from all Hearst publications.

Like the comedies, these Washington melodramas saw politics as corrupt, but they had a solution: a good man, preferably from the country rather than the city. Despite corruption, these films said, one good man could make the system work. These heroes spoke up for Democracy and the American Way in a manner that the filmmakers surely knew was corny, but they took their chances and triumphed. This belief that there would always be one good man was reflected in many subsequent films about politics.

Gabriel over the White House (1933) had a different vision, however. Directed by Gregory La Cava, best remembered for his light comedies, *Gabriel* moves from whimsical fantasy to the less amusing implication that a fascist leader could solve the nation's problems. Walter Wanger, its producer, probably had more influence on the message of the movie than La Cava did. A member of President Wilson's staff at the Paris Peace Conference, Wanger was a friend of President Roosevelt and one of Hollywood's most political producers (*The Washington Merry-Go-Round, The President Vanishes, Blockade*). Publisher William Randolph Hearst was another major influence on the film, even contributing to the script. Hearst had banned advertising for Wanger's movies in his newspapers and magazines only a year earlier, but the two men shared an enthusiasm for Roosevelt, and Hearst had recently taken an interest in filmmaking.

Their remarkable movie is the story of Jud Hammond (Walter Huston), a political hack who becomes president by making the right deals, who plans to stay in office by paying off the right people with jobs and contracts, and who shows little interest in dealing with the Depression and crime – mere "local problems," he scoffs. Hammond has an accident while taking a joy-ride in the country (symbolic of an economy out of control, say some film scholars),[6] and at this point the angel Gabriel intervenes. He transforms the hack into a benevolent leader, fully committed to solving the nation's problems by the most efficient means possible. Using radio as his communication medium (a technique FDR was just beginning to exploit), he inspires the nation, gets the powers he wants from Congress, which he then suspends, and proceeds to feed the hungry, eradicate unemployment, and end crime by declaring martial law and sending out the army to destroy the gangsters (the only cause of crime) by putting them before firing squads without benefit of trial. He then eliminates war, too, by bullying the rest of the world into joining the United States in a disarmament agreement. When the other nations comply, he blows up the entire fleet of the U.S. Navy. As soon as the problems of the nation and the world are solved, however, Gabriel disposes of the president, presumably to protect us from dictatorship.

When MGM boss Louis B. Mayer and the MPPDA's Will Hays saw an early screening of *Gabriel*, they were appalled, not because of the film's fascist implications, but because it seemed pro-Roosevelt and they were staunch Republicans. Hays warned that *Gabriel* would cause "affront," and Mayer took the film in hand, reshooting some scenes and toning others down.

The film premiered just before President Roosevelt took office. An instant hit, it was one of the big box office draws of 1933 and also won critical approval. "For its uncannily prophetic foreshadowing of the spirit of President Roosevelt's first month in office . . . for putting into film what scores of millions think our government should do," gushed *Photoplay*, "this will unquestionably be one of this year's most talked-of pictures."[7] As Mayer and Hays feared, the State Department and some members of Congress complained, but President Roosevelt enjoyed the film and saw it several times.

Film scholars now view *Gabriel* as an expression of longing for strong leadership bordering on fascism. Their case is strengthened by the fact that William Randolph Hearst, widely considered a fascist sympathizer, was a principal backer of the film. Certainly the movie proposed a dictatorship, albeit a benevolent one, and the police in the movie behave in a distinctly fascist manner. But this view is probably an exaggeration of the intentions of the filmmakers, who more likely merely wanted to encourage strong leadership and amuse the audience. In most ways, *Gabriel* was like other American political films: it saw politics as dirty, dominated by shysters, and redeemable only by a miracle, in this case the intervention of an angel. In this, as in so many other American political films, a single individual saved the nation; the masses were helpless and impotent. *Gabriel* was different from other films, however, in that it willingly, if comically, accepted the overthrow of even the pretense of democracy. In the preceding films, no such overthrow was even vaguely implied. Perhaps this made *Gabriel* a fascist film – or perhaps it was only a realistic perception of the magnitude of the crisis that the nation faced.

Producer Wanger followed *Gabriel* with *The President Vanishes* (1934), a more benign and less successful film with a more distinct leftist bias, perhaps clarifying his intent in *Gabriel*. The threat in *The President Vanishes* comes from a right-wing coalition of big businessmen, corrupt politicians, and fascist Gray Shirts plotting to drag the United States into a war in Europe in order to make profits for the arms industry. Their massive public relations program nearly suceeeds, but they are foiled when the president (Arthur Byron) fakes his own kidnapping and disappears on the very day Congress is set to declare war. Public sympathy turns to the president, and when he returns, the country is mobilized for peace. While *The President Vanishes* is an overtly anti-fascist film, it, too, reflects pessimism, about democracy. In it, the public is manipulated first one way, then the other. The truth is not important because the people are too dumb to know what it is. Better to trust a strong and benevolent leader. As in so many American political films, one man saves the day.

Although critics were less enthusiastic about *The President Vanishes* than they had been about *Gabriel*, one reviewer called it "a healthy influence,"[8] and reactions of other critics were quite intense. Audiences cheered in some theaters. Munitions dealers, on the other hand, called *The President Vanishes* "peace propaganda" and tried to have it suppressed. They succeeded only in delaying its opening.[9]

Other Visions

While some films put their faith in a strong leader, *Viva Villa* (1934) offered a revolutionary alternative. Written by Ben Hecht, directed by Jack Conway, and produced on an epic scale, by David O. Selznick, *Viva Villa* was honored with Academy Award nominations as best film and best screenplay. Its location shots, filmed in Mexico, are still impressive, but Wallace Beery's folksy Pancho Villa comes off as a horny buffoon.

The evil rich drive young Pancho to banditry until Francisco Madero, reverentially portrayed as a Mexican Abe Lincoln, asks him to join the Revolution of 1910. When Madero is killed by a cabal of evil army officers, Villa reluctantly takes his place as leader. But he is a fighter, not a politician, and he's soon bewildered by the responsibilities of government. Once he gets the land reform that Madero had promised, Villa retires to the country. Unfortunately, his boisterous ways land him in exile, and in the end he is assassinated by a man whose sister he's dishonored.

The messages of this film were mixed, to say the least. Although it supported revolution – at least in Mexico – it disapproved of revolutionaries. A few rich liberals seemed nice ("Many of us feel as badly as you do about the misery of the poor") but ineffective. In the end, however, Villa and Madero were unsuccessful. *Viva Villa* seemed to say that revolution was sometimes justifiable, but it was fraught with difficulties.

The best alternative vision and the most radical film of the thirties, *Our Daily Bread* (1934), came from King Vidor, the maker of *The Big Parade* and *The Crowd*. Improbably inspired by a *Reader's Digest* article on collective farms, this film, written by Vidor in collaboration with Elizabeth Hall, is the story of the itinerant unemployed of the Depression.

Tom and Mary, an all-American couple, flee the hopeless life of unemployment in the city to take over a bankrupt farm. They are joined by other itinerants, each of whom has a useful skill to offer. A thriving cooperative community is soon established. This utopia is nearly subverted by a blond temptress from the city who lures Tom away from the collective endeavor. His conscience soon brings him back, however, and the farm is saved when its irrigation problems are solved by a cooperative ditch-building effort. The opening of the ditch – presented in a movingly dramatic montage sequence obviously influenced by Russian films such as *Potemkin* (1925) – is the film's climax and its only great cinematic moment.

The collective politics of *Our Daily Bread* put it well out of the American mainstream, yet in other ways it was consistent with the other films of the era. It was anti-urban in its suggestion of a return to the land and to rural values, although this was an unrealistic solution in the dust bowl days of the Depression. Furthermore, threats to Tom and Mary's rural enterprise came from city forces: a banker and the blond seductress. More significantly, despite its collective rhetoric, *Our Daily Bread* insisted on the need for a strong leader. The members of the co-op decide they need "a strong boss," settling by acclamation (not election) on Tom, the film's FDR-figure, according to Andrew Bergman.[10]

Despite these lapses, *Our Daily Bread* is an impressive and unusual film. Remarkably, it was a modest success at the box office and even won some critical approval. *The New York Times* declared it "a brilliant declaration of faith in the importance of cinema as a social instrument ... a social document of amazing vitality and emotional impact," and concluded that "it is impossible to overestimate [its] significance."[11] Others called it "timely ... worthwhile ... satisfactory entertainment."[12] Most agreed on its worthiness, although some correctly pointed out that the acting and writing were turgid at best. Today it is the spirit of the film that holds up, especially in the dazzling ditch-building sequence.

Vidor went deeply into debt to fund this limited-budget production. Charles Chaplin helped him, but the studios refused to contribute, and so did the banks – not surprisingly since a bank was the "bad guy" in the film. Thus the political content of *Our Daily Bread*, by restricting the financial backing, became a limitation on its production qualities. The film's politics also caused other problems. Despite some good reviews, the right-wing press gave it a hard time. The Hearst papers denounced it as "pinko," and the *Los Angles Times* refused to accept advertising for it. But it won awards from the League of Nations and the Soviet Union and eventually found enough of an audience to turn a small profit. For all the criticism, however, the political message of *Our Daily Bread* was not much more radical than that of some Depression musicals: it was a somewhat more explicit statement about pulling together in times of adversity and recognizing each individual's contribution. Because of a weak script and cast, it hasn't held up as well as the musicals except, of course, for the irrigation ditch sequence, a production number that would have made a less rigid Busby Berkeley proud.

Another film that manifested faith in the people and in collective action, was *The General Died at Dawn* (1936), directed by Lewis Milestone and written by left-wing playwright Clifford Odets. In this movie, a mercenary sides with "the people" during the Chinese Revolution. "Your belief is in your own very limited self," he says to the enemy warlord. "Mine is in the people! One day they'll walk on earth straight, proud ... men, not animals."

More typically, Hollywood relied on strong leaders and the people were seen as stupid and sheeplike as in *Gabriel* and *The President Vanishes*. Another group of films including *The Fury* (1936) and *They*

Won't Forget (1937) expressed a fear that the people would turn into a mob. These films were part of a national campaign against lynching, which had reached a sickeningly high rate in the early thirties, but their message was as antagonistic to collective action per se as it was to lynching. For despite America's revolutionary and democratic heritage and all the "we the people" rhetoric, American filmmakers have not manifested great faith in the people who make up their audiences. Except for occasional non-mainstream movies like *Our Daily Bread*, group endeavor is rarely depicted in a positive manner. More often, the group turns into a lynch mob or passively follows venal leaders. These movie themes may have reflected the American establishment's genuine fear of revolution in the thirties. The Depression had put the masses on the move. Left-wing movements reached a high point. Roosevelt's New Deal was, in some ways, a concession to these forces and, in others, a way of buying off the masses, thus preventing revolution. And the movies played their part in all this by consistently discouraging collective movements that challenged the nation's basic political and economic structures.

The Fury and *They Won't Forget* were also reminders of Hollywood's avoidance of racial issues, a stance that, no doubt, was in part a result of the tumultuous response to *The Birth of a Nation*. It would seem logical that movies about lynchings would be anti-racist, but Hollywood caution impelled the filmmakers to choose white victims for both films despite the fact that most real-life lynching victims were black. Also, white victims were undoubtedly a better box office draw for a mostly white audience, especially when one of them was Spencer Tracy (*The Fury*).

Two other films of the era, *Black Fury* (1935) and *Black Legion* (1936), centered on American workingmen who were led into misadventure by crooks. In *Black Fury*, a miner (Paul Muni) is duped into leading a strike by agents of a company that stands to make a profit by breaking up the strike. And in *Black Legion*, Humphrey Bogart joins a KKK-like, anti-foreigner group that turns out to be a profit-making venture for its organizer. Both films played on the foolishness of the people and the ease with which they could be misled. Both also manifested what Andrew Bergman has identified as the era's tendency to blame its problems on fall guys and behind-the-scenes manipulators.[13] The strikebreaking company in *Black Fury*, the self-serving organizer in *Black Legion*, and the munitions manufacturers in *The President Vanishes* are good examples of such fall guys.

Politics in Movieland

As the politics of moviemaking got more complex, the filmmakers themselves grew more political. Warner Bros. and Hearst-owned Cosmopolitan were enthusiastically pro-FDR, while other movie moguls like Louis B. Mayer at MGM remained militantly Republican. These leanings and the disagreement about *Gabriel over the White House* may have led Hearst to shift his Cosmopolitan studio's affiliation from MGM to Warners. In 1934, the studios intervened in politics more blatantly than ever before or perhaps since.

Upton Sinclair, the socialist novelist, had won the Democratic party nomination for governor of California, and he might have been elected had it not been for a combined film and print media smear, the biggest up to that time. Apparently terrified by the popularity of socialist Sinclair, the state's leading newspapers, with the Hearst press in the forefront, accused Sinclair of being a communist, a homosexual, and an atheist. Meanwhile, the film studios produced anti-Sinclair trailers that looked like newsreels and screened them in their theaters all over the state.

Other political divisions followed. Film workers wanted to form unions, but the producers resisted; no wonder their films showed a mistrust of mobs and rarely dealt with labour relations. The Communist party reached the peak of its popularity in the thirties, too. In Hollywood, communist organizers pushed hard for the formation of unions, and many Depression-radicalized liberals joined the party. When the Spanish Civil War began in 1936, the anti-fascist cause became a rallying point for the Hollywood left. All this brought left-wing activity in the film industry to a peak in the thirties, although it was muted by wide support for FDR, a growing fear of the Nazis, and, eventually, abhorrence of Soviet-style totalitarianism.

These leftist leanings, however, rarely showed up on the screen, possibly because they would have been quashed by Hollywood's self-censors anyway. Will Hays's MPPDA had changed over the years from a toothless symbol of self-regulation to something more powerful and therefore more sinister. The strong and popular films of the early thirties had increased the authorities' concern about the social impact of films. Gangster movies were a special worry: the establishment alleged that they encouraged the lower classes to rebel.[14] There was equal concern about sexual mores.

As a consequence, the MPPDA introduced the Production Code of 1930. Although it was only advisory, the code was meant to clamp down on movies about sex, violence, and social issues. It strictly prohibited sympathetic portraits of criminals and sinners. Happy endings were permissible only if wrongdoers reformed; the unregenerate had to be punished. "No picture shall be produced," the code declared, "which will lower the standards of those who see it. Hence the sympathy of the audience should never be thrown to the side of crime, wrongdoing, evil or sin." Revenge, drug addiction and dealing, miscegenation, venereal disease, sex "perversion," and profanity were prohibited; "moral marriages" were to be the ideal. Nothing "subversive," such as a realistic portrait of slum living, was to be shown.

But even as the advisory code was toughened up, it was challenged by Mae West, the Marx Brothers, and the makers of gangster films. The Marx Brothers' disrespect for authority, especially their hilariously successful con men, and Mae West's lecherous, unmarried ladies gave deep offense to the bluenoses. West's *She Done Him Wrong* (1933), Archie Mayo's *Convention City* (1933), featuring extramarital fun and games at a salesmen's convention, and Walter Wanger's *Gabriel over the White House* especially alarmed Will Hays, who warned moviemakers away from films about sex, violence, and any political stance that might give offense.

Meanwhile, Catholic moralists formed the Legion of Decency in 1933 to fight "immorality" in the movies. By the following year, they were boasting that they had signed up 11 million supporters. The legion's advocacy of national controls led the MPPDA to attempt to preempt such action that same year by creating the Production Code Administration (PCA), headed by Joseph Breen under the supervision of Will Hays. The PCA repeated the Hays Office's earlier request that scripts be submitted for advance approval, but again the rule was frequently ignored. The PCA also tightened the code, prohibiting depiction of arson and the use of dynamite, for example. The result of this new step toward self-censorship, of course, was to mute movies that contained violence, sex, or social criticism, however great their artistic merits.

Hollywood got around constraints on violence by shifting its focus from gangsters to lawmen, but the founding of the PCA almost certainly contributed to the notable decline in the number of political films after 1934. Besides *The General Died at Dawn*, the anti-lynching movies (*The Fury, They Won't Forget*), and the movies about duped workingmen (*Black Legion, Black Fury*), there were only Cecil B. De Mille's nation-building epics (*The Plainsman* and *Union Pacific*) and a few comedies. Gregory La Cava's *My Man Godfrey* (1936), for example, reiterated the popular theme of the need for a strong leader. In this comedy, a rich family takes in a tramp (William Powell) as their butler. He straightens them out only to reveal that he, too, is rich. Another comedy, *First Lady* (1937), played on the idea of a president's wife as the power behind the scenes. There was nothing to match

Gabriel, Our Daily Bread, or the other serious political films of the beginning of the decade, however.

One of Hollywood's most political periods came to an abrupt end, perhaps because filmmakers and audiences now had a president they trusted to lead them out of the Depression or because their appetite for politics had been sated. Surely the strengthening of the Hays Office and the Production Code had a chilling effect on political moviemaking.

NOTES

1. Ray McDonald, *SUFG Bulletin*, 2nd Term, 1957.
2. Mark Roth, "Some Warners Musicals and the Spirit of the New Deal," *The Velvet Light Trap*, No. 17, Winter 1977, p. 3.
3. Andrew Bergman, *We're in the Money* (New York: New York University Press, 1971), p. 102. See also Nick Roddick, *A New Deal in Entertainment* (London: British Film Institute, 1983).
4. *Photoplay*, August 1932.
5. *The New York Times*, 9 June 1932.
6. Robert L. McConnell, "The Genesis and Ideology of *Gabriel over the White House*," in Richard Dyer MacCann and Jack C. Ellis, eds., *Cinema Examined* (New York: Dutton, 1982), p. 209.
7. *Photoplay*, June 1933.
8. *The New Republic* 26 December 1934.
9. *Photoplay*, February 1935.
10. Bergman, *We're in the Money*, pp. 78–79.
11. *The New York Times*, 25 March 1934.
12. *Film Daily*, 8 August 1934.
13. Bergman, *We're in the Money*, p. 109.
14. Ibid., p. 4.

Mr. Smith Goes to Washington (1939)

3

"We're the People"

Reel Politics in the Late Thirties

Although few political films were made in the mid-thirties, the decade ended with two of the best, *Mr. Smith Goes to Washington* and *The Grapes of Wrath*. The movies of the late 1930s were distinctly different from those of the beginning of the decade, however. They were better technically, more subtle in tone, and politically somewhat more conservative. In the early thirties, films had been questioning and pessimistic, torn between group solidarity and strong leadership as possible solutions to the crisis of the Depression. As Franklin D. Roosevelt's popularity grew and the New Deal attacked the nation's problems, movies became more optimistic as well as more simplistic, stressing traditional values and, as Andrew Bergman observes, making the New Deal "a veritable leading man."[1]

But it wasn't just the benevolent presence of FDR that dampened the political fervor of filmmakers. Hollywood was now under strong pressure from Washington. Will Hays and Joseph Breen at the PCA had managed to stave off outside demands for censorship, but a new form of government pressure emerged in 1938 when the Justice Department brought an anti-trust suit against the eight studios which, together, made two-thirds of all American films. The Justice Department charged that the studios' control of production, distribution, and exhibition (ownership of theaters) constituted a monopoly. Hollywood sweated, but the suit was dropped in 1940 when five of the studios agreed to loosen their control and allow more flexible booking in the theaters they owned. Meanwhile, another potential source of government intervention appeared: Congressman Martin Dies's House Un-American Activities Committee (HUAC) began showing interest in Hollywood in 1939, perhaps attracted by union activity there.

In addition to external political pressure, the internal structure of the film industry was changing. The volume of film production and weekly audience attendance were again on the rise, after having peaked in 1930 and declined during the worst days of the Depression. But production had become more rigidly organized and more dependent on bankers and other investors, often from conservative eastern families and institutions, which may have made producers more cautious.

Dorothy and Scarlett

Two of America's classic films, *The Wizard of Oz* and *Gone with the Wind*, were released in 1939. Both were directed by Victor Fleming and both became *Variety* "Box Office Champions." Both were also filmed in color, which may have helped them hold favor with later audiences.

The Wizard of Oz had no overt politics and or political intentions, but some latter-day critics have managed to discern political messages. The Scarecrow and the Tin Man, for example, were supposed to represent a longing for a populist alliance between farmers and workers, a dream that may have occurred to the author of the Oz books, but one that had distinctly faded by the time the film was made. The fake leadership of the Wizard, all promise without delivery, was a more apparent political theme, reflecting a common view of politicians. *The Wizard of Oz* concluded with the trite message of most Hollywood musicals: have faith in your own ability to solve your problems. Like earlier Depression musicals, however, it also suggested that group support helped.

Most people don't think of *Gone with the Wind* as being any more political than *The Wizard of Oz*, but the film that swept the Oscars and led in box office receipts for 1939 has at least minor political themes. After all, it is about the Civil War and is even more resolutely pro-southern than *The Birth of a Nation*. The sacrifice and suffering of the South are made much of; even the initially skeptical Rhett Butler (Clark Gable) rallies to the Cause in the end. The depiction of the Reconstruction is almost as horrifying as in *The Birth of a Nation*, with crude and greedy carpetbaggers swarming over the vanquished South. Like the southern gentlemen in the earlier movie, Ashley (Leslie Howard) and Frank (Scarlett's second husband) go off to a "political meeting," aparently a KKK raid, during which Frank is killed. Unlike *The Birth of a Nation*, this film does not present the KKK as the savior of the South, but its solution is conservative, as Scarlett (Vivian Leigh) eschews all forms of collective action in favor of determined individual struggle – and faith in the land. Her individualism is mitigated somewhat by the condemnation of her selfishness and by her willingness to save Tara not only for herself but also for her family and its faithful retainers.

Both *The Birth of a Nation* and *Gone with the Wind* romanticized the Old South, however, and both movies helped entrench American racism, a bias that probably had more political impact than their other messages. Critics pointed out the racism of *Gone with the Wind*, just as they had done with the earlier film, but there was less general outrage, perhaps because none of the black characters in *Gone with the Wind* were evil, and because Scarlett's mammy – played by Hattie McDaniel, who won an Oscar for the role – served as the highly sympathetic moral arbiter of the film.

Mr. Smith

Although *Gone with the Wind* and *The Wizard of Oz* weren't primarily about politics, the other great hit of 1939 was. *Mr. Smith Goes to Washington* was one of the most popular political films ever made, coming in second only to *Gone with the Wind* in 1939 box office receipts and Academy Award nominations.

Mr. Smith was directed by Frank Capra, one of Hollywood's most prolific, popular, and political directors, when he was at the height of his career. He had already made a string of hits that included *It Happened One Night* (1934), *Lost Horizon* (1937), and *You Can't Take It with You* (1938). He had shown an interest in politics with three of his earlier efforts: *Forbidden* (1932), a melodrama about a corrupt politician and a crusading reporter; *American Madness* (1932), a Depression tale of small savers threatened by bank failure; and *Mr. Deeds Goes to Town* (1936), a movie about a small-town poet (Gary Cooper) who inherits a fortune and tries to spread it around during the Depression.

Capra's films were characterized by an all-American hokiness that the director himself called "Capracorn." Others have called it populism, by which they seem to mean faith in the people, although *humanism* may be a more accurate term. *Mr. Smith*, Capra's most overtly political film, also reflected this humanism. Although written by Sidney Buchman, an admitted ex-member of the Communist Party later blacklisted for refusing to name others, no such ideological proclivities were visible in *Mr. Smith*, which was distinctively Capra's movie.

The story is set in motion by the death of a U.S. senator from a western state. Political boss Jim Taylor (Edward Arnold in one of his many "boss" roles) meets with his flunky, the governor (Guy Kibbee in one of his many "flunky" roles). Standing in shadow, the boss gives orders to his resistant, dejected flunky, who sits in the light. Later, during a chaotic family dinner, the governor complains that he is unwilling because of "howling citizens" to appoint Boss Taylor's man to the vacant Senate seat, and his children suggest that he appoint Jefferson Smith (James Stewart), the leader of the Boy Rangers. The governor likes the idea of appointing a naive nonentity to fill out the few months remaining in the Senate term, because the appointment would be popular and the appointee could be easily managed by Boss Taylor's agent in Washington, the state's senior senator, Joseph Paine (Claude Rains), who happens to be Smith's hero.

Flattered, Smith accepts the appointment, and his arrival in Washington is a classic of American political cinema. A bunch of political hacks, all familiar faces from other movies, waits to hustle him into seclusion, but he slips away for a tour of the capital, seen in a stirring montage featuring the icons of the American Republic – the Jefferson Memorial, the Washington Monument, the White House, and the Capitol – and accompanied by a patriotic medley of "The Battle Hymn of the Republic," "The Star-Spangled Banner," and the like. The tour comes to a moving conclusion in the Lincoln Memorial as Smith listens to a child reading the Gettysburg Address to an old man.

His idealism is shattered, however, by cynical Washington insiders who see him as Boss Taylor's dupe. When he stumbles into his new office, the dead senator's aide, Saunders (Jean Arthur), and her journalist pal (Thomas Mitchell) persuade him to hold a press conference, where the cruel city slickers make a fool of him. Later, when he confronts them with their misdeeds, they explain that it was their duty to expose him: "You're not a senator, you're a stooge!"

This depresses Smith, until Senator Paine advises him to try to accomplish just one worthwhile goal during the short time he has in office. The cause he chooses, a boys' ranch in his home state, isn't exactly earth-shaking, but Saunders, regretting her collusion in his humiliation, agrees to help him. Unfortunately, the land Smith wants for his boys is also part of a corrupt water project included in a bill being carried by Senator Paine for Boss Taylor.

When Taylor finds out, he first threatens and then slanders Smith, who retreats, devastated, to the Lincoln Memorial. Saunders, who by now is in love with him, finds him there and inspires him to fight back. Later, as she coaches from the gallery, he embarks on a filibuster, blocking Senate action for as long as he can speak in the hope that public opinion back home can be rallied to his cause before the bill comes up for a vote. As the filibuster gets under way, H. V. Kaltenborn, a real-life contemporary radio newscaster, explains the process to the audience and notes that "the diplomatic gallery includes envoys of two dictator powers, here to see what they can't see at home: democracy in action!"

The camera stares down at the filibustering hero, dwarfed in the immaculately reproduced Senate Chambers. Capra's message – that this is a little guy struggling against large forces – can't be missed, and it soon becomes apparent that Smith has underestimated the opposition. His message to the folks back home is suppressed by the boss, who controls the press and uses it to smear Smith with allegations of self-interest. But Smith is not alone. The vice president, presiding over a packed Senate, is a sort of benign father figure, no doubt the reason Capra cast Harry Carey in the part. He provides an anchor as well as encouragement in his facial expressions and occasional winks; his presence also makes the point that there are some good men in high office. The reporters and young Senate aides cheer Smith on in Washington while back home his Boy Rangers print a leaflet in an attempt to get the truth out. As if our sympathy needs further manipulation, the boss's thugs prevent the boys from distributing their flyers. All this is done in a fast-paced montage that culminates with an anti-Smith rally at home and the dumping of sacks of mail opposing him in the Senate chambers. Dejected, Smith is prepared to admit defeat when Senator Paine, an honourable man who is ashamed of what he has done to further his presidential ambitions, rushes out of the Senate chambers to attempt suicide. The truth comes out, and the film ends as the Senate erupts into chaos and we assume, according to cinema convention, that Smith has triumphed.

Capra's message in *Mr. Smith*, as in his other movies, is limited and simplistic: there is a problem because something isn't working properly, but the problem is minor, caused not by faults in the system or its institutions, but by bad men; good men, supported by the people, can fix things up. Even some of the bad guys, like Kibbee's governor and Rains's senator, do the right thing when they get a chance. Although the country was still in the Depression, Capra's faith in the system was unshaken, perhaps because of his own Horatio Alger-like rise from poort Sicilian immigrant to Oscar-winning Hollywood filmmaker. *Mr. Smith* wasn't even reformist, complacently suggesting that only the personnel, not the institutions, needed changing. All we needed was nicer leaders, like Abe Lincoln and Thomas Jefferson, the true populists so frequently cited in this allegedly populist film.

The film has been labeled "populist" because it seems to show faith in "the people," but its message is more complicated, perhaps darker, than that. It shows faith in one man – Smith, as Everyman – but it's hard to see how the film shows faith in a public that is so easily manipulated. Even the faith in one good man does not stand up to scrutiny. Smith is saved from losing only by the unrecognized hero of the film, Senator Paine, who gives up everything when he tries to shoot himself, the action that brings out the truth. Smith and the people are saved by Paine's crisis of conscience and bad aim.

Capra's movie presents a prototypical American view of politics, with messages and a style that recur in other movies about politics, but it also accurately observes some aspects of the workings of politics, including the process of appointing a senator, the Senate's institutional clubbiness, the filibuster as a parliamentary device, and the job of presiding over the Senate (although the vice president is rarely there in real life). It recognizes the power of the press as well as the importance of public opinion in both Smith's appointment and his legislative battle.

If *Mr. Smith* seems somewhat conservative now, moviegoers in 1939 did not see it that way. Written by a confirmed leftist (Buchman), *Mr. Smith* won the applause of the left, presumably because it showed the enemy as an evil boss with economic interests and placed its faith in common men like Smith, saying, in effect, "You *can* fight city hall."

Washington, however, hated *Mr. Smith*. When it premiered in the capital under the sponsorship of the Washington Press Club, journalists complained that the movie portrayed them as cynical hacks, a movie stereotype of the time – although in *Mr. Smith* they were allowed to redeem themselves by rallying around the hero in the end. The politicians were even more upset. One senator called it "grotesque distortion," while another denounced it as "exactly the kind of picture the dictators of totalitarian governments would like their subjects to see." Joseph Kennedy, father of the future president and then ambassador to Britain, tried to prevent the films from being shown in Europe because he thought it reinforced Nazi propaganda on the corruption of democracy and would demoralize the Allies. Efforts were made to buy up the film and suppress it, but they failed.[2]

Such strong reactions to so moderate a movie show just how narrow the limits on political films were. Only the fact that *Mr. Smith Goes to Washington* was a box office success can have encouraged Hollywood to make other political films.

Ford and Fonda

While Frank Capra was establishing James Stewart as one of America's most enduring images of the Good Man, John Ford was doing the same for Henry Fonda. These two directors repeatedly took up political themes, with Ford generally perceived as conservative and Capra as liberal. The two reassuring actors were also frequently cast in political roles, and eventually Stewart became associated with conservatism and Fonda with liberalism. All four names crop up repeatedly in the history of American political films.

Ford first worked with Fonda in 1939 on *Drums Along the Mohawk* and *Young Mr. Lincoln*. In the latter, Fonda plays the future president as a lawyer defending some nice young men who have killed a bully in self-defense, but whom a mob wants to lynch. Lincoln wins their freedom, of course, and we are instructed in respect for the law and a properly functioning judicial system. The film illustrates two of Hollywood's favorite political themes, condemning lynch mobs and providing a hero to show the people the way. As in *Mr. Smith*, the people were easily misled, perhaps a special concern of the volatile 1930s. Fortunately, a good leader saved the day.

Young Mr. Lincoln was a modest popular success and a great critical hit, winning praise from Sergei Eisenstein, the Russian cinematic innovator, as well as from generations of film scholars. They apparently admire this movie for its visual qualities rather than for the corny story or the stiff dialogue and acting. Like other biopics, *Young Mr. Lincoln* takes an exceedingly reverential attitude toward its subject, relying on our knowledge of what he would become to give the movie its portentous tone. By contrast, John Cromwell's *Abe Lincoln in Illinois* (1940), presented a portrait of the great man's personal life that was almost embarrassing, given the respectful treatment Hollywood's favorite president got in other films.

Ford and Fonda had a greater success in 1940, however, with *The Grapes of Wrath*, an adaptation of John Steinbeck's moving novel about dust bowl migrants in the Depression and a good example of filmmaking as a collaborative art. The project was initiated by its producer, Darryl F. Zanuck, who acquired the rights to the book and assigned Ford to direct it. Zanuck was also deeply involved in shaping the script, which muted Steinbeck's more radical and pessimistic social criticism. Part of a new generation of producers who pursued profit in a more calculated way than their hit-or-miss predecessors, Zanuck hoped to avoid offending the PCA or HUAC while pandering to the traditional values of audiences; Ford was the perfect director.

John Ford began working in films in 1914. He played a Klansman in *The Birth of a Nation* and had started directing by 1917. Eventually he became one of Hollywood's most prolific craftsmen, with 200 films to his credit by the time of his death in 1973. His style was distinctive enough to earn him the title of *auteur*, one who leaves a personal imprint on a film even while working within the confines of the studio system. Visual style is the most obvious signature of the autuer, but philosophical themes also emerge, like Capra's corny populism. In

Ford's films, a conservative faith in the common man and nostalgia for a simpler, agrarian past are apparent.

In their work on *The Grapes of Wrath*, Zanuck and Ford were aided by three other superb film artists. Nunnally Johnson wrote the tight script, and Alfred Newman composed a score based on a folksy version of "Red River Valley," which suited Ford's sad, sentimental style perfectly. Cinematographer Gregg Toland, best known for his remarkable work on *Citizen Kane* (1941), made an even greater contribution, using his photography to communicate what could not be made clear through dialogue. Long shots of the horizon give a sense of space and movement and the dreariness of the dust bowl. At times Toland's mobile camera pans to make visual connections and at other times it puts the viewer right in the action. The film as a whole retains a documentary quality that is radically different from the style of other films but perfectly suited to *The Grapes of Wrath*.

The movie starts with a long shot of the plains, followed by a shot of a lone man, Tom Joad (Henry Fonda). He's coming home from prison just as his family prepares to give up their farm and migrate to California. Tenant farmers, they are being driven off their land, a process described by a neighbor in a touching flashback in which the owner's agent denies responsibility for the eviction by blaming "orders from the East." "Then who do we shoot?" the neighbor demands. The film avoids fixing the blame, an example of its muted politics, but also a realistic point, since a whole system rather than any individual produces eviction. The neighbor goes on to tell of the demolition of his farm by a caterpillar and the photography emphasizes that the damage is done by a machine rather than a man, although a point is also made that the man driving it is another tenant farmer desperate for work. Again, blame is hard to fix. The whole flashback sequence is done in an eloquent montage, smoothly photographed and highly effective as a summary of the farmers' plight.

The people's despair is turned to hope by a flyer announcing "plenty of work in California: 800 pickers wanted." "There's somethin' going' on out there in the West," another neighbor declares, "and I'd like to learn what it is!" So the Joads pack up and take off in their old jalopy, but not before Ford milks the event for all the nostalgia it's worth with a long, sentimental scene in which Ma Joad (Jane Darwell in an Oscar-winning performance) burns her memorabilia, piece by piece.

On the road, the family falls on hard times. Elders die, the Joads run out of food and money, and they are harassed by border patrols in Arizona and California. Ma Joad struggles to keep the family "whole and clear," but she's working against the odds. They are aided, however, by waitresses, truckers, and other migrants, working folk who have learned to stick together.

Two key moments come as the family arrives in transient camps. Both scenes unfold through a subjective camera, so we see the camps as the Joads see them from their rickety old car. Starving children stare at them from grim huts as they enter the first camp, a hellish place run by growers. The Joads soon learn that California isn't the paradise they'd hoped for. There are too few jobs for the thousands of people who have been lured there by growers' propaganda intended to ensure a surplus of cheap labor. Despondent, the Joads move on, eventually arriving at a second camp, which turns out to be an oasis. As they enter, the camera zooms in on the sign above the gate: "Department of Agriculture." A benign attendant immacuately clad in white welcomes them in a mellow voice, explaining that the camp is a cooperative run by the federal government. The Joads are shocked by their good treatment, the absence of cops, and the idea of residents running the camp. It is transparently obvious that the camp is a symbol of the New Deal, complete with FDR-like manager.

But the pull of "the people" is too strong for Tom Joad to rest content with this oasis. He's been thinking, and he suspects that unions could help. At the first camp, Tom saw his friend Casey killed by the growers' thugs for doing union work. Drawn into the scuffle, Tom inadvertently killed one of the thugs, another reason for his restlessness. Earlier, he had wondered, "What is these reds, anyway?" Now he thinks that "these reds" might not be so bad if they help people. "If all our people got together and yelled . . ."

He finally leaves the family, apparently to become an organizer, although this is unclear. He reassures Ma Joad that he'll always be around, though, because "we're all part of the one big soul that belongs to everybody." She's stoic about it and gets the film's closing monologue: "Rich fellas come up and they die, an' their kids ain't no good, and they die out, but we keep acomin'. We're the people that live. Can't wipe us out. Can't lick us. We'll go on forever, Pa, 'cause we're the people."

The Ford-Zanuck message in *The Grapes of Wrath* was one of faith in the family, the land, and the working people, a message of longing for the past and despair for the present. Gloomy about contemporary problems, its response to them seemed to be one of resignation and faith in the people, who would go on forever. The Joads slowly figure out that they are victims of the system, but they don't know what to do about it. Even Tom's action is ambiguous. Like the Joads, the movie seems to long to return to the Jeffersonian agrarian ideal of small farms even as it concedes that this is no longer possible. Only the federal government, as represented by the clean, happy co-op camp, offers salvation. Stronger national government seems to be the film's solution of last resort if not first preference.

Steinbeck's novel, a great sensation at the time, was toned down considerably in the screenplay. His emphasis on class, for example, was replaced in the film by family and "the people" broadly defined. To conform with the cinematic tradition of happy endings, the film reversed the order of arrival in the camps: the happy camp came first in the book, second in the film. The ordering of these events in the movie also suggested greater faith in the federal government as the people's savior and stressed Tom's situation as a fugitive. Steinbeck made it clear that Tom went off to become an organizer, but this was offered only as a possibility in the film, where running from the law was his main motive for leaving. Steinbeck's suggestion that unions might be the answer to the migrants' problems was only alluded to in the film.

As the book ends, the strike has been broken, Casey has been killed, Tom has been beaten, and in the final scene, one of the young Joad women breast-feeds a starving man. It is a desperate, despairing ending, one the moviemakers couldn't accept, so the film ends in the government camp with Ma Joad's affirmative "we're the people" speech implying that all will be well. Survival, not change, is the theme. Nowhere is the system as a whole challenged; never is faith in the American way shaken. Where the book demands action, the film reassures. Questioned about the difference between film and book, John Ford admitted he had not read the book. He and his colleagues communicated their own message, not Steinbeck's, and did so in the traditional Hollywood style. "Never," Joan Mellen writes, "would a thirties screen hero with whom people were meant to identify lose confidence in America."[3]

But while *The Grapes of Wrath* may seem blandly moderate today, in 1940 it was controversial and, some said, radical. The Hearst press denounced it as communist propaganda, and even before it was completed, the makers were under pressure from growers and banks. They were so nervous that they kept their shooting locations a secret and, as we have seen, considerably muted the book's message. The Soviet Union saw *The Grapes of Wrath* as critical of American society, and used the movie for years as an indictment of capitalism. American critics and audiences liked the movie, though. It was a box office hit, and it won two Academy Awards (and three nominations). Pare Lorentz, the respected maker of the documentary, *The Plow That Broke the Plains* (1936), declared it "the first picture made in Hollywood since 1929 that deals with a current social problem."[4]

Unlike *Mr. Smith*, Ford's film dealt with a real-life problem and made a grim point about the divorce of the people from the land. The issue of migrant workers was intensely hot at the time the film was made. California growers were shifting over to native white workers for the first time. Japanese immigration had been halted, and many Mexicans had been repatriated because the dust bowl migrants provided a ready source of cheap labor. Union activity intensified with their arrival, but it took another forty years for farm workers to unionize, in part because World War II came along and changed everything.

The movies had been changing, too. While Capra and Ford focused on domestic politics, other moviemakers were turning their attention to international politics, priming for war.

NOTES

1. Andrew Bergman, *We're in the Money* (New York: New York University Press, 1971), p. xvi.
2. Frank Capra, *The Name above the Title* (New York: Macmillan, 1971), pp. 287, 292.
3. Joan Mellen, *Big Bad Wolves* (New York: Pantheon, 1977), p. 97.
4. *McCall's*, April 1940.*f*p

Citizen Kane (1941)

4

"You Provide the Prose Poems, I'll Provide the War"
Anti-Fascism and Preparation for War

Hollywood and the nation had concentrated on domestic politics through the thirties, but toward the end of the decade, they began to worry about the increasingly intrusive international situation. The Spanish Civil War caught the moviemakers' imagination, dividing and politicizing Hollywood from its beginning in 1936. Interest in the Spanish conflict was romantic for some, but others saw it as part of the wider rise of fascism. Hollywood was divided, however, about whether or not to oppose fascism actively. The debate showed up in a little flurry of anti-fascist films and many references to the need for international involvement, a position that ran counter to the isolationism that had dominated U.S. public opinion since World War I.

Internationalism: From Rio to Juarez

Latin America, too, piqued the interest of Hollywood in the 1930s, partly because the studios perceived a vast audience there, but also because they were under some pressure to increase public interest in South America and improve U.S.–Latin American relations. The Rockefeller family was a notable force behind this pressure, having acquired RKO studios partly to attain this end, which coincided with the family's economic interests. As part of their campaign to improve the image of Latin America, the Rockefellers tripled the budget of *Flying Down to Rio* (1933), a Fred Astaire-Ginger Rogers movie (their first) with no overt political content. Nelson Rockefeller later formed a committee to improve relations with Latin America, persuaded Twentieth Century-Fox to alter scenes that were less than flattering to

Latin America in Carmen Miranda's debut film, *Down Argentine Way* (1940), and encouraged Walt Disney to make the pro-Latino *Saludos Amigos* (1943) and *Three Caballeros* (1945).

Juarez (1939), a successor to *Viva Villa* (1934), was more distinctly political as well as internationalist, however. Directed by William Dieterle, who had cautiously raised the issue of anti-Semitism in *The Life of Emile Zola* (1937), *Juarez* centers on the attempt by Napoleon III (Claude Rains) to impose monarchy on Mexico by installing Maximilian (Brian Aherne) and Carlotta (Bette Davis) as its rulers. Juarez (Paul Muni) and Porfirio Diaz (improbably played by John Garfield) lead the resistance, countering the hubris and decadence of the Europeans with native democracy. They win, but they are given the Lincoln treatment, presented with such deference and dignity that they seem stiff and boring. Audience sympathy and interest shift to Maximilian and Carlotta, who agonize as their good intentions are rejected by the people they wish to help. Napoleon III, with his imperial ambitions, is the villain, while the savior is the United States. The French intervention is bad, but ours is good because we support Juarez and "the people" – and because Abraham Lincoln is invoked, even though he was dead by the time the United States took action in Mexico.

Despite its transparent politics, *Juarez* was a critical and box office success, especially overseas. The approval, however, may have been more for the message than for the movie. *The New York Times* declared it "a stirring restatement of faith in the democratic principle. . . . Ideologically flawless . . . socially valuable," but admitted that the diaologue was a little stiff.[2] Congressman Dies of HUAC, however, denounced *Juarez* as propaganda.

MGM joined the internationalists with *Idiot's Delight* (1939), adapted by Robert E. Sherwood from his own Pulitzer Prize–winning play and directed by Clarence Brown. An awkward movie that can't seem to make up its mind whether to be a melodrama or a comedy. *Idiot's Delight* is about Harry (Clark Gable), a second-rate vaudevillian reunited with his lost love, Irene (Norma Shearer), on a foreign border as war breaks out. Harry, representing isolationist America, tries to ignore the coming war while Irene at first romanticizes it. Some critics saw the film as anti-Hitler flag-waving, but *Idiot's Delight* was more pacifist than patriotic. "They will all lose," Irene says sadly of the countries at war.

Anti-Fascism: Melodrama and Satire

While one strain of politically oriented films emphasized internationalism, another was explicitly anti-fascist. One of the first anti-fascist movies was *Blockade* (1938), a tale of espionage in Civil War Spain, produced by Walter Wanger, directed by William Dieterle, and written by John Howard Lawson, a communist, union activist, and later one of the Hollywood Ten (see Chapter 7).

Set in Spain in 1936, *Blockade* follows the adventure of Marco (Henry Fonda), a peasant who rallies his neighbors to resist an invading force referred to only as "the enemy." He's soon assigned to root out saboteurs who are preventing food from getting past the enemy blockade to the starving people. *Blockade* never specifies which side is which, although its populist orientation and the military might and brutality of the "enemy" are obvious clues. The movie's main point is a warning to America. "As I sit here," a journalist writes, "I see nightmare visions of air raids sweeping over great cities . . . London . . . New York . . . San Francisco." Later, Marco sounds like Tom Joad: "We're part of something, something greater than we are." Turning to the camera in the film's final scene, he passionately cries, "Peace? Where can you find it? Our country's been turned into a battlefield. There's no safety for old people and children. . . . It's not war. War's between soldiers! It's murder, murder of innocent people. There's no sense to it. The world can stop it. Where's the conscience of the world?"

Despite *Blockade*'s refusal to name names, the movie's sympathy for Republican Spain was clear enough to draw criticism from right-wing and Catholic groups. Hollywood gave the film a nod for good intentions with Academy Award nominations for script and music, but the critics panned it ("shameless hokum") and the public ignored it. Today it is of interest mainly as evidence of the caution of Hollywood left-wingers.

Confessions of a Nazi Spy (1939), also from Warner, features Edward G. Robinson as an FBI agent who infiltrates the Nazi underground. Unabashedly anti-Nazi, the film is said to have been inspired by the studio's fury when its representative in Germany, a Jew, was beaten to death. *Confessions* was a popular and critical failure, although some reviewers praised the filmmakers for their daring. They had faced hostility while they were making this movie, and they came in for even greater hostility, especially among German-Americans, when it was released. Nazi sympathizers burned down the theater where it was shown in Milwaukee.

The most overtly anti-Nazi film of this era was Charlie Chaplin's still-popular *The Great Dictator* (1940). His earlier films consistently championed the struggle of the little guy against repression by bullies or institutions, but this movie is more specifically political. It is a gentle comedy in which Chaplin plays both a Jewish barber and his look-alike, the dictator of Tomania, Adenoid Hynkel, known as "the Furor." Hynkel is a burlesque character, but his political motives – including lust for power, hatred of Jews, and competition with his neighbors – are clear. The film ends with the little barber taking the Furor's place and addressing a resoundingly anti-isolationist, anti-fascist speech directly to the audience, like Marco in *Blockade*.

The war in Europe was well under way when *The Great Dictator* was released, but the movie was controversial nonetheless. Efforts had been made to stop its production, and there was hostility to its message. Even liberal critics dismissed it as belated, pointing out that Hitler wasn't funny anymore, and complained that it was too obvious, especially in its concluding speech. Audiences loved it, however, and made it a top box office hit in both 1940 and 1941. Hollywood honored it with five Academy Award nominations. And Franklin Roosevelt liked *The Great Dictator* so much that Chaplin was asked to reprise the little barber's big speech at the president's birthday celebration.

As unexceptionable as this and other anti-fascist films now appear, they were controversial in a pre-war America still committed to isolationism. And of course German-Americans and Nazi sympathizers objected to them. HUAC's Congressman Dies charged that all of these films were propaganda, attacked Chaplin for his left-wing sympathies, and even alleged that Shirley Temple was a communist dupe. The Senate set up a subcommittee in 1941 to investigate "any propaganda disseminated by motion pictures . . . to influence public sentiment in the direction of participation by the United States in the European War."[5]

Citizen Welles

Often proclaimed the best film of all time, *Citizen Kane* (1941) was yet another classic produced in this era, although its message was not primarily anti-fascist or, some would say, even political. Masterminded by Orson Welles, its twenty-six-year-old star, director, and co-author, *Citizen Kane* was based on the life of William Randolph Hearst, the newspaper magnate.

Power corrupts and money doesn't bring happiness, *Citizen Kane* said, a hackneyed message that Hollywood had delivered before and would send again, but it wasn't so much the message that made the film great as the technique. Kane's life is told in a series of flashbacks by a variety of witnesses, all filmed in dramatic compositions and lighting with extreme camera angles to emphasize power and impotence, an expressionistic style brilliantly executed by cinematographer Gregg Toland (*The Grapes of Wrath*).

The witnesses tell their tales to an unseen newspaper reporter who seeks to unravel the character of the late Charles Foster Kane by learning the meaning of his last word, "Rosebud."

But even though *Citizen Kane* is primarily a study of the private life of a public figure, it is political in its obsession with power and in its depiction of Kane's election campaign.

The young Charles Foster Kane begins his media career frivolously, because he thinks "it would be fun to run a newspaper," but he is idealistic when he writes the "declaration of principles" for his first issue: "(1) I will provide the people of this city with a daily newspaper that will tell them all the news honestly, (2) I will also provide them with a fighting and tireless champion of their rights as citizens and human beings." He stands in the dark, however, as he reads his declaration, a portent of things to come.

"If I don't look after the interests of the under privileged," the young crusader declares, "maybe somebody else will, maybe somebody without money or property." His politics are liberal, but elitist, a sort of noblesse oblige. In fact, he holds the people in contempt and manipulates public opinion with increasing cynicism. He stirs up a crisis in Cuba to boost newspaper sales. When his correspondent wires that there is no war, Kane responds, "You provide the prose poems, I'll provide the war!" Before long, he's openly announcing that "The people will think . . . what I tell them to think!" Kane's friend, Jed Leland (Joseph Cotten), sums up the publisher's shallow, elitist liberalism when he observes that the American worker is "turning to something called organized labor, and you're not going to like that one bit when you find out that it means he thinks he's entitled to something as his right and not your gift."

Kane runs for governor on a sort of populist-progressive platform, attacking "the machine," which is represented by Boss Jim Geddes (Ray Collins). The campaign culminates in a big rally. A massive portrait of Kane hangs over a crowded auditorium – a scene modeled after the fascist rallies of the time. The crowd is a painted backdrop, dots rather than faces. The looming visage of Kane and the blurred crowd are an apt comment on Kane's politics and the politics of personality as well. But the dark figure of Boss Jim Geddes gazes down on the rally from the back of the auditorium. Just as Kane is within reach of victory, Geddes demands that he drop out of the race. If he refuses, Geddes will tell the press that Kane has been keeping a mistress, a revelation that would cost him both the election and his family. Kane stubbornly refuses to quit. The story of his "love nest" is published and Kane loses both his wife and the election – all for love, Jed Leland says. "He married for love. That's why he went into politics. It seems we weren't enough. He wanted all the voters to love him, too." Welles concludes this segment of *Kane* with his most succinct and cynical comment on politics and the media as Kane's newspaper prepares alternative headlines for the day after the election: "Kane Elected" and "Fraud at Polls."

Kane now retreats to exercise his formidable power in private life, much as Hearst did, pushing the career of his mistress and building his palace, Xanadu, which closely resembles Hearst's famous estate, San Simeon. His politics, referred to only indirectly in the latter part of the film, move to the right and are ultimately discredited when he poses with Hitler in Germany and returns to the United States to announce that there will be no war. These scenes come as newsreel footage at the beginning of the movie, so we know where Kane is headed all along.

They provide a hint of anti-fascism, although *Citizen Kane* is more clearly an anti-elitist, anti-authoritarian reiteration of the American myth that power doesn't make people happy, that power corrupts. *Kane* is more cynical than earlier films, because it offers no salvation. The good characters in the movie couldn't stand up to Kane, the reporters couldn't figure him out, and the people continued to buy his newspapers without protest, rejecting him politically for the wrong reasons – because of his love nest, not his egotistical elitism.

Citizen Kane was far from the first American movie to deal with political corruption. Others, from the nearly contemporary *Mr. Smith* back to *The Birth of a Nation*, and beyond, had raised the issue. But *Kane* was different because Welles refused to offer simple solutions. Another distinction is *Kane*'s focus on the corrupt man himself. Instead of a Jefferson Smith or Tom Joad, we get Charles Foster Kane, a nasty man whom we don't like but for whom we feel some sympathy because of his lost childhood and his youthful exuberance and good intentions. Although "Rosebud" provides a simplistic explanation of Kane's character, the film's closing shot focuses on a "No Trespassing" sign outside Kane's lavish estate, suggesting we can't really know what makes people tick anyway. Welles insisted on a complex portrait of a human being and was willing to let the viewers reach their own conclusions.

Audiences, however, were less than enthusiastic, and *Citizen Kane* was not a great box office success, despite positive, if qualified, reviews. Writing for *McCall's*, Pare Lorentz praised the technique, but felt that Welles's acting wasn't strong enough to carry a film about so unsympathetic a character.[6] Other critics called *Kane* "a magnificent sleigh-ride" and "a curious adventure in narration."[7] Bosley Crowther of *The New York Times* acclaimed the film, saying it was "as realistic as a slap in the face," but he expressed reservations about the "undefined character" of the "eminent publisher." Despite this quibble, however, he ranked it among the year's ten best films.[8] Other reviewers praised *Kane*'s maturity, but some thought it flashy, superficial, and trite. The New York Film critics liked the movie well enough to vote it best film of the year, and it was nominated for six Academy Awards. It won only a single Oscar, however, for writing; in the other categories it was beaten by John Ford's *How Green Was My Valley* and Howard Hawks's patriotic film, *Sergeant York*.

Citizen Kane was applauded at its New York City press showing, despite its criticism of the press, but the Hearst newspapers assaulted the film vigorously. They'd begun doing so while it was being made, with Hearst gossip columnist Louella Parsons campaigning to get RKO to "junk the project."[9] Once it was released, the attacks escalated, focusing especially on its writer, Herman Mankiewicz, who had been friendly with Hearst and Davies. The publisher himself made threats, but some actions to suppress the film may have been taken without his instigation. There was trouble with the PCA over scenes in a brothel, resulting in the deletion of a character called Madam Georgie and the toning down of a scene with dancing girls so that they are not so obviously whores. Louis B. Mayer and others tried unsuccessfully to buy up all the negatives of the film, and theater chains, including Warner Bros., refused to screen it until RKO, Welles' studio, threatened legal action.

Citizen Kane had made a stylistic and political splash. Besides its gleeful attack on one of America's most powerful men, *Kane* almost off-handedly condemned Hitler and ridiculed the foolishness of people like Kane who thought war could be avoided. This was perhaps a cheap shot by 1941, but as we have already seen, it made for controversy. Beyond that, *Citizen Kane* marked an advance for political films because of the complexity of Kane's character and because of its broad, if pessimistic, attack on power and capitalism.

Frank Capra's *Meet John Doe* (1941) expresses similar pessimism, as corrupt political bosses and media moguls nearly succeed in getting their dupe, a bum played by Gary Cooper, elected president. They are foiled not by "the people," who love the phony candidate, but by John Doe himself, in a happy ending that twisted the original meaning of the story so much that its authors sued.

Perhaps alarmed by the rise of Hitler and Mussolini, both Capra and Welles expressed a fear of demogoguery. Neither of these filmmakers, however, seemed optimistic about whether America could resist it. But by 1941, after years of isolationism, America was finally shifting its attention from domestic to international politics.

NOTES

1. Allen L. Woll, *The Latin Image in American Film* (Los Angeles: UCLA Press, 1978), pp. 55–56.

2. *The New York Times*, 26 April 1939.
3. *The Spectator*, 24 November 1939.
4. John E. O'Connor, *The Hollywood Indian* (Trenton: New Jersey State Museum, 1980).
5. Colin Shindler, *Hollywood Goes to War* (London: Routledge & Kegan Paul, 1979), p. 31.
6. *McCall's*, June 1941.
7. *Monthly Film Herald*, 12 April 1941.
8. *The New York Times*, 2 May 1941.
9. Charles J. Maland, *American Visions*, (New York: Arno Press, 1977), p. 307.

"We've Been Shaken Out of the Magnolias"
Hollywood at War

Hollywood was enthusiastic when the United States finally entered World War II. With the nation united around a single cause, right wing critics were silenced and audiences were easier to please. Before Pearl Harbor, Warners had been the most political and most pro-Roosevelt studio, and the political left had been the chief advocates of intervention. But now all the studios and people across the political spectrum rallied around the flag, turning out entertainment films that supported the cause, making training films, and joining the campaign to sell war bonds.

At this point, domestic politics and social issues all but disappeared from American films except as background in such movies as *The Glass Key* (1942), a murder mystery complicated by machine politics, and *In This Our Life* (1942), a family melodrama with a racial theme. Throughout the war years, filmmakers stuck with optimistic stories of heroism, patriotism and anti-fascism. And, thanks to the rapid production of the studio system, these movies were hitting the screens within months of America's declaration of war.

From Casablanca to the Rhine

The greatest classic to emerge from the era was Warners' *Casablanca* (1942), directed by Michael Curtiz and written by Howard Koch, a team that had already expressed themselves on isolationism and preparedness in *The Sea Hawk* (1940). *Casablanca* made a more urgent case for involvement, though, with the cynical American expatriate Rick (Humphrey Bogart) reluctantly joining the Free French and

Mission to Moscow (1943)

sacrificing Ilsa (Ingrid Bergman), his true love, to another freedom fighter (Paul Henreid). "If it's December 1941 in Casablanca, what time is it in New York?" Rick asks. "I bet they're asleep in New York. I bet they're asleep all over America." Waking up was clearly the right thing to do, in case anybody still doubted it in 1942. Gracefully presented in a seductively romantic story laced with humor and adventure, *Casablanca*'s strong political message went down well, and the movie was a box office and critical hit, winning Oscars for best picture, director, and script.

Encouraged by the success of *Casablanca* as well as their own politics and the active urging of President Roosevelt, the Warner brothers churned out war movies for the next couple of years. James Cagney took the lead in the patriotic but otherwise relatively apolitical, *Yankee Doodle Dandy* (1942), also directed by Michael Curtiz. Bogart was back in *All Through the Night* (1942), fighting saboteurs and spies on the home front. Erroll Flynn joined the war effort in a string of straightforward adventure stories: *Desperate Journey* (1942), *Northern Pursuit* (1943), *Edge of Darkness* (1943), and *Objective Burma* (1944). In 1943, *Action in the North Atlantic*, *Air Force*, and *Destination Tokyo* came from Warners at the request of President Roosevelt. These films were straightforward, inspirational calls for support in the war effort. Some of them condoned collective action and egalitarianism, but these normally left-wing themes had suddenly become widely acceptable because of the war. In the early 1940s, oppression and military necessity justified both collectivism (we had to stick together) and egalitarianism (we needed everybody, regardless of class or race). Anyway, there was usually a WASP leader to guide the cross-section of society that made up the little bands of warriors.

Although Warner Bros. took the lead, other studios joined the cause. At United Artists, Ernst Lubitsch wrote, directed and produced *To Be or Not to Be* (1942), a black comedy about a troupe of actors caught up in anti-Nazi espionage. Paramount produced *For Whom the Bell Tolls* (1943), based on Hemingway's novel about the Spanish Civil War, although even in 1943 the studio shied away from politics and emphasized the love story. Less shy were three propagandistic anti-Nazi movies: RKO's *Hitler's Children* (1943), Paramount's *The Hitler Gang* (1944), and MGM's *Hitler's Madman* (1943). MGM also produced *Mrs. Miniver* (1942) and *Thirty Seconds over Tokyo* (1944). Only a few of these films, including these two MGM productions and *Casablanca*, were hits with audiences and critics.

One of the most memorable was *Watch on the Rhine*, a Warners production adapted by Dashiell Hammett from the play by Lillian Hellman and directed by Herman Shumlin. Kurt Muller, a German freedom fighter superbly played by Paul Lukas, brings his wife, Sarah

(Bette Davis), and their children home to her family in pre-war America. "I am an anti-fascist," he explains to his in-laws when they ask about his profession and his failure to settle down in one place. But even in America, the Mullers are not safe. A Rumanian houseguest learns that Kurt plans to return to Germany with money for the resistance. The Rumanian threatens to betray Kurt to his Nazi friends at the German embassy. When the Americans learn of the Rumanian's plot, they try to buy him off. "The new world has left the room," the Rumanian says when he finds himself alone with Kurt and Sarah. "[They] are Americans," Kurt responds. "They do not understand our world, and if they are fortunate, they never will." But the Americans aid the freedom fighter. "We've been shaken out of the magnolias," the matriarch declares.

Although the anti-fascist theme of *Watch on the Rhine* was old hat by 1942, the movie stood out for its quality and subtlety. Unlike other anti-fascist films, it couldn't be labeled anti-German because the hero was German and it was clear that there were others like him. In sharp contrast with the other anti-fascist films, *Watch on the Rhine* made a modest attempt to understand the enemy. The only dedicated Nazi in the film was a villainous fanatic, but the others who supported his party were given reasons for doing so, mostly having to do with greed or the will to survive. "I do not say that you want to understand me, Mrs. Muller," the Rumanian tells Sarah. "I say only that you do understand me." Although some latter-day viewers infer that the hero of *Watch on the Rhine* is Jewish, the plight of Germany's Jews is not mentioned in this movie.

While Bette Davis waits for the return of her German hero, Ginger Rogers and her housemates, a cross-section of American womanhood, also await the return of their men in *Tender Comrade* (1943). Edward Dmytryk and Dalton Trumbo, both later members of the Hollywood Ten, directed and wrote this story of a group of war wives who work in an aircraft factory and live together in a co-op. The film focuses on their home life, complete with refugee German housekeeper, and teaches several strong lessons about the need for sacrifice, the dangers of hoarding, the reasons for rationing, the importance of keeping mum about troop movements, and the tragedy of the "murder" of German democracy. Ginger Rogers says, "Share and share alike, that's the meaning of democracy" – a line that would later be offered as testimony of "communist content" – as the women solve their individual problems while working together toward a common goal.

Even Alfred Hitchcock joined the anti-fascist struggle with *Lifeboat* (1944), written by John Steinbeck and Jo Swerling. Like many other movies of the era, *Lifeboat* features a microcosm of humanity – a group of survivors set adrift in a small craft after their ship is sunk by a

German submarine. Tallulah Bankhead plays a glamorous journalist whose chief concern during the disaster is the great photos she's getting – until her camera goes overboard. But she eventually joins the group effort by giving her furs to a freezing mother and offering her jewels for use as a fishing lure. An industrialist automatically and autocratically assumes leadership of the band of suvivors, but he is soon displaced by one of the lifeboat's proles, a sailor whose socialist sympathies prompt Bankhead to accuse him of being "a fellow traveler." The group grows dispirited as the lifeboat drifts, and eventually they begin to depend on the strong and confident leadership of the German U-boat captain (Walter Slezak), whom they have rescued. When it finally dawns on them that they've drifted into fascism and been misled by this strong leader, they kill him (lynching was okay for Nazis), concluding *Lifeboat*'s tidy, if somewhat belated, morality tale.

And On to Moscow

As the war went on, a few movies crossed the line into more overt propaganda. President Roosevelt urged them on, pressing first for films about the Asian front, then for movies about our European Allies, especially Russia. *Mission to Moscow* (1943) was made, Jack Warner said, at the specific request of Roosevelt, who wanted to "flatter" Stalin and "keep [him] fighting"[1] as well as to educate the American public. Directed by Michael Curtiz and written by Howard Koch, the team that had made *Casablanca*, the pro-Russian movie was as bad as their earlier film was good.

Mission to Moscow starred Walter Huston as Joseph E. Davies, the real-life American ambassador to the Soviet Union from 1936 to 1941. Davies himself introduces the movie with praise for the Warner brothers, "those great American patriots." Then we see Huston as Davies, happily fishing before President Roosevelt calls him out of retirement to take on an urgent assignment. On his way to Moscow, Davies passes through Germany and is appalled at the regimentation and authoritarianism that held sway there. He watches grimly as Jews wearing identification tags are marched by. The cruel totalitarianism of the enemy is thrown into sharp relief when the ambassador reaches the Russian border, where cheerful soldiers and happy women engineers welcome their American friends with food and laughter. Davies is impressed by the wisdom of the Russian leaders and the bravery of the people while his wife visits women who work in factories, schools, and mines. These details, by the way, were probably not intended to make points for feminism but rather encourage American women to work during the war – another propaganda goal. Davies is like an aging Jefferson Smith who never wakes up to what's going on around him in this glowing portrait of Russia that is strictly party-line propaganda. The purges of the thirties are presented as unimportant exercises carried out only for purposes of internal security. The Hitler-Stalin Nonaggression Pact of 1939 is blamed on American isolationism and European appeasement. Russia's occupation of Finland is explained away as a strategic necessity for which the Soviets had asked – and received – Finland's permission.

Bogged down with narration and stagy explanations of American policy and Soviet politics, and very awkwardly done, *Mission to Moscow* failed as entertainment as well as analysis. The movie industry's trade press nevertheless gave the movie grovelingly good reviews and pointed out the significance of movies "flexing their muscles in human crisis."[2] Bosley Crowther proclaimed it "the most important picture on a political subject any American studio has ever made," but criticized its glowing portrait of the USSR and its sloppy history.[3] Others were less kind, calling it "a mishmash" and "a lot of rot" and denouncing its "cuddly, reverential treatment" of FDR,[4] who was already being given the Abe Lincoln treatment in American films. The Hearst press and Republican presidential candidate Thomas E. Dewey condemned its pro-communism while liberals objected to its Stalinist portrait of Trotsky, and the U.S. Congress was irate at being labeled "a hotbed of profiteering isolationists."[5] Audiences avoided the movie, and Hollywood's most serious attempt at sending a message – approved and encouraged by the President of the United States – bombed.

Samuel Goldwyn didn't do much better with his World War II message movie. *The North Star* (1943), directed by Lewis Milestone and written by Lillian Hellman, is set in a happy and charming Russian village (populated by Dana Andrews, Walter Huston, and Walter Brennan) that is overwhelmed by Nazis (led by Erich von Stroheim). Goldwyn said it was about "people who think and act as do Americans,"[6] and the clear intent was to make the American public more enthusiastic about their Soviet allies. *Time* magazine loyally declared *The North Star* "a cinemilestone"[7] for its portrait of Russian struggle, but the Hearst press dismissed it as communist propaganda, and audiences showed little interest.

MGM and RKO responded to Roosevelt's urgings with *Song of Russia* (1943) and *Days of Glory* (1944), both hyping our Russian allies. Like *Mission to Moscow* and *The North Star*, they flopped, probably not so much because of what they said as because they were bad movies. When American filmmakers tried hardest to make political points, they failed most dismally, perhaps because they were trying too hard to please Washington and not hard enough to please their audiences.

Winding Down the War

As the fighting on the European front drew to a close, Hollywood shifted its attention to the war in the Pacific. In *The Fighting Seabees* (1944) and Edward Dmytryk's *Back to Bataan* (1945), both starring John Wayne, the racist portrayal of the enemy was even more extreme than the depiction of the villainous Nazis of the anti-fascist films.

But by 1944 Hollywood was also looking forward to peacetime with films like *Hail the Conquering Hero*. Preston Sturges wrote and directed this comedy about a hero's son (Eddie Bracken) who is discharged from the marines because he has hay fever. Unable to face the folks back home, he sets out to drown his sorrows, but he is saved by a group of sympathetic marines who decorate him with borrowed medals and send him home. After being welcomed as a hero and drafted as a candidate for mayor, he confesses, but the townspeople are so unaccustomed to hearing the truth from politicians that they continue to believe he's a hero and elect him mayor anyway.

Sturges had never been very positive about politics. His first film, *The Great McGinty* (1940) was about a bum who gained favor with a political boss but ruined his career when true love turned him honest. Sturges later made fun of Hollywood's social concerns in *Sullivan's Travels*. *Hail The Conquering Hero*, however, was basic Capracorn. In this movie, the innocent triumphs for no apparent reason except that he is good, in contrast to the incumbent mayor, who is inept, pretentious, and hypocritical. Even the mayor's wife turns against him, and the well-meaning man who usually runs against the mayor denounces his own dullness and steps aside in favor of the young hero. Room must be made for the returning warriors, the movie tells us. More disturbingly, it also informs us that politics is like love: "You don't need reason." The sophisticated Sturges may have been working with his tongue in his cheek, but audiences loved his film nonetheless.

Wilson was a loftier, if more ponderous, contemplation of post-war politics on an international level. The big biopic of the year was produced for Twentieth Century-Fox by Darryl Zanuck, written by Lamar Trotti, and directed by Henry King. Zanuck, who was determined to make an epic, spent $5 million (a great deal of money in 1944) and employed a cast of 13,000, but *Wilson* was really a one-man movie, starring Alexander Knox as the president. "Sometimes the life of a man mirrors the life of a nation," the film's prologue announces, but

Wilson was not so much about the man as about the peace treaty ending World War I and the need for international cooperation, "the dream of a world united against the dreadful waste of war." Zanuck's epic argued that the League of Nations and collective security might have prevented World War II.

Wilson deserves credit for taking politics seriously, but while the movie's intentions were good, it was long and dull. Personalities, social issues, and political processes were radically oversimplified, and Wilson himself got the Lincoln treatment: he was wise and good while the Europeans were greedy and vindictive and the American isolationists who opposed the League were fools. Right and wrong were never doubted, although the happy ending never came. *Wilson* implied that America had to make that happy ending through the United Nations or face the consequences.

The movie was successful despite its lecturing. Wilson's family and colleagues approved of it, and the film was a top box attraction, winning four major Academy Awards and critical favor. *The New York Times* hoped this "careful and tasteful" motion picture would "inspire millions," and judged it one of the ten best films of the year. The *Times* called its politics "authentic," singling out the exciting scenes at the party convention where Wilson first wins the presidential nomination. Still, the reviewer conceded that the movie was chauvinistic in that it presented an exclusively American viewpoint and gave no credit to European leaders or perspectives.[8]

Not everyone agreed with this assessment, however. *Wilson* created almost as much of a furor in 1944 as *Mission to Moscow* had incited the year before. Republicans and isolationists denounced it as propaganda for FDR's 1944 re-election campaign. Darryl Zanuck, its producer, denied the charge, pointing out that he was himself a Republican who had supported Wendell Willkie, Roosevelt's opponent, in 1940. The film, he said, was his "personal crusade for world peace"[9] and "damned nonpartisan."[10] Still, *Wilson* was not shown to the armed forces because it was judged too partisan in an election year. Protests against this ban led to an act of Congress relaxing restrictions on military screenings. Perhaps in part because of all the controversy, a million people went to see *Wilson* within five weeks of its release, and it earned over $3 million in two years. That was a lot of money in those days, but not enough to cover the $5 million that Zanuck had spent on the epic. The loss, combined with the controversy, may have discouraged Twentieth Century–Fox from making other movies on similar themes.

Retreat from Politics

From *All Quiet on the Western Front* to *Wilson*, America and Hollywood had been through a depression and a war, both of which challenged the nation's way of life and traditional values. These challenges and changes were reflected in the movies, although films may have changed less than did the nation and their audiences. Hollywood tended to cling conservatively to myths about the people, democracy, and great men, rarely questioning the entrenched values, much less the system as a whole. Hollywood's faith in the people was qualified, however, by fear that they could be manipulated and even turned into a mob, as in the anti-lynching movies. Although motion pictures were cynical about politicians, especially fictional ones, who were invariably portrayed as evil, venal, or silly men, Hollywood longed for a strong leader. They relied to some extent on revered historical figures, from Lincoln to Roosevelt and even Wilson and Juarez. But if a great man didn't come along, John Doe would do – someone who was naive, innocent, and previously apolitical, who could iron out minor problems and make the system function properly. Only a few movies like *Our Daily Bread*, *The Grapes of Wrath*, and *Citizen Kane* offered substantial critiques of American society and politics, and even these voices were silenced when the nation went to war and Hollywood dropped all negative images of domestic life to campaign for internationalism and against fascism.

With few exceptions, the propagandistic wartime movies were flops, and most of the exceptions were controversial. As a consequence, Hollywood grew increasingly cautious about sending political messages, for even when quality and profits were highest, the movies came under attack from the politicians who did not share the filmmakers' point of view. Both the House of Representatives and the Senate, for example, accused Hollywood of encouraging war, promoting FDR, or leaning to the left (never the right). Those who made such charges represented a minority, however. Instead of retreating, political filmmakers might have relied on the immense popularity of Roosevelt, the New Deal, and the war effort to sustain the production of more left-leaning films. Of course, the Production Code Administration also kept the pressure on, although a few filmmakers challenged its rules. As early as 1943, Howard Hughes let immoral people have a happy ending in *The Outlaw*, starring Jane Russell.

The close scrutiny of the censors and the intense attacks of the politicians indicated how influential they thought the movies were. And if the tremendous size of the audience was a measure of the influence of films, they were right. But even as their audience was at its largest, filmmakers retreated from political topics. On the one hand, this retreat may have reflected the mood of the country after long years of depression and war. On the other hand, the sheer size of audiences may have led filmmakers to seek maximum profits by avoiding controversial topics. Most likely, producers and studios refused to support political projects because of their wartime disasters and their nervousness about interference from Washington. But the worst was yet to come.

NOTES

1. Rudy Behlmer, ed., *Inside Warner Bros., 1935–1951* (New York: Viking, 1985), p. 290.
2. Cited in Colin Shindler, *Hollywood Goes to War* (London: Routledge & Kegan Paul, 1979), pp. 58–59.
3. *The New York Times*, 30 April 1944.
4. Cited in *Monthly Film Bulletin*, 5 May 1944.
5. David Culbert, ed., *Mission to Moscow* (Madison: University of Wisconsin Press, 1975), p. 16.
6. Ron Harris, *The Thousand Eyes Magazine*, Volume 2, No. 3, 1976, p. 16.
7. *Time*, 2 August 1943.
8. *The New York Times*, 2 August 1944.
9. Thomas J. Knock, "History in Lightning: The Forgotton Film, *Wilson*," in Peter C. Rollins, ed., *Hollywood as Historian* (Lexington: University Press of Kentucky, 1983), p. 95.
10. *Collier's*, 22 July 1944.

"There Are No Leaders but Yourselves"

Post-War Optimism, Liberalism, and Corruption

Hollywood's audience reached a high point in the "golden years" following World War II and then started a long decline from which it has yet to recover. From 1946 to 1948, an average of 90 million people went to the movies every week, but by 1950 weekly attendance had plummeted to 50 million. As it moved from fat times to lean times, from security to insecurity, the film industry experienced more changes in those few years than in any other period in its history. Not surprisingly, this turbulence was apparent in the political films of the era, which started with optimistic crusading, grew increasingly cynical, and then moved away from political topics almost completely.

Hollywood and America started the post-war years cheerfully enough. The United States had won the war, and its economy was strong again, making it the most powerful nation in the world. The government rewarded its triumphant veterans with cheap loans for education and homes. People spent their wartime savings on cars, refrigerators, washers, and television sets. The suburbs burgeoned and a baby boom started. But the good times weren't perfect. President Roosevelt, the dominant political figure of over a decade, was gone, replaced by a man who was as yet unproven. Inflation, labor unrest, and a recession resulting from reduced military spending caused economic jitters for a nation that had not yet forgotten the Depression. Veterans had problems coming home; women had problems staying home after being pushed out of the work force when the men returned from the war. Racial tension increased as blacks, more assertive after their wartime experience, moved out of the South and grew impatient for equality. External threats were even more frightening. The Soviet Union expanded into Eastern Europe; guerrilla wars broke out in Greece and Turkey; China went communist; and in 1949, Russia

All the King's Men (1949)

exploded an atom bomb and America began to worry about Soviet spies.

By 1947, Hollywood had become a special target for the anti-communist crusaders. Investigations continued through the mid-1950s, and Hollywood's once-solid resistance began to crumble. The Production Code, still rigorously applied despite challenges like *The Outlaw*, was supplemented with a list of instructions cautioning against criticisms of capitalism or glorification of "the collective" or "the common man."[1] Meanwhile, in 1944, the Justice Department renewed legal action against the eight major film companies for delaying implementation of the pre-war agreement to reduce their near-monopoly on production, distribution, and exhibition. Five years later, the studios were ordered to divest themselves of their theater chains but allowed to retain control of production and distribution. They had five years to implement the change which, when completed, denied them their captive exhibitors and thus their captive audiences. Theater owners competed for films by bidding and could refuse to show studio productions that they perceived as inferior or controversial. This development seemed to discourage the studios from taking risks on political subjects, for few were produced after divestiture was implemented in 1954, but it also gave independent producers access to audiences. As a result, independents were the major source of political films by the late 1950s.

Light and Dark

As the nation and the film industry fluctuated between extremes of optimism and dread, so did the movies. The musicals of the late forties and early fifties expressed the optimistic viewpoint while the style that came to be known as *film noir* expressed the dread.

From *Meet Me in St. Louis* through *Easter Parade*, *On the Town*, and *Singin' in the Rain*, Hollywood sang and danced its way through the post-war era, led by Judy Garland, Gene Kelly, and Fred Astaire. MGM studios virtually specialized in the genre. Less political than the musicals of the early thirties, these movies presented an almost perfect world in which problems could be solved simply by making an effort.

Film noir was just the reverse, as dark in its mood as in its lighting. In movies like *The Strange Love of Martha Ivers*, *The Postman Always Rings Twice*, and *The Lady from Shanghai*, dangerous women (Barbara Stanwyck, Lana Turner, Rita Hayworth) lured weak men (Van Heflin, John Garfield, Orson Welles) to their fate, often aided and abetted by charming villains. Although not overtly political, these movies reflected the post-war sense of social breakdown and dislocation and commented on class structure through their use of rich villains and poor victims. There was nothing reformist about these films, however. They portrayed a big, bad world where sinners – especially grasping women – were punished. Among these motion pictures, only Abraham Polonsky's *Force of Evil* (1948) stands out as a forthright condemnation of the corrupting qualities of capitalism.

Another little group of post-war movies combined the optimism and pessimism of the times in their treatment of social issues. Their look and point-of-view often resembled *film noir*, but their resolution was almost always more optimistic as good people overcame adversity through love, understanding, or individual effort. One of the first and most important of these social problem films was *The Best Years of Our Lives* (1946), a melodrama about three soldiers adjusting to civilian life. This sad and moving film criticized the treatment of returning vets by callous civilians bent on business as usual, but it offered no solutions other than the assurance that the love of a good woman and the passage of time would heal all wounds. *Pride of the Marines* (1945) and *Till the End of Time* (1946) tackled the same subject, but *The Best Years of Our Lives*, produced by Samuel Goldwyn, was the most successful of these films, becoming the top box office attraction of 1947, winning the approbation of the critics, and sweeping the Academy Awards.

Director Edward Dmytryk combined the problems of veterans with racial bigotry in *Crossfire* (1947), the story of a demented ex-soldier who murders a Jew. Anti-Semitism is also the theme of Elia Kazan's *Gentleman's Agreement* (1947). In this movie, Gregory Peck plays a writer who pretends to be Jewish for eight weeks. He confronts crass prejudice in hotels and eventually condemns even those who claim to disapprove of anti-Semitism but who say nothing and thereby condone it. "Don't treat me to any more lessons in tolerance. I'm sick of it!" his fiancée pouts when he accuses her of being one of the latter. She denounces her own hypocrisy in time for a happy ending, though, as Gregory Peck returns to being WASP and the lovers are reunited.

In *Pinky* (1949), Kazan dealt with the problems of a young black woman trying to pass as white. Prejudice against blacks was also the subject of *Home of the Brave* (1949), directed by Mark Robson, and *Intruder in the Dust* (1949), an adaptation of William Faulkner's novel. *Home of the Brave* dealt with the discrimination suffered by a black GI, while *Intruder* reiterated the anti-lynching theme of the thirties but faced up to the fact that most of the victims were black. The image of American Indians was rehabilitated in *Devil's Doorway* (1949) with Robert Taylor as an Indian Civil War veteran victimized by prejudice, and in *Broken Arrow* (1950), with Jeff Chandler playing Cochise and

James Stewart as the government agent who understands him. Hollywood had at last returned to the noble savages of *The Vanishing American*, although by the fifties, they appeared to be pretty much like the rest of us and usually ended up settling down on farms, as in Robert Aldrich's *Apache* (1954). Hispanics received less attention, but Joseph Losey, later a target of the HUAC witch-hunters, directed *The Lawless* (1950), an update of *The Grapes of Wrath* centering on Mexican-American migrants, and Elia Kazan cast Marlon Brando as the lead in *Viva Zapata!* (1952), to which we will return.

Similar well-intentioned movies about racism appeared throughout the fifties. In 1950, Sidney Poitier made his debut in *No Way Out*, while Ginger Rogers and Ronald Reagan did their bit in the anti-KKK *Storm Warning*. Even *Giant* (1956), a precursor of *Dallas* and *Dynasty*, starring Rock Hudson, Elizabeth Taylor, and James Dean, preached a mild sermon about equality for women and Hispanics ("Juana's a great little gal, but . . ."). Poitier was back in *The Defiant Ones* (1958), and the *Pinky* story got a reprise in *Imitation of Life* (1959). A different social problem, juvenile delinquency, had its day in 1955 in *The Blackboard Jungle* and *Rebel Without a Cause*.

Most of these movies seem transparently didactic today. They rarely got beneath the surface of the problems they tackled, and their solutions were invariably based on the assumption that we're all alike anyway. Veterans, Jews, blacks, Indians, Hispanics, and juvenile delinquents were all portrayed as human beings in need of understanding. Prejudice was bad, according to these films, but solution was simple because the problem went no deeper than ignorance. Racism was not institutional but personal; delinquency was not social but individual.

Although many of these films seem naive today, they were taken seriously in the fifties, and some of them were big hits. *The Best Years of Our Lives, Crossfire, Gentleman's Agreement*, and *Pinky* all did well with the public and the critics and won Academy Award nominations. Both *Best Years* and *Gentleman's Agreement* won the Oscar as best picture. These movies were also highly controversial, however. A Texas theater owner was jailed for screening *Pinky*. *The Blackboard Jungle* was condemned as communist propaganda because it presented a negative picture of the United States. So were several other problem films including Edward Dmytryk's *Crossfire*, Abraham Polonsky's *Force of Evil*, Elia Kazan's *Gentleman's Agreement* and *Pinky*, and Stanley Kramer's *Home of the Brave* and *The Defiant Ones*. These movies seem mild now, but they were testing the limits then, and at least one study found that films like *Crossfire, Gentleman's Agreement*, and *Pinky* had a slightly positive effect on viewers' tolerance of the minority groups that were their subjects. The oversimplifications of these problem films is put into historical context by Leonard Quart and

Albert Auster, who argue that they are "yet another sign of the overwhelming optimism of the era; an optimism which refused to see any problem as insoluble."[2]

Walking Away from Politics

With the Justice Department anti-trust suit in progress and congressional investigations beginning in 1947, Hollywood tended to steer clear of politics and limit its messages to tolerance and understanding. Filmmakers rarely exercised their power to fight back. It must have seemed easier just to keep quiet for a while and wait for the politicians to go away, and so Hollywood avoided political films, except for a few comedies and stories about bosses or martyrs, all fairly safe bets.

Some, like *The Senator Was Indiscreet* (1947), were throwbacks to the thirties. Directed by George S. Kaufman and written by Charles MacArthur, a team responsible for many thirties comedies, this broad satire was produced by Nunnally Johnson, who wrote the script for *The Grapes of Wrath*. William Powell plays a senator who seeks his party's presidential nomination but loses out when he misplaces his little black book, which is full of dark secrets about the party. It was a standard portrait of dirty politics.

It took Frank Capra to push the movie view of politics into the post-war era with his prescient *State of the Union* (1948). Like his earlier film, *It's a Wonderful Life*, this movie lacked the frothy Capracorn that had marked his work during the 1930s. The post-war world seemed more dangerous to Capra, and his solutions were neither simple nor happy.

In *State of the Uniion*, Grant Matthews (Spencer Tracy) is a rich airplane manufacturer and all-round good guy who is drawn into politics by his mistress, Kay Thorndyke (Angela Lansbury), a powerful Republican publishing heiress with a lust for power. Matthews, a populist and an idealist, is eager to bring his good works to government. When he becomes a candidate for president, Matthews needs his estranged wife (Katharine Hepburn) by his side, and she voluntarily complies. Not a normal politician, Matthews says just what he thinks, but this only increases his popularity. He advocates world government and condemns interest groups for caring only about themselves and not the greater good. Thorndyke, his publisher-mentor, puts him under the guidance of a cynical and corrupt political hack (Adolphe Menjou), who introduces Matthews to some harsh political realities: "The only difference between Democrats and Republicans is that they're in and we're out." When the candidate is impressed by public admiration, the hack is incredulous. "Those letters are just from *people*," he sneers, "not state chairmen!" He soon has his candidate stumping for support from labor, farmers, business, ethnics, southerners, and professional politicians. Pushed by the publisher and the hack, Matthews begins to want the nomination enough to make any deal to get it.

He is kept loyal to his own principles by his wife and her ally, a wisecracking, good-hearted journalist (Van Johnson). These two, but especially Hepburn as the wife, function as Capra's voice in *State of the Union*, encouraging the candidate to say what he thinks and put his faith in "the common man." Capra also makes his standard "populist" points by giving waiters and maids a chance to express their faith in Matthews. But the candidate is seduced and ready to sell out until he sees his wife sell out herself by making a televised speech about him that she doesn't believe. In the end, he recoils with disgust and announces that he will dog the politicians to make them tell the truth, but he will not be a candidate himself. Husband and wife are reunited; publisher and hack move on to their next victim.

State of the Union stirred up almost as much controversy as Capra's *Mr. Smith*, partly because, unlike other fictional political films up to that time, it named real people and real parties. Some saw it as pro-Truman because it seemed to attack the old, Harding-style Republican machine. Capra may have felt sympathy for Truman as the closest the nation has come to putting one of his idealized common men in the White House, but Truman was hardly free of the taint of machine politics. At any rate, the controversy failed to stimulate public interest in *State of the Union*, which was only a mild success despite good reviews.

State of the Union deserved better because it is noticeably more sophisticated than earlier political films. Capra's portrait of interest group politics and his hint at the future importance of television put the film ahead of its time, but he had also moved away from his earlier faith in the common man and his depictions of good-hearted citizens triumphing over corrupt politicians. Here he presented a political world ruled by a power elite represented by publisher Lansbury, party hack Menjou, and a gaggle of character actors who spoke for various vested interests. In the thirties, Mr. Smith had stood, fought, and won; in the late forties, Grant Matthews saved his integrity by walking away. The people supported him, but they were not strong enough to defeat the organizational elite – a cynical view of politics that was all the more powerful coming from Frank Capra.

Capra wasn't the only cynic, however. Billy Wilder directed and co-wrote an acute satire on American politics in *A Foreign Affair* (1948). In this comedy, Jean Arthur is a member of a congressional delegation investigating the morale of American troops in post-war Berlin. She gets involved with an army captain (John Lund) whose German mistress (Marlene Dietrich) provides a sharp contrast between American naiveté and European world-weariness.

The most successful post-war political comedy, however, was *Born Yesterday* (1950), directed by George Cukor. After a shot of the Capitol tells us where we are, we meet Harry (Broderick Crawford), a junk man who has become a big time "dealer in scrap metals" in Washington and who has attempted to further his own interests by bribing some congressmen. With him is Billie (Judy Holliday), his crass mistress. Harry persuades Paul (William Holden), a reporter, to coach Billie and make her more presentable; Paul agrees in order to spy on Harry. "Harry's a menace," Paul instructs Billie. "The whole history of the world is the story of the struggle between the selfish and the unselfish. . . . All that's bad around us is bred by selfishness. Sometimes selfishness is a cause, an organized force, even a government, and then it's called fascism." Paul, on the other hand, represents intellect, enlightenment, altruism, even democracy – plus he's cute. He wins Billie's affection, and she helps him expose Harry. Good triumphs over evil, and *Born Yesterday* makes it clear that Harry is out of date when even his cynical attorney tells him that despite "a few bad apples," congressmen are basically honest. Cukor's film was well received by both the public and the critics and is still a favorite, thanks largely to Judy Holliday's performance, for which she won an Oscar.

Broderick Crawford had won an Academy Award the year before for his portrayal of Willie Stark in *All the King's Men*, a fictionalized version of the career of Huey Long, the populist demagogue who dominated Louisiana politics for a generation. Robert Rossen, one of Hollywood's most progressive filmmakers, wrote and directed the movie based on Robert Penn Warren's novel. Its populism was more complicated than that of Frank Capra's earlier films in that it had a dark side – the public's tolerance of corruption and propensity to fascism.

Willie Stark begins as an idealistic man of the people. He runs for office but loses to the corrupt local organization, so he adapts and comes to terms with the machine: "I'd make a deal with the devil if it'll help me carry out my program." When he becomes governor, he fulfills his promises, building roads and hospitals for the rural folk who elected him. The ends seem to justify the means, and we're on his side, but not for long. Willie soon becomes cynical and corrupt, a demagogue who misleads and manipulates his people, misusing and wasting their tax money on useless projects. He crudely compromises the old elite, represented by an affluent, educated, liberal family, when he takes their daughter (Joanne Dru) as his mistress and their son (John Ireland) as his aide. The adoring masses are symbolized by another of Stark's aides (Mercedes McCambridge), who is blindly in love with him and resolutely loyal. These three are sympathetic characters, but it is apparent that their own weakness has betrayed them. Willie Stark is murdered in the end, punished for his transgressions, as was Huey Long.

Power corrupts, this movie tells us – not a new theme in American political films, but one that was frequently reiterated after the war. *All the King's Men* also warned against putting too much faith in leaders. The film was careful, however, to make it clear that the fault was not only in the leaders but also in the corrupt and decadent society that accepted them. Fascism could arise in America, in other words, if the masses put their faith in the wrong leaders.

Aside from the Academy Award-winning performances of Broderick Crawford and Mercedes McCambridge, Rossen's preachy film hasn't held up well over time. Some critics noted its preachiness in 1949, but others admired the film; the *Motion Picture Herald* even praised it for *not* preaching or moralizing. *The New York Times* thought it was "raw, racy ... pictorial journalism," a "rip-roaring film," and included it among the year's ten best.[3]

All the King's Men was followed by other films about dirty politics. *The Washington Story* (1952) was a fairly standard tale of corruption and muckraking journalism while *A Lion Is in the Streets* (1953) reiterated the condemnation of demagoguery first sounded in *All the King's Men*. *Lion* stars James Cagney as Hank Martin, the ambitious man of the people who betrays his own supporters to win the favor of the machine. When even this fails, he leads an armed mob on the state capitol to demand that the legislature resolve a tie vote for the governorship in his favor. Hank's wife and an aristocratic friend, both college-educated liberals, take his side until he goes too far. Then his wife reveals one of his dirty secrets, and a woman whose husband he has misused finally kills him in revenge. The dangers of strong leaders and mobs are emphasized in *A Lion Is in the Streets*, but the condemnation of society is not as complete as in *All the King's Men*. Good people see through Hank all along; some walk away and others, including his wife, finally help to destroy him. But even though this film showed some faith in society and the political system, it was not as successful as *All the King's Men*, perhaps because it was too similar.

Elia Kazan's *Viva Zapata!* (1952), written by John Steinbeck, was superficially unlike all these films, yet it's final message was similar: power corrupts. Marlon Brando plays Emiliano Zapata, the peasant who became one of Mexico's great revolutionary heroes, not out of any profound political beliefs, according to the film, but to win land for his people. The revolution succeeds, but like Pancho Villa before him

(*Villa*, 1934), Zapata loses his faith in other leaders and reluctantly accepts the presidency after another round of fighting. He is encouraged in all this by Fernando (Joseph Wiseman), a bizarre-looking political manipulator who is dressed in black and apparently intended as a stereotypical Marxist revolutionary. Zapata soon feels he is being corrupted by power, like other leaders before him, so he resigns and returns to his people where eventually, inevitably, he must again lead a guerrilla revolution. The new rulers know how to end this one, however. "Cut off the head of the snake, and the body will die," Fernando advises. "Kill Zapata, and your problem's solved." Zapata, however, has trained his people not to need him. "You've always looked for leaders," he instructs them, "strong men without faults. There aren't any. They're only men like yourselves. They change. They desert. They die. There are no leaders but yourselves. A strong people is the only lasting strength." Zapata goes Christ-like to his death, apparently knowing that he has been betrayed but that his spirit will be an inspiration to his people. "Sometimes," an army officer observes "a dead man can be a terrible enemy."

Viva Zapata! was nominated for five Academy Awards and was a modest box office success. Both of those facts may be surprising for a movie about a Mexican revolutionary released at the height of McCarthyism in the conservative 1950s, but this film's message was more romantic than revolutionary, and the movie never came to terms with the root causes of the Mexican Revolution; its class conflict was obscured by the film's emphasis on straightforward corruption. Evil men subverted the revolution, presumably in their own interests, and Kazan later claimed that these characters made the movie anti-communist. In the end, *Viva Zapata!* was a mishmash of elitist hero-worship and soppy reliance on "the people."

As in *State of the Union*, *All the King's Men*, and *A Lion Is in the Streets*, the bottom line in *Viva Zapata!* was that power corrupts. Like Grant Matthews, Emiliano Zapata had to walk away from power to retain his integrity. Such conclusions condemned not only power but politics as well, saying that good men couldn't remain involved with government. Even at their most optimistic, these films could promise only that evil leaders like Willie Stark and Hank Martin would be destroyed if they went too far. Earlier films had criticized the corruption of politics and politicians, but they always provided a solution, usually in the form of a heroic leader or "the people." The movies of the late forties and early fifties were more profoundly cynical. Great leaders like Roosevelt, good programs like the New Deal, even faith in the people, were no longer enough. Post-war optimism had already turned to pessimism, even cynicism, especially about politics. This bleak view would dominate political films for three decades.

NOTES

1. Ayn Rand, "Screen Guide for Americans," in John Cogley, ed., *Report on Blacklisting I: The Movies* (New York: Fund for the Republic, 1956).
2. Leonard Quart and Albert Auster, *American Film and Society Since 1945* (New York: Praeger, 1984).
3. *Motion Picture Herald*, 5 November 1949; *The New York Times*, 9 November 1949.

My Son John (1952)

7

"Sooner or Later One Has to Take Sides"

The Anti-Communist Crusade

The anti-political films of the late forties and early fifties played to an apolitical nation, a nation that chose a nonpolitician, the moderately conservative Dwight Eisenhower, to serve as its president from 1952 to 1960. This was a prosperous time for America, a time for big cars, television sets, suburban houses, and large families. Joan Mellen, author of *Big Bad Wolves*, suggests that the films of the fifties reflected this prosperity in their "glorification and reinforcement of individual success and crass material gain."[1] But Americans in the early fifties also had to come to terms wth an increasingly urban and corporate nation. The old emphasis on individualism had to be tempered to suit the new organizational context, which demanded conformity and consensus, and this change, too, showed up in the movies. America in the fifties was also adjusting to being a world power. The cold war grew hot in Korea in 1950 and cold again when that "limited war" ended in stalemate in 1953. At home the threat of communism produced fear that bordered on paranoia, and that fear reinforced consensus and conformity and gave birth to a fervid anti-communism that culminated in the career of Senator Joseph McCarthy.

As it tried to adapt to these changes, the film industry worried about the economic impact of the studios' divestiture of their theater chains and, even more, about television. Weekly movie attendance dropped from 90 million a week in 1948 to 40 million in 1958. TV broke the habit of regular moviegoing. A worried Hollywood tried to lure audiences back with extravagant historical epics and technical innovations that TV couldn't match, like VistaVision and 3-D. "Movies are better than ever," a desperate advertising campaign declared.

The result of these elaborate efforts and declining box office receipts was fewer, more costly films designed to draw huge audiences. Annual production fell from 383 films in 1950 to 154 in 1960. And the more spectacular Hollywood films became, the less political they were, at least in terms of overt and contemporary politics. The epics, westerns, and science fiction movies of the era often had political content, however. Michael Wood points out that the persecution of minorities is the theme of *Quo Vadis*, *The Robe*, and *Ben Hur*, while Stanley Kubrick's *Spartacus* delivers a lesson about revolution.[2] Other film historians have noted the allegorical politics of westerns like *High Noon* and sci-fi movies like *The Thing* and *Invasion of the Body Snatchers*.

More and more, the studios avoided explicitly political films, however, since they did not draw in the huge audiences the studios needed. Independent filmmakers like Stanley Kramer made a few political films during the fifties, and the lack of studio controls may have let the independents express their ideas more freely, but their political output remained modest, because the caution of investors and distributors made it hard to raise the necessary money.

As it turned out, however, Hollywood had another reason to avoid political films.

HUAC and Hollywood

The House Un-American Activities Committee discovered Hollywood in 1939 when it held its first hearing on subversion in the film industry. The committee returned in 1947 to begin investigations that resulted in a *cause célèbre*, the Hollywood Ten – a group of moviemakers who were jailed on a charge of contempt of Congress for refusing to talk about their political activities. The Hollywood Ten included Edward Dmytryk, Dalton Trumbo, and John Howard Lawson. Hollywood at first rallied to their defense, then cravenly backed off and introduced the infamous blacklist, systematically refusing to employ men and women who had allegedly supported leftist causes. The investigations continued until well into the fifties, destroying many careers, helping others, and influencing the kinds of movies that were, and were not, made.

The film industry was not the only major American institution that was investigated by the anti-communist crusaders, but it was a special attraction because of the massive press coverage it produced and because of the presumed power of the movies. Besides, Hollywood really was a center of liberal and even communist political activity. The Communist party had made the industry a special organizing target in 1936, a move that reflected Lenin's belief in the power of cinema. Proclaiming that movies are "the weapon of mass culture," the party organizers urged their recruits to at least "keep anti-Soviet agitprop" out of the movies they worked on.[3] The Communist party had some short-term recruiting success during the Depression, the New Deal years, and the Spanish Civil War, but news of Stalin's purges and the Nazi-Soviet Nonaggression Pact stopped its advances. In the 1950s, HUAC finished it off.

Communist infiltration of Hollywood was never very successful, however, and the investigators probably knew it. They found a lot of film people who leaned to the left, but they never came up with much evidence of undue party influence on the movies. They kept looking, however, because they were less interested in reality than in publicity, and glamorous Hollywood provided plenty of that. Besides, the investigations gave ambitious, conservative congressmen like Richard Nixon a chance to attack people they didn't like much anyway – for many of Hollywood's elite were rich, Jewish, liberal, Democratic, and intellectually arrogant.

The HUAC investigations provided an opportunity for pipsqueak politicians to bring mighty Hollywood to its knees, and they did. Dozens were jailed, usually for contempt of Congress – in other words, for refusing to testify against their friends. Others were forced to inform on friends and co-workers in order to save their own careers. Many were ruined by blacklisting. A rich and mighty industry caved in, turned itself inside out, surrendered its workers to the committee's witch-hunters, and denied employment to talented people because of alleged past associations with communism.

No segment of the industry held out against HUAC, but then, Hollywood has never been brave in the face of adverse public opinion, perhaps not surprisingly given its dependence on the public. Even the unions joined the purge, after initially resisting. "Do they [HUAC] expect us to constitute ourselves as a little FBI of our own and determine just who is a commie and who isn't?" Ronald Reagan reasonably demanded as president of the Screen Actors Guild (SAG), but soon he, too, was testifying that there were cliques in SAG that "follow the Communist party line."[4] Liberals joined the purge, too, and Hollywood Jews became particularly vigorous anti-communists because they were afraid the attacks would turn anti-Semitic.[5] Once the united front was broken, every member of the film industry was on his or her own.

Some, like director Elia Kazan, cooperated fully. Others, like writer Dalton Trumbo, resisted and went to jail. Still others, like playwright Lillian Hellman, talked about their own activities but refused to name others.

Ironically, the investigators found little evidence of subversion in the testimony of those who were willing to talk. Walt Disney alleged that the Cartoonists Guild had tried to "subvert" Mickey Mouse. Ginger

Rogers's mother testified that her daughter had been given the line, "Share and share alike – that's democracy," in *Tender Comrade* (see Chapter 5), a film written by Dalton Trumbo and directed by Edward Dmytryk, both members of the Hollywood Ten. Conservative novelist Ayn Rand cited "a suspicious number of smiling children" in *Song of Russia* and also pointed out certain suspicious elements in *Mission to Moscow* and *The North Star*.[6] All three movies were transparently pro-Russian, however, because they had been made with government encouragement to strengthen the U.S.-Soviet alliance during World War II. They weren't hits, and they were poor evidence of a communist conspiracy.

For all their efforts, HUAC never came up with much evidence of communist propaganda in American movies, much less a massive conspiracy. Most of those accused had worked on patriotic war movies as well as projects that reflected a liberal ideology. In fact, Hollywood's radicals never got much beyond defending President Roosevelt and attacking fascism. Dorothy Jones's detailed analysis of 300 films on which Hollywood "Reds" worked revealed that some were "vaguely liberal," but none contained actual communist propaganda. Further-more, "none of the 159 films credited over a period of years to the Hollywood Ten contained communist propaganda" or were cited by the conservative MPAA for such content. Jones argued that the collegial method of making films fragmented responsibility and muted any propaganda, while "the habitual caution of moviemakers with respect to film content" and the "self-regulating practices of the motion picture industry as carried on by the Motion Picture Association" were further preventatives.[7]

HUAC, however, did not require evidence to act. Many progressive film-workers were driven out of the industry after the 1947 hearings, and many more followed after another round of hearings that began in 1951. A few committed suicide, some were imprisoned, others went into exile, and many merely went underground. Those who continued working avoided political subjects or social issues. Professor Jones discovered that while fully 28 percent of Hollywood productions in 1947 dealt with "social and psychological themes," only 9.2 percent fit into this category by 1954. She concluded that the HUAC attack was based less on real concern with the communist threat than on a "fear . . . of movies getting serious about social and political problems."[8] Besides digging through Hollywood's past, the investigations intended to influence its future, and they did.

Hollywood Joins the Anti-Communist Crusade

Hollywood made at least thirty-three anti-communist films between 1947 and 1954,[9] although many more scored anti-red points allegorically or featured communist villains. These productions, peaking in number just after the 1947 and 1951 hearings, suggest that the film industry got the hint when HUAC asked director Leo McCarey, a cooperative witness, if he thought Hollywood made enough anti-communist films.

First off the starting block was *The Iron Curtain* (1948), a box office failure produced by Darryl Zanuck and directed by William Wellman. This was a traditional espionage story in which the communist characters were so villainous that outraged leftists picketed it when it opened. The following year saw the release of three box office flops: *The Red Menace*, *The Red Danube*, and *I Married a Communist*, a Howard Hughes production starring Robert Ryan, which *Time* magazine referred to as "a celluloid bullet aimed at the USSR."[10] This movie also attacked the West Coast dockworkers union, which then had communist leaders, and it was allegedly used to test the politics of various directors, thirteen of whom refused to work on it.[11] When the film failed, Hughes withdrew it, edited it so as to deemphasize its politics, and then released it as *The Woman on Pier 13*, but it was no more successful. Despite their failure, these movies entrenched the "dirty commie" stereotype. Sleazy, immoral, often fat and effeminate, these characters left no doubt that they were bad guys, and audiences saw them over and over in the fifties, just as they had seen the same stereotypes as Nazis a decade earlier.

A somewhat less overtly anti-communist film, *The Fountainhead*, was also released in 1949. This one was directed, perhaps surprisingly, by King Vidor, the progressive maker of *The Big Parade* and *Our Daily Bread*. The principal source of the conservatism in *The Fountainhead*, however, was not Vidor but the reactionary author of the story, Ayn Rand. She was a leader of the arch-conservative, anti-communist Motion Picture Alliance for the Preservation of American Ideals and the formulator of the "Screen Guide for Americans." Published to coincide with the 1947 HUAC hearings as a supplement to the MPAA's production code, Rand's guide advised filmmakers not to "smear the free-enterprise system . . . success" or "industrialists," not to "deify the 'common man,' " and not to "glorify the collective."[12]

The Fountainhead reflects these directives in its story of Howard Roark (Gary Cooper), an avant-garde architect who is nearly hounded out of his profession by traditionalists and conformists. He gets a few jobs and becomes a modest success, but when his design for a public housing project is altered, he blows up the building. At the trial that follows, he makes an impassioned plea for artistic integrity and individual rights. Incredibly, the jurors swallow this dynamiter's line and let him off.

The Fountainhead was a clear expression of Rand's right-wing libertarianism. The enemy was the public, whipped up by cynical media manipulators. The declared intent of one of them, improbably an architecture critic, was to raise the collective and destroy the individual. But despite the movie's condemnation of the masses and public opinion, in the end Roark demanded public approval for his act of destruction and got it from the jury and a courtroom audience.

Thanks to its often ludicrous sexuality, *The Fountainhead* has become a camp classic, but contemporary critics didn't think it was funny. "The most asinine and inept movie that has come from Hollywood for years," sneered *The New Yorker*[13]; "long-winded, complicated preachment ... pretentious ... turgid ... twaddle," agreed *The New York Times*.[14] The critics certainly didn't feel compelled to please HUAC by praising a right-wing film.

The Fountainhead was unusually indirect, however, in its attack on communism. Far more typical was *Big Jim McLain* (1952) with John Wayne as a HUAC agent purging communists from Hawaii. Production of these anti-communist films peaked with thirteen in 1952 alone, just a year after HUAC renewed its investigation. One of the best of these was *My Son John*, Leo McCarey's response to HUAC.

McCarey's movie is about the all-American Jefferson family, played by familiar actors in familiar parts. Dean Jagger is the American Legionnaire father, Helen Hayes the devoutly Catholic mother, and Robert Walker their misled son John. When the intellectual, college-educated John comes home for a visit and makes sarcastic remarks about the American Legion, his father questions John's Americanism. Then a visit from the FBI worries Mom, who is reassured when John swears his loyalty on her Bible. "John stands for everything I stand for," she explains. "He's just a liberal. Saint Paul was a liberal." Dad isn't so sure, though. "How's your supper coming?" he asks his wife, sending her scurrying away so he can have a man-to-man talk with his son. They argue, John makes some anti-American remarks, and Dad hits him with a Bible. When John returns to Washington, his mother follows him to return a key he has left behind. Learning from the FBI that the key is for the apartment of a female spy, Mom sneaks away, finds that the key works, and confronts her son. He confesses to having an affair, but denies that he is a spy. The unbelieving mother turns him in to the FBI, then with rosary in hand, tearfully begs him to confess. "Take him away," she says when he refuses. "You have to be punished,

John." The FBI agent urges him to "Use whatever free will you have. Give up. Name names." John escapes, then remorsefully phones the FBI and agrees to turn himself in and become an informer. On his way, the communists shoot up his taxi, which crashes ostentatiously on the steps of the Lincoln Memorial. Fortunately, he has left a tape-recorded confession, which is melodramatically played for the graduating class at his alma mater.

Like other films of this cycle, *My Son John* casts suspicion on intellectuals and liberals, who are perceived as easy dupes for communists. The film disapproves of John for rushing off to see his egghead professor when he first comes home instead of staying with his parents, who represent the traditional American values of patriotism, religion, and family. John is advised to emulate the simple-minded patriotism of his father and "think with your heart, not your head," as his mother puts it. Nobody in this film does much thinking, however. The parents are deadheads, and the communists, although they are supposedly intellectuals, have lost all capacity to think for themselves. That's okay, though, because the trustworthy FBI is ever-present to take care of things, even though one agent admits that their methods are often criticized by "those with something to hide."

My Son John was better than most of the anti-communist movies, although its thinking was muddled and its plot was jumbled, possibly because Robert Walker died before the film was completed. The critics noted both flaws. Bosley Crowther called it "cultural vigilantism." The father was a drunk and the mother a "stool pigeon" who took the FBI's word over that of her own son. Further, the film endorsed the father's "stubborn bigotry" and took "a snide attitude toward intellectuals."[15] But even though the critics didn't like *My Son John*, Hollywood signaled its approval by nominating McCarey's original story for an Academy Award, perhaps for HUAC's benefit. McCarey himself described his movie as the story of a typical American family in which "one of the kids gets too bright." Remarkably, he thought the film had a happy ending, saying, "I've never yet ended a film on a note of futility."[16] John is dead and his family is broken, but McCarey saw John's tape-recorded speech as a kind of redemption. Better dead than red!

My Son John was one of the last of the crusading anti-communist films. By 1954, Senator McCarthy had brought about his own downfall through his investigation of the army and his attacks on the president. HUAC also faded away. The cold war went on and so did the blacklist, but few anti-communist movies were made after 1953, partly because the pressure was off and also because audiences had not flocked to the earlier films.

One of the last of the cycle, a film that was both behind and ahead of its time, was *The Quiet American* (1957), an adaptation of Graham Greene's novel, given a significant twist by writer-director Joseph Mankiewicz. The scene is Vietnam in the early fifties, with the French fighting a communist-nationalist revolution. The narrator (Michael Redgrave) is a British journalist cynically observing the decline of European imperialism and the rise of American power and the Third World. He tells the story of an American, improbably and badly played by Audie Murphy. Caught between the two men and the worlds they represent is a Vietnamese girl (Georgia Moll) who spurns the European when she falls in love with the American.

The film follows Greene's novel closely at first. The American arrives in Saigon spouting off his professor's theory about the need for "a third force" that is neither imperialist nor communist. The journalist presumes he is an agent. In the book, this is true and he is destroyed when his plot goes awry, but Mankiewicz balked at this anti-American message. "I have no politics," the European journalist says, but a nasty communist agent persuades him that the American is aiding terrorist murderers and insists that "sooner or later, one has to take sides." The reporter gives in, losing his professional objectivity and aiding the communists, not only to prevent terrorism but also to destroy his rival. The American turns out to be innocent, of course. He's merely a do-gooder who imports food, not bombs. A French policeman explains that "the idea had to be murdered," apparently meaning that aid was as threatening to communists as military intervention.

A few critics liked the *The Quiet American*. Arthur Knight thought Mankiewicz had improved a weak, anti-American book,[17] but *Variety* dismissed it as "too talky" and "literate . . . a toughie to sell to mass audiences."[18]

The anti-communist movies failed less because of their message than because of their sledgehammer delivery. Critics regularly complained about "mouthing ideologies" and slimy communist villains too evil to be credible. They probably also disliked the portrait of intellectuals, which critics consider themselves to be, as easy dupes. Audiences and critics alike saw that these movies oversimplified communism and failed to show why nice guys like Robert Walker were attracted to it. These films, in fact, may have hurt anti-communism more than they helped it.

In Other Words

But Hollywood did not enlist en masse in HUAC's holy war. Dissenters survived and even dared to speak out against the cold war and HUAC's witch-hunt, although they often did so indirectly or allegorically.

High Noon (1952) was a western, but according to Carl Foreman, who wrote it, "What *High Noon* was about at the time, was Hollywood and no other place but Hollywood."[19] Producer Stanley Kramer, a leading Hollywood liberal, and Foreman, who was soon to be blacklisted, were commenting on the filmmakers' abandonment of their colleagues who were under attack by HUAC. This film is about a sheriff (Gary Cooper) who gets no help from the townspeople when a vengeful gang of killers comes after him. No cavalry arrives representing the federal government, nor do the people rally around their sheriff, as in the populist movies of the thirties. *High Noon* is a bleak story of one man's courage in a cowardly society. Its left-leaning politics were smoothly folded into a movie that became a hit with audiences and critics and picked up Oscars for Cooper's performance and Dmitri Tiompkin's music.

Meanwhile, those who had cooperated with HUAC defended themselves in works like *On the Waterfront* (1954), written by Budd Schulberg, featuring Lee J. Cobb and Leif Erickson, and directed by Elia Kazan, all of whom had named names. Kazan had joined the crusade against communism with *Viva Zapata!* (1952) and *Man on a Tightrope* (1953), in which a Czechoslovakian circus owner tries to escape from communism, but *On the Waterfront* was not so much an anti-communist movie as a vindication of informers. Making an informer into a hero, however, was no mean feat. Stool pigeons had always been disdained in American folklore and movies.

Terry Malloy (Marlon Brando) is the informer in *On the Waterfront*. His girl friend (Eva Marie Saint) and a priest (Karl Malden) urge him to tell a government investigator (Leif Erickson) the truth about the corrupt activities of a union boss (Lee J. Cobb). Terry must choose between his loyalty to friends and co-workers and a higher order represented by the girl, the priest, and the investigator. His choice is simplified when the mob rubs out not only Terry's brother (Rod Steiger), but his pigeons as well.

"The message is clear," Victor Navasky writes. "The injunction against informing is all right as a guideline for an adolescent gang, but it won't do for adults who are obliged to look at each situation in its own moral context. (What's ratting for them is telling the truth for you.) Squealing is relative."[20] Besides, Terry really has no choice, and the audience has no option but to sympathize with him. Not only must he avenge the murder of his brother and loss of his pigeons, but he must fight the corrupt union, win the girl, and please the priest and the investigator.

Beyond its justification of informing, *On the Waterfront* is politically orthodox. Like other movies about politics, it praises individual action and a benign government. It never occurs to Terry, for example, to rally the troops and reform the union from within; collective action simply is not an option. Instead, like a good corporate liberal, he puts himself in the hands of the federal agents. Still, Kazan managed to make *On the Waterfront* and his other socially conscious films complex enough for their messages to be palatable. The public and the critics liked *On the Waterfront*, and it swept the Oscars. Of course, Hollywood's enthusiasm might be explained in part by the number of informers there and also by the fact that some liberals approved of the film's gritty portrait of the working class.

An even grittier movie about the working class was made the same year, however. Funded by a mine workers union, *Salt of the Earth* was a collaborative effort by blacklisted filmmakers including its director, Herbert Biberman. Except for Rosaura Revueltas, a Mexican movie star, and a few American character actors like Will Geer (who later played Grandpa Walton on television), the cast was made up of miners and their families.

In *Salt of the Earth* the Mexican American zinc miners go on strike because Anglo workers in their company's other mines have better pay and working conditions. The company says it "can't afford equality," however, and it uses cheap Mexican labor to keep the Anglos in line. While the men strike over salaries and working conditions, the women meet and independently decide to strike over housing and sanitation in the company town. The men shrug these demands off, saying they're not as important as working conditions, but when a court order prohibits them from picketing and the women replace them, they take over the housework and soon agree to include the women's demands in the bargaining.

The close vote to put the women on the picket line is the turning point that solidifies the community. The miners are aided by their international union and others, but the film makes it clear that they are essentially on their own and treats them with great reverence. Only the company men and the sheriff (Will Geer) come off badly; they are caricatured in a turnabout of Hollywood tradition. The oversimplification of these characters is a weak point of the movie, as is the acting of some of the amateurs in the cast.

Salt of the Earth was remarkable for being staunchly feminist when no movies, liberal or conservative, were feminist, but it was also remarkable that a leftist film was made at all at the height of McCarthyism. It comes as no surprise, then, that the production process was often disrupted. The filmmakers were harassed by gun-carrying townspeople on location, and the Mexican actress who played the lead was deported three times during the shooting of the film. After it was completed, distributors boycotted it and the projectionists union refused to screen it. In the end, *Salt of the Earth* was screened in only eleven theaters, most of them in New York and Los Angeles, and then it was not seen again for a decade. Even now, the film is shown mainly in union halls and at leftist conferences, and it is not listed in most film reference books.

Not surprisingly, *Salt of the Earth* was attacked out of all proportion to the size of its audiences. The American Legion condemned it, and the cinemas showing it were picketed. Film historian Andrew Dowdy remembers being "warned to park blocks away . . . because FBImen were taking down license plate numbers at the theater."[21] *Variety* screamed that the Russians had to be prevented from getting prints or they would use the movie as anti-American propaganda,[22] but other reviews were more balanced. The *New York Herald Tribune* thought the film was good, despite its "loaded" message.[23] *Time* conceded that "within the propagandistic limits it sets," it was "a vigorous work of art" from which "social anger hisses."[24] Whatever its flaws, *Salt of the Earth* provided an alternative vision of workers and unions and were particularly notable for its feminism. Many Americans shared its political perspective, a perspective that they rarely saw on film. Nor did most of them see *Salt of the Earth*. And Hollywood, of course, took note of its fate.

But that did not prevent a parting shot from the left: Daniel Taradash's *Storm Center* (1956), "a sure loser as the only attack on HUAC ever made in a Hollywood studio," according to Andrew Dowdy.[25] In this movie, Bette Davis plays a librarian who refuses to remove from her library a book called *The Communist Dream*. She is accused of belonging to communist front groups and fired, but a boy gets carried away and burns the library down. *Storm Center* attacked the inquisitorial, guilt-by-association techniques of HUAC, but the message of free speech was so oversimplified that even the Daughters of the American Revolution endorsed it, and the movie was an unqualified flop. *Storm Center* was not Hollywood's last word on the deep trauma of the investigations, the pain of which is still not forgotten. But by the mid-fifties, other things were happening in the nation and in the movies.

NOTES

1. Joan Mellen, *Big Bad Wolves* (New York: Pantheon, 1977), p. 189.
2. Michael Wood, *America in the Movies* (New York: Basic Books, 1975), p. 184.
3. Victor Navasky, *Naming Names* (New York: Penguin, 1983), p. 78.
4. *San Jose Mercury News*, 25 August 1985.
5. Navasky, *Names*, p. 146.
6. Ibid., pp. 79–80.

7. Dorothy Jones, "Communism in the Movies," in John Cogley ed., *Report on Blacklisting I: The Movies* (New York: Fund for the Republic, 1956).
8. Ibid., p. 216.
9. Ibid., pp. 300–01.
10. *Time*, 17 October 1949.
11. Colin Shindler, *Hollywood at War* (London: Routledge & Kegan Paul, 1979), p. 121.
12. Cited in John Cogley, ed., *Report on Blacklisting I: The Movies* (New York: Fund for the Republic, 1956), p. 11.
13. *The New Yorker*, 16 July 1949.
14. *The New York Times*, 9 July 1949.
15. Ibid., 9 April 1952.
16. Quoted in *Variety*, 26 March 1952.
17. *Saturday Review*, 25 January 1958.
18. *Variety*, 22 January 1958.
19. Peter Biskind, *Seeing is Believing* (London: Pluto Press, 1984), p. 49.
20. Navasky, *Names*, p. 210.
21. Andrew Dowdy, *The Films of the Fifties* (New York: Morrow, 1973), p. 35.
22. *Variety*, 17 March 1954.
23. Cited in Dowdy, *Fifties*, p. 34.
24. *Time*, 29 March 1954.
25. Dowdy, *Fifties*, p. 184.

8

"Everything Isn't Black and White"
Beyond HUAC – Centrist Politics in the Fifties

The forces of conformity and consensus were so strong in the fifties that they dominate our memories and images of the decade. Post-war optimism and faith in the future had been strengthened by prosperity and widespread support for the moderate conservatism of President Eisenhower. But the nation was not as placid as it seemed. International politics was dominated by the cold war, and the sense of American hegemony was fading. In 1956, America stood by as the Soviet Union invaded Hungary and, in the eyes of many, abandoned its European allies in the Suez. Russia launched Sputnik the following year, and America felt technologically inferior for the first time in decades. When Fidel Castro signed a trade agreement with the Soviet Union in 1959, communism seemed to have arrived at America's doorstep. And the threat of nuclear war loomed over all the events of the decade.

Even as the world became a more dangerous place, the paranoia of HUAC and Senator Joseph McCarthy fell into discredit, and domestic politics became more complex as liberals grew braver and new social movements emerged. The civil rights movement gained momentum and by 1957 was in the forefront of American politics, where it would stay for two decades. Rock and roll and the Beat movement drove a significant wedge between generations, and journalists pounded the wedge in deeper by mocking the bland conformity of suburbia and the organization men in their gray flannel suits.

All these changes were mirrored and sometimes predicted by the movies. Social issue films peaked in the late forties, but kept appearing right through the fifties. Among them were an increasing number of movies about rebellious teenagers, like *The Wild One* (1953) and *Rebel Without a Cause* (1955). Meanwhile, as we have seen, filmmakers engaged in a modest debate about the cold war, HUAC, and their own

Advise and Consent (1962)

obligations in movies that ranged all the way from *I Married a Communist* to *High Noon* and from *On the Waterfront* to *Storm Center*. But this was also a time when new genres emerged and old ones changed as the power of the studios and the production code broke down.

The PCA and the Blue Moon

Filmmakers had been challenging the production code for some time, but perhaps surprisingly, they became more daring in the conservative, conformist fifties. Otto Preminger managed to get his sex comedy, *The Moon is Blue* (1953), screened without code approval despite dialogue that seemed scandalous in those days. He then took on the forbidden subject of drug abuse in *The Man with the Golden Arm* (1955) and got away with that, too. In 1956, the Production Code Administration (PCA), bowing to pressure from the film industry, amended the code to permit the subjects of drugs, abortion, prostitution, kidnapping, and miscegenation. And after that, the remaining rules quickly crumbled. Films about homosexuals began to appear. They were subtle at first (*Tea and Sympathy*, 1958), but they soon grew bolder (*Suddenly Last Summer*, 1960). Gradually, fewer and fewer "sinners" were punished.

Most of the code-shattering filmmakers were liberals, but their defiance of the old rules probably had more to do with finding an audience than with the Bill of Rights. Television had taken over middle-of-the-road family entertainment, and moviemakers had to be more daring to sell tickets. They made epics and introduced new techniques (3-D, CinemaScope, VistaVision), but they also made more adult movies, sometimes challenging the intellect, though more often merely titillating with controversial subjects, especially sex.

Changing Genres

While some filmmakers challenged the production code in the 1950s, others remolded the old movie genres to suit the changing times. War movies, for example, underwent a transformation after World War II. Peter Biskind points out that World War II films were written mostly by ideologues of the left like Lillian Hellman, Dalton Trumbo, and John Howard Lawson. These writers "were preoccupied with articulating war aims – democracy, freedom, brotherhood – and went out of their way to explain why we fought." Films about the Korean War, however, were apolitical adventures, because the moviemakers "didn't know why we fought, and what's more, they didn't care."[1] Biskind goes on to describe three different political perspectives in the war movies of the fifties. *Attack* (1956) and *Paths of Glory* (1957) were leftist films criticizing war and the military while *The Court-Martial of Billy Mitchell* (1955) was a conservative condemnation of bureaucracy. The mainstream political ideology of the decade, however, was expressed in the centrist *Strategic Air Command* (1955).

In this film, Dutch (James Stewart) is a baseball player and U.S. Air Force reservist who is recalled to temporary duty. Over the objections of his wife (June Allyson), he signs up permanently. "Sally," he explains, "if there was a war on, you wouldn't question any of this."

"But that's just it," she answers. "There isn't."

"But there is a kind of war," Dutch drawls. "We've got to stay ready to fight without fighting. That's even tougher. That's why I made the decision." When a bad arm makes it impossible for Dutch to fly, he refuses a ground job, and Sally wins, but a general (Frank Lovejoy) gets to deliver a big speech pleading for public support for "good conditions" for the men of the air force and their dependents so they get "the best men." Dutch, Sally, and the air force all win, providing a centrist solution, but only after the husband and wife express their willingness to sacrifice their selfish preferences to the greater cause – the consensus, as represented by a benign military. In the process, the film educated its audience on the accepted policy of the day. As in the other war films of the fifties, the focus had also shifted from groups of enlisted men to the officer elite, in whom the nation was to place its trust.

While war movies changed, another genre grew in prominence in the fifties. The popularity of science fiction movies fed on the new interest in outer space and the anxiety about atomic power. Also, in an era when direct political commentary was dangerous, science fiction offered a rich source of allegory. Whether they were mutants of radiation or invaders from another planet, the aliens in these movies could represent any force at all, from technology gone mad to communist infiltration.

As with war movies, Peter Biskind sees right, left, and center in sci-fi. While the centrist movies reassured us that we were in good hands, the left and right used sci-fi to deliver utopian and anti-utopian messages and to warn us not only about invaders but also about the ineptitude of our rulers. Proponents of all three perspectives seemed to agree on the need for vigilance. Right-wing sci-fi was paranoid about infiltration (*The Thing*, 1951; *Them!* 1954) and about people hopelessly searching for utopias (*Forbidden Planet*, 1956) and getting into things they should have kept out of. Science and government often saved the day, as in *Them!* and *Forbidden Planet*, but sometimes they were inept and average guys became heroes, as in *The Thing*. Left-wing sci-fi, on the other hand, had benign aliens offering utopia only to be rejected by dumb humans (*The Day the Earth Stood Still*, 1951). Biskind quotes Jack Arnold, the director of *It Came from Outer Space* (1953), who admitted that he "wanted to have some meaning to it all. I think science fiction films are a marvelous medium for telling a story, creating a mood, and delivering whatever kind of social message should be delivered. . . . If ten per cent of the audience grasped it, then I was very successful."[2] In centrist sci-fi, danger usually came when nature went berserk (*The Black Scorpion*, 1957; *The Creature from the Black Lagoon*, 1954). Radiation, a new worry in the fifties, was often at fault, but these movies trusted good scientists or the government to come to the rescue. Alien pods turn normal people into unfeeling automatons in Don Siegel's *Invasion of the Body Snatchers* (1956). Although now seen by some film scholars as a leftist condemnation of the stifling conformity of the fifties, few doubted that the film was a rightist denunciation of communist mind-control when it was first released. The ending, to which Siegel purportedly objected, was centrist, however, with the federal government stepping in to save the day. The invasions and disasters of sci-fi were a particularly convenient medium for centrist messages because they "dramatized the necessity of consensus, of pulling together," according to Biskind.[3] Happy endings, provided by government, science, or the military reassured us that we were in good hands.

Angry Men and Aging Bosses

But the ultimate centrist political movie of the fifties, according to Biskind, was neither a war story nor a sci-fi adventure: it was the drama *Twelve Angry Men* (1957), directed by Sidney Lumet and written by Reginald Rose. The men of the title are members of a jury, a convenient cross-section of American males. They vote 11 to 1 to convict the defendant, but they are gradually turned around by the lone dissenter, a liberal architect plagued by doubt (Henry Fonda). He is vehemently opposed by two reactionaries (Ed Begley and Lee J. Cobb) and a cold-minded stockbroker (E. G. Marshall), but he wins them over and justice prevails, or so we assume. The court system works in this film, but only because of the presence of one good man. Although this one liberal dissenter prevails, it is also important that all of the others agreed with him in the end, providing a centrist solution typical of the conformist fifties.

The Last Hurrah (1958) was less distinctly contemporary than

Twelve Angry Men, but although it reminisced about the good old days of machine politics, it also had something to say about politics in the coming decade. Based on Edwin O'Connor's novel about an aging boss, *The Last Hurrah* was directed by John Ford, whose treatment oozes with nostalgia for a simpler past in which family and community stood at the center of American life. Although the film was sympathetic to the machine, Boston's Mayor Curley thought the fictional city of the movie was sufficiently like his own to attempt to have it suppressed.

Ford's caring machine is led by Frank Skeffington, played by Spencer Tracy, whose mere presence signifies goodness. In case that isn't enough, the filmmakers throw in several touching scenes in which Skeffington helps his people solve their problems. The machine is shown to be corrupt only on a small scale, and the point is repeatedly made that politics is a means of social mobility for Irish immigrants like Skeffington. The town's leading banker, a Yankee aristocrat (Basil Rathbone), refuses to lend the city money for a housing project that Skeffington needs to ensure his reelection, saying "the banks don't consider the city a good risk under the current administration."

"The city is no longer yours," Skeffington reponds, "it's ours. That's what really bothers you."

But he's wrong. The power of the machine is crumbling, partly from sheer age, a point made both visually and verbally. The old Yankee aristocracy meets at the Plymouth Club and decides to dump Skeffington and run a slick but vacuous media candidate who will attract the emerging urban middle class, the children of Skeffington's supporters. The editor of the local newspaper (John Carradine) attacks Skeffington in front-page editorials and bans photographs of the incumbent mayor while running a series on his opponent's life. "Politics is the best spectator sport in the country," Skeffington says as he tries to make the most of his rallies and speeches. But he knows that his old-fashioned campaign style is "on the way out. It'll all be TV," he explains. His bland opponent puts his family on TV in a scene reminiscent of Richard Nixon's famous "Checkers" speech, complete with dog, and wins the election as Skeffington dies.

The critics found *The Last Hurrah* sentimental, old-fashioned, and oversimplified, although a few thought it gave a good sense of how politics worked. Slow and one-sided as it was, Fords's film built up a rich portrait of machine politics that could have been improved by a less saintly Skeffington and a more credible opponent. The younger candidate was so ludicrous that his victory looked like a condemnation of the gullibility of voters – and of TV, which may have reflected the filmmakers' attitude toward the competing medium and its audience. Still, the rehabilitation of the machine after fifty years of stereotyping as evil and corrupt was no mean feat. *The Last Hurrah* showed how the machine helped immigrants become assimilated and how it cared for people, humanizing and personalizing their government. Sociologists were writing about these functions of the machines in the fifties; *The Last Hurrah* illustrated them.

Despite its sentimentality, the movie respected politics and politicians, treating them as caring, well-meaning, and distinctly human people. The younger generation of politicians came off less well, of course, as did the old aristocracy. The portrait of this Anglo elite, meeting at their Plymouth Club to plot against the upstart Irish, gave *The Last Hurrah* added depth in that it made the class basis of political conflict clear, something few other American political films have accomplished. Condemnation of the elite was not balanced by faith in the masses, however. No respect was shown for the voters in *The Last Hurrah*, no Capra-like trust in the people. Rather, they seemed to get what they deserved when the media candidate won the election.

This kind of pessimism about the power of television and the gullibility of the people became the theme of several American movies in the 1950s. Elia Kazan took it up in *A Face in the Crowd* (1957), written by his *On the Waterfront* collaborator Budd Schulberg. In this movie, lonesome Rhodes (Andy Griffith) is a bum who is discovered by a local radio station and catapulted into stardom as a singer and populist philosopher. He ends up grooming a dull conservative candidate for president in return for the promise of becoming secretary for national morale if the candidate wins. Rhodes is cynical, using his talent and the television medium only to gain sex, wealth, and power. The politicians are equally cynical, using Rhodes and his methods to sell themselves rather than their programs to the voters. Although the film's token intellectual (Walter Matthau) eventually determines to destroy Rhodes, the demagogue is done in when a spurned lover (Patricia Neal) leaves a microphone on after he thinks he's off the air. His insulting remarks turn his audience against him, and his fame and power dissipate overnight.

Kazan was commenting more on the superficial power of television than on politics, but *A Face in the Crowd* made it clear that politicians would use that power and that the public would be duped unless good people told the truth – and there weren't many of them around. Like Ford, Kazan seemed pessimistic about the people.

Priming for the Sixties

Unlike Kazan and Ford, Stanley Kramer saw the people as victims rather than simply as dupes. One of Hollywood's most consistent liberals, Kramer started as producer of *Home of the Brave* (1949), a film about the racism experienced by a black war veteran. He went on to produce Arthur Miller's *Death of a Salesman* (1951), *High Noon* (1952), *The Wild One* (1954), and *The Defiant Ones* (1958), which he also directed. In 1959, he made *On the Beach*, an early disaster movie based on Nevil Shute's best-selling novel in which the last survivors of a nuclear holocaust, a cross-section of humanity played by an all-star cast, await the clouds of death, mostly with dignity.

On the Beach opened portentously with "a global premiere" in seventeen cities, including Moscow. It was treated as a profound statement on the need to come to terms with the atomic future, a theme that had been touched on by sci-fi films but never by a big-budget movie with stars like Gregory Peck, Ava Gardner, and Fred Astaire. It became the film people talked about and felt they had to see, but critics liked it, too. Arthur Knight of *The Saturday Review* praised Kramer for his social concern and awareness,[4] and others declared the movie "brilliantly directed" and "deeply moving."[5] A few, however, pointed out that it left audiences feeling helpless because it gave no clue as to what could be done to prevent the holocaust. They also observed that the end of the world was more bland than horrifying in *On the Beach*. *Time* noted "what really is horrible about the end of the world: boy does not get girl."[6]

Kramer followed *On the Beach* with *Inherit the Wind* (1960), the story of the Scopes trial, which involved the teaching of Darwin's theory of evolution in Tennessee schools. An impassioned plea for free speech, praising the good citizens who stand up for the persecuted teacher at the risk of angering the mob, the film said as much about the fifties as it did about the trial. Kramer next turned to persecution and prosecution on a grander scale with *Judgment at Nuremberg* (1961), which tells the story of the Holocaust through the trial of German war criminals. He dealt with anti-Semitism again in *Ship of Fools* (1965), and he took on race relations with *Guess Who's Coming to Dinner* (1967).

Some reviewers thought Kramer's films were overly sentimental and simplistic, and they certainly seem so now, but they were popular hits, often garnering Academy Awards and nominations, and they were almost always treated respectfully as "must see" movies. Remarkably, Kramer managed to elicit this response despite his consistently liberal perspective. His use of all-star casts helped, and the softness of his liberalism made his messages easy to swallow. He never demanded much more than tolerance, and he rarely called on people to do much more than stand up for the rights of others, although this may have seemed like a lot in the post-McCarthy fifties and early sixties. Kramer's movies surely contributed to the development of the social consciousness of the sixties activists, a generation of Americans who were teenagers when Kramer was most prolific. The first of a long line of movies dealing with nuclear apocalypse, *On the Beach* shaped attitudes about the bomb, but his other movies, each of which confronted a major contemporary social issue, gave instruction in tolerance and at least implied that something should be done. From *The Defiant Ones* to *Guess Who's Coming to Dinner*, Kramer's movies were seen and talked about, and they surely left their mark.

While Kramer was worrying about the future, other moviemakers were reviving the past in one of the last of the big and positive political biopics, *Sunrise at Campobello* (1960), directed by Vincent J. Donohue and written by Dore Schary. The film concentrated on the beginning of Franklin Delano Roosevelt's career and his battle with polio. Unlike other political films from *State of the Union* onward, however, *Sunrise* saw politics as a worthwhile pursuit and showed good people fighting to overcome personal adversity in order to participate. Later biopics became darker and more complex – and the nation's view of FDR did, too – but *Sunrise at Campobello* was a straightforward, perhaps anachronistic, presentation of the president as hero.

More contemporary themes were taken up by other political films of the early sixties. *Exodus* (1960), directed by Otto Preminger and written by Dalton Trumbo, was a popular epic of the founding of modern Israel. Elia Kazan's less successful *Wild River* (1960) dealt with the eradication of traditional rural life by progress in the form of federal dam-builders. *The Ugly American* (1962), George Englund's movie about communism and nationalism, was a flop despite the star power of Marlon Brando and its prescient focus on southeast Asia.

Audiences had never shown much enthusiasm for anti-communist films, but they welcomed unorthodox treatments of the ideological struggle. Billy Wilder had a hit with *One, Two, Three* (1961), a satire of the cold war starring James Cagney and daring for the times. Even more unorthodox was John Frankenheimer's *The Manchurian Candidate* (1962), one of the first and most successful political thrillers. A brainwashed veteran of the Korean War (Lawrence Harvey) is programmed to assassinate on command while a gravel-voiced McCarthy type (James Gregory) rabble-rouses, declaring he has "lists" of communists in government agencies, at one point coming up with the number 57 when he glimpses the "57 Varieties" label on a bottle of Heinz catsup. Linking the two men is the veteran's mother, who is also the demagogue's wife and mastermind (Angela Lansbury in an Oscar-nominated performance that reprises her manipulative mistress in *State of the Union*). A shocking conclusion reveals that the communist agent who controls the programmed assassin is his mother; the right wing turns out to be a front for subversion, a nice twist and one that was courageous in 1962. Frankenheimer's brilliant film brought the anti-communist cycle to an end by adding complexity and confusion to everybody's motives, simultaneously establishing the thriller as a major form for political movies.

Mr. Anderson Goes to Washington

Melodrama combined with realism in *Advise and Consent* (1962), a political movie in the Hollywood tradition but with a skillful evocation of the Washington scene and a more probable plot than most such films. Based on the novel by Washington journalist Allen Drury, *Advise and Consent* was directed by Otto Preminger, who toned down the novel's conservatism.

In this film, Robert Leffingwell (Henry Fonda) is the presidential appointee for secretary of state, awaiting approval by the Senate, which must advise and consent. Right-wingers label him soft on communism and denounce his "egg-headed arrogance." We are on Leffingwell's side from the outset, not only because he's played by Henry Fonda, but because his chief opponent is the reactionary old southerner, Seab Cooley, portrayed with great relish by Charles Laughton. Pushing from the left is the ruthless and dogmatic Senator Van Ackerman (George Grizzard), who is willing to violate all the rules to make Leffingwell secretary of state. Leader of a national pro-disarmament group, Van Ackerman is always surrounded by zombie-like aides (communist automatons?). Caught between them all is the senate majority leader (Walter Pidgeon), an honorable man who only wishes to get his president the ratification he wants, even though he knows it won't be easy.

Van Ackerman wants to chair the subcommittee that will hold the hearing on Leffingwell's nomination, but although he's the logical choice, he is rejected because his ambition has led him to violate the Senate's unwritten rules of conduct. ("He doesn't belong here," the Senate leaders say. "No tact.") They choose young Brig Anderson (Don Murray) to chair the hearings because "*he* knows how to be a senator."

Anderson seems perfect: he is clean-cut and polite, a more mature and sophisticated version of Mr. Smith; he has a nice family, plays by the rules, and honors his elders, but he turns out to be a bit rigid. Senator Cooley (Laughton) dredges up evidence that Leffingwell was once a member of a communist cell. Leffingwell denies the association, but when Anderson learns he has lied, he turns against him despite pressure from the president and the majority leader, who understand that "We all make mistakes" in youth and that "everything isn't black and white." But Brig Anderson, the pure young idealist, plans to denounce Leffingwell until a mysterious caller threatens to expose Brig's past homosexual affair unless he supports the confirmation. Unable to cope with the truth about himself and unwilling to compromise his position on Leffingwell, Brig commits suicide.

The Senate deliberations proceed, but as the vice president (Lew Ayres) prepares to cast the tie-breaking vote, the president dies and the issue is moot. It turns out that the evil Van Ackerman was behind the blackmail, and he is scourged by his fellow senators. "Fortunately this country is able to survive patriots like you," the majority leader tells him. "We can tolerate about anything, but you've dishonored us." Senator Cooley, however, is still in the club because he played by the rules.

Although it was made in 1962, *Advise and Consent* carries a 1950s message of consensus: characters who do not fit or will not play by the rules are destroyed. Like earlier movies, this one says that politics is a dirty business, but *Advise and Consent* is more interesting, sophisticated, and morally complex than its predecessors. The human side of politics is clear; the majority leader and the Senate regulars are good men who live by a code of honor, even if that code is morally ambiguous. Nobody is pure, not the president or the secretary of state or the clean-cut young senator, not the left or the right, yet some are well-intentioned and play the game with honor. Pidgeon's majority leader and Ayres's vice president give the film moral weight because we like them and trust them, as we did Harry Carey in *Mr. Smith*.

Advise and Consent also provides painless instruction on the way the political process works. A group of diplomats' wives in the gallery, for example, allows the filmmakers to explain how the Senate operates. The repartee between the majority leader and his mistress also provides a distinctly grown-up perspective on politics.

The New York Times saw *Advise and Consent* as a cynical movie about dishonourable men, including the president.[7] Pauline Kael wrote it off as a "mindless 'inside' story of Washington shenanigans" and an "overwrought melodrama,"[8] but other critics liked it, noting the accurate depiction of the workings of the Senate. As in many political films, the melodrama was there for entertainment, but it turned out to be the weak point of the film, while the political machinations and procedures were stronger. Still, they wouldn't have been as interesting without the moral conflict introduced by the melodrama.

Real-life politicians took a great interest in *Advise and Consent*. Although Martin Luther King refused an offer to play a senator, three senators did appear in it, and President Kennedy entertained the filmmakers at the White House while the movie was being made. Some senators didn't like the final product, however. "I don't think it will be wholesome for either our people or those abroad," declared Strom Thurmond.[9] As usual, the real-life politicians over-reacted. *Advise and Consent* not only gave a strong sense of how politics worked, it also insisted that most politicians were decent men. Mr. Anderson's Washington of 1962, however, was different from the city that Mr. Smith visited in 1939. Politics had become more complicated, and innocence was no longer allowed to triumph.

On toward Camelot

Political movies had changed during the 1950s. They had begun to deal with discrimination, they had confronted the cold war, and they had learned to look at the communist threat and the anti-communist crusade from a new perspective. The result was a substantial body of political films from an era that is commonly perceived as dull and apolitical. Films like *State of the Union*, *The Last Hurrah* and *Advise and Consent* had new and different things to say. Generally more cynical, they were also more complex, sophisticated and realistic. Unlike the redemptive politics of some twenties movies or the longing for strong leaders of the thirties or even the up-lifting triumphs of the people and their innocent leaders best captured by Frank Capra, the political films of this era saw good men destroyed. The message of the fifties was more a warning than a rallying cry, however. Politics was viewed as a dangerous game in these movies, but at least there were a few good men – and even women – around, although they were advised to mute their individualism and fit into the consensus. Only *Salt of the Earth* offered collective action as a solution, and that movie was suppressed.

And while the film rolled, America went from Truman to Eisenhower to Kennedy, from post-war optimism to fifties paranoia and conformity, and finally, to Camelot. Political films had grown more sophisticated by the Kennedy years, but the liberalism that Kennedy inspired did not catch up with either the nation or its filmmakers until after his assassination in 1963.

NOTES

1. Peter Biskind, *Seeing is Believing* (London: Pluto Press, 1983), p. 59.
2. Ibid., p. 159.
3. Ibid., p. 102.
4. *Saturday Review*, 24 October 1959.
5. Cited in *Variety*, 23 December 1959.

6. *Time*, 28 December 1959.
7. *The New York Times*, 7 June 1962.
8. Pauline Kael, *5001 Nights at the Movies* (New York: Holt, Rinehart and Winston, 1982), p. 6.
9. *Time*, 30 March 1962.

Dr. Strangelove (1964)

"Power Is Not a Toy"

The Sixties – From Dr. No *and* Dr. Strangelove *to the Counterculture*

America's youngest president took office in January 1961, ushering in a new political era. John F. Kennedy's tragic death less than three years later has perhaps caused us to exaggerate his stature as a leader but even so, his presidency signaled a change. The roots of that change were not so much in his politics as in his image.

Kennedy, a moderate Democrat more interested in foreign than domestic policy, charged that there was a "missile gap" between the United States and the U.S.S.R. and promised to get America moving again. He did, increasing military spending and launching the space program. He also introduced a boldly active cold war interventionism that included the disastrous invasion of Cuba at the Bay of Pigs, a nuclear confrontation with the Soviet Union over missiles based in Cuba, and the beginnings of U.S. involvement in Vietnam. Whereas in the fifties we had been paranoid about the communist threat, the sixties produced in us a cocky confidence that we could beat the communists at their own game.

Kennedy was not so active or interested, however, in such issues as civil rights, urban decay, and poverty. These were issues for which the sixties would be remembered, but they emerged during and after Kennedy's term in office. He awoke to them as the nation did, but his close election and an uncooperative Congress made domestic politics more treacherous for him and he moved much more slowly on these issues. It was left to his successor, Lyndon B. Johnson, to develop and implement the programs that distinguished the era, assisted by the political momentum of the spirit Kennedy had awakened and by his martyrdom.

For Kennedy's great gift to the nation was not a program but a spirit. He was young, active, witty, and articulate whereas Eisenhower had been old, tongue-tied, and cautious. Kennedy's family, with their good looks, sophistication, and sheer joy in living, gave Americans new role models. The handsome, vigorous president inspired hopes and aspirations that resulted in the Peace Corps and the space program.

While the Kennedy spirit helped liberalize the nation, the civil rights movement provided political momentum, driving both Kennedy and Johnson to the left. Martin Luther King, Jr., led the great march on Washington in 1963. The following year saw riots in several urban ghettos. Johnson responded with his Great Society legislation, but there was also a bitter white backlash. Meanwhile, a wave of student activism started in 1964, evolved into the radical New Left, then into the anti-war movement, and eventually into an anti-materialist youth counterculture made up of hippies and flower children.

Where were the movies? In 1962, *Advise and Consent* caught some of the Kennedy's joy in politics, although its conclusion was as consensus-oriented as that of any fifties movie and as confident that the system worked as *Mr. Smith*. That same year, *The Manchurian Candidate* expressed some of the wit of the era by putting down McCarthyism, but it managed to do so safely by portraying the red-baiters as the real reds. In 1963, *P.T. 109*, an action movie about the World War II exploits of John Kennedy (Cliff Robertson), simultaneously contributed to and cashed in on the young president's popularity. For the most part, however, Hollywood lagged behind the nation, perhaps because it was a bad time for the film industry.

By 1960, average weekly attendance had dropped to 40 million, half what it had been in the forties, and by 1970 it had fallen to only 20 million. The number of movie theaters declined, and so did the number of films made, bottoming out with 154 in 1960. RKO went out of business, and MGM quit making movies. Surviving film companies were absorbed by corporate conglomerates like TransAmerica (United Artists) and Gulf & Western (Paramount). The moviemakers grew more cautious and profit-conscious, producing fewer films as they concentrated, without great success, on blockbusters.

The movies launched a surprising revival later in the 1960s, however, even as television replaced the motion picture as America's primary entertainment medium. Television took over the middle of the road, freeing movies to search for more selective audiences and thus to take more chances, even on politics. This risk-taking was limited, though, by the studios' corporate conservatism and profit orientation, which now forced them to take lucrative TV sales into consideration when making movies. The continued dominance of a few major distributors was also a constraint, but independent producers like Stanley Kramer could win wide distribution by first proving their films during "art house" runs in New York and Los Angeles. The number of independent producers grew as distribution opportunities appeared, and liberal filmmakers began to take advantage of the nation's new political mood. Stanley Kramer, Sidney Lumet, Stanley Kubrick, and Martin Ritt became more active, and others, like Dalton Trumbo and Abraham Polonsky, returned to work after having been blacklisted. They were joined by a new generation of politically oriented filmmakers, including Robert Altman, John Frankenheimer, Alan Pakula, Mike Nichols, and Arthur Penn.

There were new audiences, too. Some filmmakers began to exploit the large numbers of young ticket buyers, a move that resulted not only in beach-blanket movies but also in such classics as *Bonnie and Clyde* and *The Graduate*. Others aimed at the increasingly larger and more sophisticated art house audience in big cities and university towns, an audience that was capable of making "small" movies profitable. The beach-blanket audience and the more sophisticated art house audiences even merged to support a few independent productions with counter-culture themes, like *Easy Rider*, making them big hits.

In the liberal 1960s, the production code finally succumbed to defiant filmmakers, civil libertarians, court decisions, changing politics, and the need for movies to attract audiences by giving them what they couldn't get on TV. By 1966, the code was advisory rather than mandatory, but it still recommended rewarding virtue, condemning vice, and dealing cautiously with sex. For the first time, it also suggested limits on violence. In 1968, the code was replaced by the more liberal rating system, which limited film audiences to specified age groups, mainly to protect the young from sex, violence, and obscene language. Film-makers were undoubtedly happy to be free of the code's restrictions, but investors and the public still served as censors, rejecting subjects that offended or angered large groups of people.

Although Hollywood was slow to pick up the politics of the sixties, a number of political films in 1964 marked the beginning of a period during which American filmmakers strongly criticized the dominant values of their society. The American Film Institute subject index of films of the 1960s lists more than seventy movies that touch on political themes. Of course, that's only half as many as were made in the 1920s, but keep in mind that far fewer films were made in the sixties.[1]

From *Dr. No* to *Dr. Strangelove*

Although the politics of the 1960s is remembered as liberal, or even radical, one of the most durable movie symbols of the era was neither, but did reflect the general fear of nuclear war and the Kennedy administration's reliance on CIA intervention.

James Bond was a British secret agent created by novelist Ian Fleming, whose books President Kennedy enjoyed. The first Bond movie, *Dr. No* (1962), was such a hit that a dozen more followed, with Sean Connery and later Roger Moore as the suave and witty spy. The political content of the Bond movies was simplistic at best, but they did suit the political mood of the nation. Joan Mellen declares them "the key image of the decade," reflecting the "macho politics" of the Kennedy era[2] as superspy Bond foiled villainous plots for world domination or destruction almost single-handedly. To some extent, the Bond movies were a vestige of the cold war, but their view was somewhat more complex in that the Soviet Union was not always the enemy. More often, the menace was China or an evil genius like Dr. No who played the superpowers off against one another, thus expressing the public's fear that something might go wrong in the delicate balance of power and bring apocalypse. The solution in these films always resulted from the appearance of a superhero. All we had to do, they suggested, was let the CIA or the British secret service take care of business, a notion that was shared by the Kennedy administration with its penchant for brisk and brutal intervention by the CIA or Special Forces and international brinkmanship. Some CIA plots, in fact, like the attempted assassination of Cuban Premier Fidel Castro, went even further than the Bond movies, in which action was mostly defensive rather than offensive.

The Bond films and many copycat movies were spoofs that toyed with international disaster, but other motion pictures of the era took the subject seriously, suggesting that worldwide disaster might come not from evil enemies but from within. Some even suggested that the final holocaust could result from an accident. These were the movies that somewhat belatedly brought Hollywood into the politics of the sixties.

The first, *Seven Days in May* (1964), was a thriller written by Rod Serling, best known today for his *Twilight Zone* TV series, and directed by John Frankenheimer. In this movie, a wise, liberal president (Fredric March) signs a nuclear nonproliferation treaty with the Soviet Union, but a group of right-wing generals, led by Burt Lancaster, plots a coup. The president's aides (Kirk Douglas and Martin Balsam) discover the conspiracy, and when the president reveals their treachery to the nation, the coup falls apart. Gerling and Frankenheimer thus turned American paranoia inside out, suggesting that the threat could come from within and from the right. They also created heroes (March, Douglas, Balsam) who saved the day by appealing to the public through televised appeals, thus reassuring moviegoers that the masses had a role to play in the political process, an unusual message in American political films other than those of Frank Capra. *Seven Days in May* did well at the box office and was praised by most critics. Bosley Crowther thought it proved democracy worked, and Arthur Knight was excited to see Hollywood, "the sleeping giant ... waking up again" and dealing with contemporary issues after the escapism of the fifties.[3] But despite its comforting message that the system worked, politicians worried about the impression *Seven Days in May* would give abroad, demanding that the export version be clearly labeled "fictional," lest "ignorant foreigners" think such right-wing coups were possible in the United States.[4]

In *Fail Safe* (1964), directed by Sidney Lumet and written by the formerly blacklisted Walter Bernstein, the threat results from a technological accident: an American bomber heads for Moscow because of a mechanical glitch. As in *Seven Days in May*, however, level-headed human beings solve the problem. The president, reassuringly played by Henry Fonda, negotiates his way out of the mess, finally ordering U.S. planes to bomb New York City to assure the Russians of fair play and to avoid wider destruction. Rational men capable of thinking the unthinkable – as strategists of nuclear war were doing at the time – somehow made even the sacrifice of New York seem necessary. Some critics praised *Fail Safe* for showing how "intelligent men trying to use their wits and their techniques correct an error,"[5] but others thought the movie was platitudinous, and it stirred little enthusiasm at the box office. *Fail Safe* also suffered from comparison to another, more devastating film about nuclear war that made all other movies on the subject seem naive.

Dr. Strangelove or: How I Learned to Stop Worrying and Love the Bomb (1964), written by Stanley Kubrick, Terry Southern, and Peter George and directed by Kubrick, was a critical and box office hit even though it proclaimed that the world had gone mad and was bound for destruction. *Strangelove* opens with a lyrical scene of a bomber being refueled in midair, perhaps an allusion to a similar scene in *Strategic Air Command* (1955), but this time "Try a Little Tenderness" is the musical accompaniment and the tone is satirical, providing a suitable prologue to Kubrick's scathing movie. During a simple military exercise, a fleet of American bombers is sent toward the Soviet Union, but some of the bombers do not respond to a command to return to base. It turns out that the mad commander of Burpleson Air Force Base, General Jack D. Ripper (Sterling Hayden), has initiated a real attack on the Soviet Union. He hopes to force President Merkin Muffley (Peter Sellers) to proceed with the assault rather than suffer Soviet retaliation. Muffley orders Ripper to send the coded call-back orders to the planes, but the general refuses. The president sends the army to seize Burpleson Air Force Base, but Ripper tells his men they are under attack by subversives in American uniforms. While the battle at the base goes on, the bombers get closer and closer to their target and the president summons his cabinet to the war room. As the tension builds, Kubrick cuts between Ripper at the base, Muffley in the war room, and a bomber commanded by Major Kong (Slim Pickens).

General Buck Turgidson (George C. Scott) advises an all-out pre-emptive attack, but President Muffley calls the Soviet ambassador to the war room instead and uses the hot line to warn the Russian premier, who informs him that a secret doomsday device will destroy the entire world if the Soviet Union is attacked. Confronted with apocalypse, the two leaders cooperate in shooting down the American bombers – all except the one piloted by Major Kong. Damaged in the attack, Kong's plane flies too low for radar detection and proceeds to its target to the tune of "When Johnny Comes Marching Home." Meanwhile Dr. Strangelove (Peter Sellers in a multiple role) arrives in the war room. Speaking in a heavy German accent and giving Nazi salutes with a gloved hand he can't control, Strangelove advises the president and cabinet on survival after the holocaust, raving about life in caves and mines, drooling over his planned male-female ratio, and referring to the president as "Mein Fuehrer" in a caricature of Werner von Braun, the German expatriate missile designer. Major Kong's B-52 gets through, however, and the film ends in lyrical shots of mushroom clouds accompanied by "I'll Be Seeing You," the sentimental World War II song.

Dr. Strangelove is relentlessly, almost bewilderingly cynical and satirical, and it has no completely sympathetic characters. Scientists and the military take the toughest beating. Science is represented by the mad Nazi, Dr. Strangelove, and the military is embodied in Turgidson ("war is too important to be left to politicians") and Ripper, a lunatic who is convinced that everybody is after his "precious bodily fluids." These three characters also represent different male sexual fears. Major Kong, the ingenious cowboy pilot, would have been the hero in any conventional movie, but cheering for him in this movie would mean rooting for apocalypse. *Strangelove* does not even offer a reasonable liberal as hero. The president is well meaning but ineffectual. So is his military counterpart, a visiting British officer (Peter Sellers again) attempting to stop the insane General Ripper. In other words, liberal faith in good men, even a rational president willing to communicate with the Soviets, is dismissed as derisively as is conservative faith in the military. And *Strangelove* attacks technology as well as human folly and fallability. Slick machines, without hearts or minds, go out of control in the hands of insane, careless, or incompetent humans. The U.S. Air Force later denied that such accidents could happen, but Terry Southern, one of the film's authors, declared that its intent was "to blast smugness . . . over a foolproof system which may not be."[6]

Most disturbingly, *Strangelove* issued a warning without offering any hope of salvation. *Seven Days in May* and *Fail Safe* also condemned the military and expressed concern about the safety of technology, but they offered human heroes and a political system that worked. *Strangelove's* condemnation was more sweeping and offered no hope at all. "It is not war that has been laughed to scorn," Pauline Kael wrote, "but the possibility of sane action."[7] Like Kael, other critics were alarmed at *Strangelove's* ultimate message. The *Washington Post's* reviewer worried that "no communist could dream of a more effective anti-American film to spread abroad than this one,"[8] but critics conceded the brilliance of the film, and its skillful combination of comedy and politics went down well at the box office. *Strangelove* won Academy Award nominations (but no Oscars) for best picture, director, writers, and actor (Sellers), the first political film to gain such approval since the forties.

Not since the sci-fi films of the 1950s, had the consequences of nuclear technology been so directly addressed. *Strangelove, Fail Safe, Seven Days in May*, and an earlier film, *On the Beach*, played to and expressed public concern about nuclear war and kept the subject on the nation's agenda. They helped shape a generation's attitudes, and they may have contributed to Lyndon B. Johnson's electoral victory in 1964. Johnson presented himself as the "peace candidate," whereas his right-wing Republican opponent, Barry Goldwater, an officer in the U.S. Air Force Reserve, was portrayed as a warmonger and virtual Strangelove.

America moved toward detente as it worried about nuclear war, and so did Hollywood. *Fail Safe* suggested we could negotiate with the Russians, while *Strangelove* sent up the hotline and satirized the Soviets as viciously as it did our own leaders, but both movies helped to modify the old fifties' image of evil communists, as did other films of the sixties. *Doctor Zhivago* (1965), for example, was a romantic tale of the Russian Revolution in which all communists were Stalinist villains, but the eponymous hero (Omar Sharif) remained resolutely sympathetic with the revolution. *The Russians Are Coming! The Russians Are Coming!* (1966), however, is a self-consciously liberal comedy in which a Soviet submarine runs aground in New England and its nine crew members are perceived as invaders by wacky villagers. "I do not wish to hate anybody," says the handsome Russian (John Phillip Law) to the pretty American (Eva Marie Saint). "It doesn't make sense to hate people," she responds, delivering the movie's message of reconciliation.

Mainstream Politics

While some movies confronted new international realities, others were more traditional in their treatment of politics. *Kisses for My President* (1964), for example, was a thirties-style sex comedy featuring Fred MacMurray as "first husband" to a woman president (Polly Bergen). *The Best Man* (1964), by contrast, was considerably sharper and more contemporary, thanks to Franklin Schaffner's direction and Gore Vidal's adaptation of his own play.

In *The Best Man*, the scene is a convention to select a presidential nominee, implicitly to succeed Lyndon Johnson, since the film's titles play over portraits of all the presidents through LBJ. Bill Russell (Henry Fonda again) is the intellectual former secretary of state, an Adlai Stevenson-style liberal and presumably the best man. His wife (Margaret Leighton), an independent and intellectual woman, rallies to his side, like Hepburn in *State of the Union*, setting aside marital problems for the greater cause. "Politics make strange bedfellows," she wryly comments. Russell's opponent, Joe Kantwell (Cliff Robertson), is a ruthless ideologue and true believer who combines the image of John Kennedy with the politics of Richard Nixon. Kantwell is scornfully dismissed for having built his career on the pursuit of "an imaginary communist mafia," an indication of how much American and Hollywood politics had changed in just ten years.

The unscrupulous Kantwell threatens to reveal that Russell once had a nervous breakdown unless he withdraws from the race. Russell's supporters urge him to retaliate by accusing Kantwell of being a homosexual. Russell is incredulous ("That ugly wife, those ugly children!") and refuses to smear his opponent, insisting that he wants to win the nomination because of his stand on political issues. Small corruptions, he insists, destroy character. Russell himself, however, has misled the public about his "happy" marriage, given speeches he hasn't read ("I'll surprise myself"), and manipulated the press.

If Kantwell embodies the ruthless ideologue and Russell the conscientious liberal, political pragmatism is represented by ex-president Hockstadter. Lee Tracy was nominated for an Academy Award for best supporting actor for his portrayal of this Truman-like pol who declares that he doesn't personally care whether Kantwell "has carnal knowledge of a McCormick reaper," but he demands that Russell use whatever he's got against his opponent. "Power is not a toy we give to children," he explains. "It's a weapon and a strong man uses it." Disdaining Russell's squeamishness, he asserts that "to want power is corruption already" and that "there are no ends" [to justify means]. It's normal to fool the people, Hockstadter warns Kantwell, but it's "serious when you start fooling yourself." He fails to persuade the ideologue to back down, however, and when Russell still won't fight back, he refuses to support him. "It's not that you're a bastard," Hockstadter says disgustedly, "it's that you're a stupid bastard." In the end Russell martyrs himself to stop Kantwell, withdrawing from competition and releasing his delegates with a request that they vote for a third candidate. "Men without faces tend to get elected president, and power or personal responsibility tend to fill in the features," he assures us. These may be the best men, but the conclusion is subverted by the film's clear prejudice in favor of Russell-Fonda, the man who is too good for politics.

In an era of increasing interest in politics, *The Best Man* caught enough of the excitement of the game to engage mild public interest and win mixed reviews, although most critics pointed out that Russell-Fonda was altogether too scrupulous and that the film's ends-means morality was less than profound.[9] The State Department worried about the reaction of Soviet audiences, but director Schaffner said the issue didn't matter because the Soviets "don't understand politics", by which he presumably meant electoral politics, as in *The Best Man*.[10]

Like *Advise and Consent* (1962), *The Best Man* was an inside view of politics. Both films played on its seaminess, featuring blackmail based, disturbingly, on homosexuality, but in both films, the political institutions finally worked, and the process and system triumphed. Both films also disparaged ideologues and lauded team players. And in both, Henry Fonda played the good man with a tainted past who had to give up politics, although his character in *The Best Man* did so more decisively.

Like *State of the Union* (1948), *The Best Man* set out the choice between personal integrity and political ambition and opted for integrity. Such martyrdom to idealism "is a central liberal dramatic tradition," according to Richard Maltby,[11] but the choice would have been stronger if Russell's stand on political issues had been clearer rather than simply "good" by implication and in comparison to the abhorrent politics of his opponents. *The Best Man* cynically rejects politics as dirty and hypocritical, thus falling back on a Hollywood cliché. The Fonda character doesn't even trust the public enough to appeal to them, as a Capra hero would have done, and his aloofness gives the film an overall tone of elitism and condescension toward politics, perhaps reflecting the attitude of its privileged author, Gore Vidal, who himself dropped out of politics after an unsuccessful congressional candidacy. This elitism is mitigated by the suspicion that perhaps Russell-Fonda isn't the best man after all; he seems rather too good, too self-consciously superior. In the end, we are instructed that the probable nominee will live up to his position and all will be well, a reassuring conclusion that has been confirmed by any number of real-life presidents.

Hollywood Discovers Minorities

Race relations and the war in Vietnam dominated the politics of the sixties like no other issue, yet Hollywood avoided both issues until late
in the decade. Only John Wayne took on the Vietnam War in *The Green Berets* (1968); the rest of Hollywood waited until the war was over to address it directly, apparently assuming that an issue which polarized the nation would also polarize audiences and offend too many people to turn a profit. The same rationale had applied to films about race since the tumultuous response to *The Birth of a Nation*, although there had been honorable exceptions, from *Arrowsmith* to *In This Our Life*, *The Defiant Ones*, and *To Kill a Mockingbird*.

In the sixties, however, Hollywood discovered that race could sell tickets. Minority issues were hot, and a vaguely liberal national consensus on civil rights had developed; as long as filmmakers played safely within that consensus they could appear controversial yet please the majority. This trend accelerated when the film industry belatedly noticed that minorities themselves constituted a substantial potential audience.

One of the first successful films on racism was *In the Heat of the Night* (1967), written by Stirling Silliphant and directed by Norman Jewison. The story of a racist southern sheriff (Rod Steiger) and a black northern lawman (Sidney Poitier) who are forced to work together, *In the Heat of the Night* made fun of the southerner's racist attitude toward the clearly superior northern black man. The film was an all-round hit and won Academy Awards for best motion picture, script, and actor (Steiger).

Another contender in the 1967 Oscar race was also anti-racist: Stanley Kramer's *Guess Who's Coming to Dinner*, which starred Katharine Hepburn and Spencer Tracy as parents whose daughter is about to marry a black doctor (Poitier). Audiences loved this comedy, and it was 1968's second highest grossing film. Both Kramer and Hepburn won Oscars, but critics were hard on the movie, pointing out that the problems of its affluent families were irrelevant in an era of ghetto riots.

Sidney Poitier was ridiculed for playing cuddly, acceptable blacks in this and other sixties films, yet his screen presence surely helped prepare white audiences for integration, even if some were shocked when they found out that not all blacks were like Poitier. He also helped create an audience for subsequent virtually all black films like *The Learning Tree*, *Watermelon Man*, *Cotton Comes to Harlem*, *Shaft*, and *Sounder*. Although few of these films were explicitly political, they helped build black pride and educate white audiences, and thus they contributed, if modestly, to integration.

Indians were also treated better in the sixties, although fifties films like *Broken Arrow* had started the trend. Hollywood doyen John Ford made up for his past portraits of bloodthirsty savages with *Cheyenne Autumn*. Far more radically, blacklist victim Abraham Polonsky suggested in *Tell Them Willie Boy Is Here* (1969) that Indians and other minorities should go their own separatist way, trusting no one, least of all white liberals. The film centers on a manhunt as a sheriff (Robert Redford) chases an American Indian (Robert Blake) who is wanted for a killing. Under pressure caused by an impending presidential visit, the posse and the press turn into a frenzied mob. The white liberal schoolmarm (Susan Clark) who would have brought reconciliation in earlier films, here is shown to be silly, ineffectual, and condescending in her wish to care for the Indians. *Little Big Man* and *Soldier Blue* (both 1970) continued the revision of American history by interpreting the fate of the Indians as genocide; both films also alluded to the American involvement in Vietnam.

To their credit, most of these movies about blacks and Indians unequivocally condemned white racism, but they did so in a sanitized way calculated not to offend white audiences. Their racist characters were such crude caricatures that whites could join in the condemnation without feeling guilt about their own racism. The liberalism of these films was thus well within the national consensus of the time.

The Coming of the Counterculture

Meanwhile, a youthful counterculture was emerging. With roots in the beatniks of the fifties and the student protests of the sixties, and further stimulated by the civil rights and anti-war movements, the counterculture was an anti-materialist, youth-oriented phenomenon that expressed itself politically as the New Left and socially as the flower children, or hippies.

The first movie to catch the spirit of this counterculture may have been *Bonnie and Clyde* (1967), a box office success that was denounced by some critics for its romanticization of violence. Based on the exploits of two real-life Depression criminals, the film follows two young people (Faye Dunaway and Warren Beatty) as they drift into crime, partly as

an act of rebellion against their elders. At one point, Bonnie and Clyde
are welcomed as heroes in a migrant camp reminiscent of the one in
The Grapes of Wrath, but otherwise, this movie is not explicitly
political. Rather, many regard it as an allegory of youthful disaffection
and rebellion against authority in the sixties. *The Graduate* (1967), a
big box office and critical hit directed by Mike Nichols, played on the
same theme.

Wild in the Streets (1968) took the generational conflict one step
further in the tale of a rock star who uses his popularity to gain political
power as young people take over the country. The voting age and then
the age for office-holding are reduced to fourteen. Adults are sent to
"retirement" camps. In the end, yet another youth coup is plotted as
seven-year-olds prepare to rebel against their teenage elders. *Wild in the
Streets* managed to simultaneously exploit and send up the youth
culture, which was already turning sour.

In *Easy Rider* (1969), the counterculture's biggest box office hit, two
hippies (Dennis Hopper and Peter Fonda) judge the state of the nation
during a motorcycle odyssey enhanced by drugs. "This used to be a
helluva country," says their sidekick (Jack Nicholson). "I can't
understand what's going on." The saint-like hippie leader (Fonda)
bestows approval on people who live freely and independently, but
admits in the end that he and his friend, if not his generation and the
country, have failed: "We blew it." Although *Easy Rider* criticizes
conformity, materialism, and authority, it is less political than it seemed
at the time. Its most revolutionary effect in 1969 was to demonstrate to
the big studios that an independent production and a film about the
counterculture could make money.

By 1968, the counterculture was falling apart. It had finally become
clear that drugs led to addiction instead of liberation. The Manson
family made communes a nightmare. Martin Luther King, Jr., was
murdered, and the civil rights movement was weakened by calls for
black power and cultural separatism. The hopeful politics of the anti-
war movement was shattered by the assassination of Robert Kennedy
and riots at the Democratic convention in Chicago, and the New Left
moved from sit-ins to revolution. Richard Nixon was elected president.

Perhaps the film that best summed up the political aspects of the
counterculture and its demise was *Medium Cool* (1969), a low-budget
independent production directed by left-leaning cinematographer
Haskell Wexler (*The Best Man*). A TV news crew films an auto accident
as the movie begins. Only after they have shot their footage do they call
for help for the victims, establishing one of Wexler's themes, the
exploitative nature of the media. John (Robert Forster), the cameraman,
senses the coldness of his work and feels alienated from it, as he does
from his playboy life-style. He films a passionate group of black

militants and quits his job when he learns that his station is turning over his footage to law-enforcement officers. Meanwhile, apparently longing for a traditional family relationship, he gets involved with an Appalachian woman and her son. The boy disappears, and the couple search for him on the violent streets of Chicago during the 1968 Democratic convention.

The street conflict is real. Wexler set his film in Chicago so the story could be played out with the convention as a backdrop. His reputation as a radical was already sufficient that police hassled him and his crew during the making of the movie, but the footage they got makes a remarkable blend of fact and fiction, successfully heightening the tension of the film as we hear one of his crew shouting, "Watch out, Haskell. This is for real!" It was real enough that the Department of Justice requisitioned Wexler's footage during its investigation of the riots. *Medium Cool* ends somewhat gratuitously in an auto crash, with the camera pulling back to reveal Wexler and his crew filming the wreck, a self-conscious application of his point about the disengagement of the media. This disengagement, or failure to connect, was the central point of *Medium Cool*, not black militancy, street riots, or convention politics, all of which were in the film only as background details. Wexler was saying that traditional politics had failed, that it had ended in the isolation and death of his protagonists. He refused to let them find solace in the counterculture politics of the sixties or the "Me Decade" that was to come.

The critics were divided about *Medium Cool*. Vincent Canby of *The New York Times* called it "technically brilliant" and perhaps even "a kind of cinematic *Guernica*," and others thought it was "dazzling" and "thoughtful," but Penelope Gilliatt in *The New Yorker* dismissed it as "awkward and even pretentious ... a slashing indictment of car driving."[12] Audiences made *Medium Cool* a box office success, however. Its immediacy pulled them in, compensating for its virtually nonexistent plot with the sheer intensity of the moment, and its sense of outrage and alienation was perfectly in tune with the mood of 1969. Many people considered *Medium Cool* the only truly contemporary film of the era.

The success of *Easy Rider* and *Medium Cool* sparked the interest of the studios, which tried to cash in on the counterculture in 1970 with movies like *The Strawberry Statement*, *Getting Straight*, and *RPM*. Their subject was student protest, but all three trivialized it ludicrously, and only *Getting Straight*, a comedy starring Elliott Gould, did well at the box office.

Other films addressed the anti-war sympathies of the era. Franklin Schaffner's highly entertaining *Planet of the Apes* (1968) and its sequels despicted life on earth after a nuclear holocaust, with apes ruling and human beings reduced to slaves. *Patton* (1969), written by Francis Ford Coppola and also directed by Schaffner, presented the World War II general as a sort of mad genius, useful in war but in need of containment by calmer superiors. Winner of three Oscars, *Patton* was a huge box office hit, satisfying both those who praised and those who damned the military. *M*A*S*H* (1970), directed by Robert Altman, and *Catch-22* (1970), directed by Mike Nichols from Joseph Heller's novel, both made vicious fun of the military, while *Johnny Got His Gun* (1971), written and directed by blacklist victim Dalton Trumbo, delivered a more serious anti-war message about a paraplegic veteran of World War I. Trumbo's film was the least popular of these. Audiences were prepared to laugh cynically at war, but not to examine its consequences too closely.

Besides these films, *Joe* (1970), about a bigoted blue-collar worker who is both attracted and repelled by the counterculture, and *WUSA* (1970), about a right-wing radio station, dealt with fascism in contemporary America. Jane Fonda, Peter Boyle, and Donald Sutherland made *Steelyard Blues* (1972), an anti-authoritarian comedy about a group of sixties rebels. And a French film about political assassination in Greece, *Z* (1968), directed by Costa-Gavras, won major Academy Award nominations and ranked fifth in box office receipts for 1970. Francis Ford Coppola capped the era with *The Godfather* (1971), a dark contemplation of the American dream seen through the lives of a Mafia family.

NOTES

1. Kenneth W. Munden, *Subject Index to Films of the 1960s* (New York: Bowker, 1971).
2. Joan Mellen, *Big Bad Wolves* (New York: Pantheon, 1977), pp. 249, 251.
3. *The New York Times*, 20 February 1964; *Saturday Review*, 14 February 1964.
4. *Variety*, 13 May 1964.
5. *The New York Times*, 16 September 1964.
6. Lawrence Suid, "The Pentagon and Hollywood," in John E. O'Connor and Martin A. Jackson, eds., *American History/American Film* (New York: Frederick Unger, 1979), p. 225.
7. Pauline Kael, *Kiss Kiss, Bang Bang* (New York: Bantam, 1969), p. 79.
8. Quoted in Mason Wiley and Damien Bona, *Inside Oscar* (New York: Ballantine Books, 1986), p. 368.
9. *Time*, 10 April 1964; *Saturday Review*, 4 April 1964.
10. Quoted in *Variety*, 15 September 1964.
11. Richard Maltby, *Harmless Entertainment: Hollywood and the Ideology of Consensus* (London: Scarecrow, 1983), p. 306.
12. *The New York Times*, 31 August 1968; *Saturday Review*, 6 September 1969; *The New Yorker*, 13 September 1969.

"How Do You Know They'll Print It?"

Cynicism and Paranoia in the Seventies

The American invasion of Cambodia in 1970 produced the most widespread anti-war demonstrations of the era, but they were probably the last gasp of the movement, just as the invasion was the last desperate military gambit of President Richard Nixon and Secretary of State Henry Kissinger. Afterward, the war wound down, finally ending with the fall of Saigon in 1975. Before that, Nixon had enjoyed a landslide reelection victory only to face the protracted agony of the Watergate scandal. His 1973 resignation began an era of almost total disillusionment with politics and put the uninspired Gerald Ford into the White House. The political activism of the sixties gave way to what Tom Wolfe labeled the "Me Decade." Self-interest and political apathy replaced involvement.

The film industry was also retrenching after the big studios suffered record losses between 1969 and 1972. Coincidentally, these had been among the industry's most political years, but the high volume of political films was not sufficiently linked with financial losses to discourage further productions. Some, like *Che!*, an awful film about the Cuban revolutionary, lost money. Others – including *Easy Rider*, *Medium Cool*, and *Z* – were sufficiently profitable to make the studios take notice, while big productions like *Hello, Dolly* and *Ryan's Daughter*, lost more money than most of the political films cost, so the studios were not totally discouraged and independent filmmakers were positively encouraged.

But while the output of political films at the end of the sixties and the beginning of the seventies was high, Hollywood's approach to politics remained cautious except in the hands of independents like Haskell Wexler and Europeans like Costa-Gavras. Many of the films of this highly political era dealt delicately or indirectly with contemporary issues. Most of the anti-war movies, for example, were set during wars

The Candidate (1972)

other than the one in which the country was then engaged. More remarkably, virtually no movies dealt directly with the political process, except perhaps *Wild in the Streets*. Then, in 1972, Joseph Sargent made *The Man*, in which the president pro tem of the Senate (James Earl Jones) becomes America's first black president when the incumbent dies and the vice president (Lew Ayres) is disabled by a stroke. At first reluctant to exercise his power, the new president finally does so as the film concludes affirmatively. *The Man* was a sixties-style political melodrama, but 1972 also brought another film with a more contemporary political perspective.

Mr. Redford Goes to Washington

Robert Redford was the star, producer, and prime mover in *The Candidate* (1972), the first and best film of the seventies to deal with political campaigns. Although the film uncannily anticipated the career of Edmund G. "Jerry" Brown, writer Jeremy Larner and director Michael Ritchie based it on their experiences in the 1970 campaign of John Tunney, the Kennedyesque senator from California. Several incidents in the film were drawn from the Tunney campaign, and the senator was allowed to okay the script "so it wouldn't be a knife job on him," according to Ritchie.[1]

The Candidate begins on election night in an unnamed state, as a losing candidate addresses his supporters. His manager (Peter Boyle) is already on his way to another campaign, showing a colleague a photo of young Bill McKay (Robert Redford) in *Time* magazine. The manager is warned that McKay couldn't possibly beat Crocker Jarmon (Don Porter), the powerful incumbent senator from California, but he nevertheless goes to McKay's ramshackle poverty law office. From McKay's directions to his staff, we learn of the good causes the handsome son of a former governor works on, but he tells the manager that he's happy with what he's doing and he's not interested in politics. "You're happy?" the manager asks. "Okay. Clams are happy. You saved some trees, you got a clinic opened. Does that make you feel good? Meanwhile, Jarmon sits on his committees and carves up the land, the oil, the taxes. . . ." Tempted, McKay asks what's in it for the manager, who murmurs something about "an air card, a phone card, a thousand dollars a week." It's only a job to him, he says, but he appeals to McKay, the crusader, by offering him a forum for his causes and by promising him that he'll lose the election. "Of course you'll have to register," McKay's wife warns as he agrees. Like many post-sixties activists, McKay is an idealist and a crusader, but he is naive, apathetic about traditional politics and somewhat suspicious of it.

In the beginning, the campaign is forthright and issue-oriented as McKay bluntly answers questions on controversial issues like abortion and busing at his first press conference. "Jesus!" a reporter exclaims. "That's a first," another declares as McKay admits he doesn't know enough to answer a question. But when he says he'd fire the Board of Regents of the University of California only to be told that senators do not have that power, McKay begins to recognize his need to be briefed on issues, and after that he grows more dependent on his manager and staff.

The manager takes the candidate to a media man (Allan Garfield), who is enthusiastic about McKay's youth and virility as contrasted with the age and weariness of his opponent. The voters, he says, will look at Jarmon and think "the crock . . . can't get it up anymore." So the media packaging begins, first with a haircut, then with new suits and ties, and finally with carefully filmed and edited television ads. In the first ads, McKay talks about issues, but when he sees the results, he realizes that issues don't work in commercials, and so do we. The edited, music-backed ads are much better. "You're showing your face," the media man explains. "That's what we have to sell first." McKay keeps trying to talk about the issues as he is filmed meeting people, but the results are incoherent. "Maybe we can use a line or two out of context," sighs the consultant.

Nobody else wants to run against Jarmon, and McKay wins his party primary easily, but then, manipulated by the manager and his opinion polls, he begins to want to win the election. "You're only reaching the people who agree with you already," the manager says, "You're gonna lose." "But I'm supposed to lose," the candidate replies. "Yeah," says the manager, "but if you keep going this way, you won't only lose, you'll be humiliated, and so will your ideas." We can see that McKay is being manipulated, but we're seduced along with him. Soon he's making all the compromises necessary to win, rehearsing for press conferences and softening his tone on issues. We watch as his advance men prepare a rally, cynically guaranteeing a crowd by scheduling the event during the busy lunch hour and blocking off streets. Eventually, McKay grows so accustomed to being packaged that when he goes on television he points at his coat and asks whether to button it or not: "Is this open?" Told to change his tie, he first asks why, then gives up with a resigned "Never mind."

One of the themes of *The Candidate* is the power of the media, deftly introduced through actual footage of Hubert Humphrey, George McGovern, and John Tunney at a big banquet. As McKay rises to give his maiden speech, however, the TV lights are switched off and a voice in the background says, "Okay, we got all we need." Later, McKay tries to get some free coverage, changing his schedule to rush to a forest fire in Malibu. "It's perfect," his breathless staff says, showing no concern about the disaster. When he gets there, McKay begins talking about environmental policy, but he is interrupted when his powerful opponent arrives by helicopter and the press dashes away to question him. Jarmon points up the power of incumbency with the reminder that he chairs a Senate committee and has a direct line to the president. He promises to do something immediately, and McKay can only smile ruefully.

As the campaign grows more desperate, McKay is persuaded to swallow his pride and solicit the support of his father, the ex-governor, whose politics disgust him. "Did you really run your own [campaign]?" the son asks the father (Melvyn Douglas) as they walk in the woods groping for reconciliation. "Shit, yes," the old man says. "What's it like to campaign in this state these days?" "I wouldn't know," his son answers. When the young McKay debates his opponent, he grows frustrated with the glib platitudes he's been instructed to mouth and returns to his old style, bringing up all the tough issues they haven't discussed. Chastised by his staff and thoroughly demoralized, he returns to his dressing room, but his spirits are revived when his father arrives to endorse him. "Son," the old man says, "you're a politician" – the ultimate insult to young McKay. Still thinking about the debate, the candidate wonders "if anyone understood what I was trying to do." "Don't worry, son," his father says not very reassuringly. "It won't make any difference."

Eventually, the campaign completely swallows the candidate. He follows directions, not knowing where he is or what he's doing, and he has little real contact with people. His campaign staff has grown so large that he doesn't know them all. Groupies in search of autographs and sex treat him like a star, while strangers slug him or harangue him, even in toilets. He seldom argues with his aides, and when he does, he loses. He becomes an automaton, doing whatever they tell him. "I don't know what her name is, but she's sending a check," he reports after carrying out an order to phone a contributor.

McKay's campaign finally gains momentum and gels, however. At a meeting with the leader of a union similar to the Teamsters, the old Bill comes out as he condemns the union for what it has done to the farm workers, but the leader endorses him anyway, and at a rally of the union members he gives the speech that ignites the campaign. "There has to be a better way," he cries. In rhythmic references to the division between black and white, old and young, rich and poor, he demands change without being specific. It's a media speech, but it works. The upturn is accompanied by a stirring musical crescendo – the same music that underscored Crocker Jarmon's moving, patriotic speeches. The two candidates have become alike. The campaign rushes on, full of incidents that illustrate the humor, cynicism, intensity, and excitement of politics as well as its techniques, from advertising to getting out the vote. McKay is stunned, however, when he wins. "What do we do now?" he asks his manager, but before he gets the answer, he's swept away by cheering supporters. The door closes, and the camera lingers on a deserted white room.

The Candidate didn't set box offices afire, but it turned a profit and advanced the careers of Robert Redford, Michael Ritche, and Jeremy Larner, who won an Oscar for his script. Most reviewers liked the film, although Andrew Sarris denounced its "winning is losing puerilities."[2] Vincent Canby agreed, commenting on its "perverse and puritanical" view of politics. "If a candidate wants to win," he wrote, "he must be suspect. Ambition itself is bad. . . . We put great store by the kind of modesty that insures defeat and that, only then, is revealed to be a form of arrogance. The best man should lose, or he isn't the best man." But he conceded that *The Candidate* was "one of the few truly funny American political comedies ever made" and praised its style for being "as nervous and frenetic as the campaign itself."[3] Even politicians were impressed with *The Candidate*. California's Jerry Brown allegedly wanted to buy advertising time for his campaign during its television broadcast, but was dissuaded by his staff, who argued that the public would misunderstand. Brown and others liked the movie's humor, but they also appreciated its depiction of campaign techniques and of the seductive power of politics.

From advertising to winning endorsements and cajoling key groups, *The Candidate* is a veritable campaign primer, deficient only in its treatment of fund-raising. Presumably for simplicity's sake, the movie also ignores the Vietnam War.

This movie succeeds in catching the spirit of a campaign and the way it sweeps away not only the candidate but everybody around him. We watch McKay sell out, but we cheer him on because we, too, want him to win. We laugh at the cynicism of the campaigners and of the "now what?" ending, but all this cynicism is softened by the casting of Robert Redford as the candidate. He may be naive, but he means well, and in the end, we still like him, which makes it easier for us to understand how decent people get drawn into the political process and forget their good intentions.

The Candidate also marked a change in the way movies saw politics. Before World War II, filmmakers insisted that individuals could make a difference; heroes and heroines could fight the system and win, often by calling on the support of the people. But soon after the war, movies began to worry about the corrupting nature of power as good men became evil (*All The King's Men, A Lion Is in the Streets*) or had to walk away from politics to preserve their honor (*State of the Union*, *Viva Zapata!*). Still later, individuals had to adapt to the system and play as members of the team (*Advise and Consent*, *The Best Man*). But in *The Candidate*, the system was bigger than the individuals. The process itself dominates, and individuals were swept along by it. *The Best Man*, on the one hand, worried about means and ends, as Bill Russell contemplated the degree to which he was willing to compromise his values for his ambitions, and he eventually chose to leave the game. *The Candidate*, on the other hand, "phrased the essential political dilemma for activists in the early seventies," according to James Monaco. "Electoral politics is cooptative and ultimately severely compromising. But 'street' politics seems futile."[5] Bill McKay's only choice was whether to play. Once he joined the game, his choices had all been made. As entertaining and seductive as *The Candidate* was, its message about politics was less than encouraging.

Paranoia

The Candidate's sense of being overwhelmed by the system was mild, however, compared to the political messages of other films of the mid-seventies. Francis Ford Coppola followed *The Godfather* with *The Godfather, Part II* (1974), an even bleaker view of American society in which his Mafia family goes corporate and falls apart. Meanwhile, Roman Polanski's *Chinatown* (1974) took up corrupt water politics in Los Angeles, one of Hollywood's favorite themes, with a godfatherlike businessman (John Huston) pulling all the strings. In all three movies, economic interests were the dominant powers, and politicians were mere puppets.

Executive Action (1973), based on the works of conspiracy theorist Mark Lane and written by Dalton Trumbo, was even more paranoid with its theory that a right-wing conspiracy had President John F. Kennedy assassinated to prevent his family from perpetuating itself in power and moving the country to the left. The squeamishness of corporate interests holds the conspirators back briefly, but when big business finally gives its blessing, the plot proceeds. Newsreel footage and factual details made *Executive Action* seem realistic, but too much didactic dialogue defeated it with critics and at the box office.

Executive Action ends with an ominous report of the deaths of eighteen material witnesses within three years of Kennedy's assassination, an observation that also inspired *The Parallax View* (1974). In this film, a crusading reporter (Warren Beatty) stumbles onto a corporate assassination bureau when he notices that all the witnesses to a political killing are being eliminated. He infiltrates the Parallax Corporation, which at first seems to be training him as an assassin but later sets him up as the fall guy for another agent. The film begins and ends with investigative commissions dismissing charges of conspiracy in assassinations and concluding that the killer (in both cases the wrong man) acted alone, exactly as the Warren Commission did after the Kennedy assassination.

Director Alan Pakula called *The Parallax View* "a cautionary tale of 'native fascism,' " but with its ominous music, dark lighting, and obscure villain, it was basically up-dating the political thriller. Pakula also declared this his film marked "the death of the hero,"[6] since his protagonist was overwhelmed by the faceless organization. The Beatty character was not merely coopted, like Bill McKay in *The Candidate*; he was destroyed by the system. Even in the cynical seventies, however, audiences apparently weren't ready to give up on heroes and happy endings, for *The Parallax View* failed at the box office.

Another paranoid thriller appeared the following year. It was *Three Days of the Condor*, directed by Sydney Pollack and co-authored by Lorenzo Semple, Jr., one of the scenarists of *The Parallax View*. Robert Redford is back as a slightly scruffy CIA researcher who chances onto some dangerous information that results in his entire office being wiped out, a massacre he escapes only by a fluke. He phones his superiors, who promise him safety if he comes in, but when the friend sent to reassure him is murdered, he grows wary. Isolated and able to trust no one, be becomes paranoid. In the end, he figures out that a renegade organization has penetrated the CIA, but since he doesn't know whom to trust, he takes his story to *The New York Times*. This promises a happy ending until a CIA operative (Cliff Robertson) says to Redford, "How do you know they'll print it?" The doubt in Redford's face leaves us uncertain about the film's ending. Is even *The New York Times* controlled?

Three Days of the Condor was not as paranoid as *The Parallax View*, however. Its bad guys were deviant cases, and it did have good guys, although it was hard to know who they were. It also suggested that a good man could fight the system by appealing to the public through the press – or could he? The seed of doubt planted at the very end satisfied both supporters and critics of the system who could believe or disbelieve that the *Times* would print the Condor's story. This ambiguous ending may have helped make *Condor* one of the all-time political box office hits, although audiences may have been drawn more by the star power of Robert Redford.

The success of *Three Days of the Condor* was surpassed, however, by that of *All the President's Men*, another well-made Redford film. Although this movie was presented as a thriller, audiences consciously saw it as a political movie. Fascinated by the story of Nixon's fall from power, Redford acquired the rights to the book by Bob Woodward and Carl Bernstein. He then recruited director Alan Pakula, who brought to all of his films an ominous sense of doom through the clever use of lighting, editing, and music. Aided by writer William Goldman and cinematographer Gordon Willis, Pakula gave this same tone to *All the President's Men*.

The filmmakers faced a problem, however, when they set out to make a movie of events that were only three years old. Audiences had read the story in the newspapers, watched the Senate hearings on television, and heard Nixon deny his involvement, and they had made a best-seller of the book by the young reporters who started the Watergate investigation. The filmmakers were gambling that the nation was sufficiently obsessed with the story to make their movie a success, too. But as Pakula said, the story consisted of "one phone call after another. How do you make that interesting?"[7] With megastars Robert Redford and Dustin Hoffman in the lead roles, they decided to play the story as a thriller. *All the President's Men* could not be a whodunit, of course, since the public already knew the answer. It was more of a how-they-done-it, focusing on the young reporters and how they gradually and painstakingly got their story. The thriller elements helped to make entertainment out of slogging journalistic drudgery.

The action begins with the Watergate burglary, a story assigned to junior *Washington Post* reporter Bob Woodward (Redford). Carl Bernstein (Dustin Hoffman) muscles in as co-author, and when their story looks bigger than burglary, editor Ben Bradlee (Jason Robards, Jr.) resists demands to put a national reporter on it. The big-time editors and reporters, we are told, would be less likely to dig into the story because they've been coopted by their subjects, lunching at the same posh restaurants as the president's men. This battle between the little guys and the elite puts us firmly on the side of the young reporters and their tough editor. They experience self-doubt when other papers ignore the story, missing the security of pack journalism, but they persist.

These pressures are made visual by the film's techniques, which constantly isolate and dwarf the reporters. As they drive away from the newspaper building, for example, their car seems to be swallowed up by the city. As they plow through reams of research material at the Library of Congress, the camera looks down on them, and they appear to the audience as tiny figures encircled by an endless maze, an image that suggests the impossibility of their huge task. At another point, Woodward sits alone at his typewriter while his television screen shows a crowd at the Republican convention chanting, "Four more years!"

The sound track, too, constantly underlines their isolation with ominous music.

The two battling journalists gradually get their story not from the president's men but from low- and middle-level workers in the Campaign to Re-Elect the President (CREEP) – except for Deep Throat (Hal Holbrook), the mysterious high-level informant whose face is never shown and who insists on secret meetings. Like the Parallax Corporation or the Condor's CIA, CREEP is powerful, unapproachable, and somehow dangerous. The low-level informants are terrified, and even Deep Throat is obviously fearful. Film technique makes this fear palpable when Deep Throat meets Woodward deep inside a murky parking garage in a scene complete with creepy footsteps and thriller lighting. But while the investigation takes place in half-light and long shots with high camera angles, the revelations take place in the bright newsroom, with the camera closer and lower. Pakula says the "hard light of truth is in that newsroom; no shadows there."[8] At the end of the movie, we hear the guns saluting Nixon's inauguration on a television set in the newsroom, but the shots are gradually drowned out by the clacking of a lone Teletype pounding out reports of the conviction of the president's men. By telling the truth to the people, two little guys have brought down the president and his men – an even more upbeat ending than even Capra provided – and this time the story was true.

The crtics were almost unanimously ecstatic about *All the President's Men*, praising its accurate treatment of journalism although mainly admiring it as a thriller. Vincent Canby called it "the thinking man's *Jaws*."[9] Woodward and Bernstein became role models for American youth as journalism schools turned away applicants and newspapers were swamped by investigative reporters. Only Sylvester Stallone's *Rocky*, another movie about a little guy making good, beat *All the President's Men* at the box office in 1976. No other purely political film has done better at the box office than this one, which ranked as one of *Variety*'s 100 "Box Office Champions" 1984. Audiences responded to a well-made film with big stars, but they must also have wanted to relive the recent trauma of Watergate and learn more about it. The film was nominated for Academy Awards for best film and direction. Goldman won an Oscar for his script, and Jason Robard took the award for supporting actor.

Yet the political message of *All the President's Men* was far from profound. The movie said that politics is corrupt and that bad men can gain great power, but it also said that brave individuals, a free press, and public opinion can bring the evil men down – the traditional Hollywood view. The fact that the movie played down politics and concluded reassuringly may partly account for its success. Whereas *The*

Parallax View had said that evil was all-pervasive, *President's Men* said that wickedness could be exposed and defeated. The Condor's faith in the integrity of the press was vindicated. And this movie also delivered a message about heroes. If *The Parallax View* dealt with the vanishing hero, *All the President's Men* was about his reappearance.

Our "heroes," however, seem more devoted to advancing their careers than to saving their country from the forces of darkness. They chortle with glee when they find wrongdoing in high places. They publish their findings knowing innocent people will be hurt, and the movie does not justify their action. They manipulate people and use their colleagues. Their tricks finally lead them to make a big mistake about the confirmation of some information. When Bernstein meets Donald Segretti (Robert Walden), the Nixon operative smirks about his "dirty tricks" just as the reporter smirks about the dirt he's digging up. They're interchangeable careerists.

Pakula's journalists still come off as heroes, but the message of *All the President's Men* is not entirely comforting. If two junior reporters have to save the country all by themselves, surely democratic institutions and the press are working imperfectly. It was good fortune that Bob Woodward was in that police court and that he had a fanatical colleague and a stubbornly courageous editor, but the defense of democracy would have failed if just one of them had been diverted. Furthermore, playing the story as a thriller implied an ominous and evil power although it remained undefined. Was it as malevolent and omnipotent as it seemed? What were the CREEP workers so frightened of and what actually happened to them? Who were the president's men and what exactly did they do? Their actions may have been an accumulation of small corruptions not entirely unlike those practiced by Woodward and Bernstein, but Pakula made them seem purely malign, perhaps even worse than they were. The president's men became a faceless conspiracy like the Parallax Corporation. This treatment, however, probably had more to do with making an entertaining and profitable movie than with sending a message.

Rocky and Jimmy

Jimmy Carter was elected president in 1976, the year of *All the President's Men* and *Rocky*. According to scriptwriter William Goldman, Ronald Reagan thought that *All the President's Men* "cost Gerald Ford the presidency against Jimmy Carter, because the film's release in April of '76 and its long run flushed to the surface again all the realities of Watergate that the Republicans had tried so hard to bury. We are talking," Goldman boasted, "about a movie that . . . just might have changed the entire course of American history."[10] Appropriately, it was the first film screened in the Carter White House.

But Reagan and Goldman not withstanding, *Rocky* may have had as much to do with Carter's election as *All the President's Men* did. Both movies were about little guys who became heroes, just as Carter rose from the obscurity of Georgia politics to the presidency. Like movie politicians from Mr. Smith onward, Carter presented himself as a nonpolitician, carrying his own luggage, sleeping in the homes of voters, and swearing never to tell a lie; and the nation longed for a nonpolitician like Jimmy Carter in 1976.

NOTES

1. James Monaco, *American Film Now* (New York: Oxford University Press, 1979), p. 356.
2. Andrew Sarris, *Politics and Cinema* (New York: Columbia University Press, 1978), p. 20.
3. *The New York Times*, 30 June 1972.
4. Monaco, *Film Now*, p. 356.
5. Ibid.
6. Alan Pakula, Guardian Lecture, National Film Theatre, London, 25 February 1986.
7. Ibid.
8. Ibid.
9. *The New York Times*, 3 August 1976.
10. William Goldman, *Adventures in the Screen Trade* (London: Futura, 1985), p. 147.

11

"It Don't Worry Me"

The Revenge of the Blacklist and the Emergence of Disillusionment

Thrillers dominated the political films of the sixties and seventies, thanks to popularity of movies like *The Manchurian Candidate* and *Three Days of the Condor*. Only a few films like *The Best Man* and *The Candidate* focused on the political process itself. Unfortunately, the interest of filmmakers in politics during this period lagged behind that of the nation, with the number of political films increasing only later, as the nation grew more alienated and apathetic. The films of the sixties did succeed, however, in shattering the consensus patterns of the fifties, and they did open the door to more political films with more diverse points of view. In addition to political thrillers and movies like *The Candidate*, the mid-seventies brought three other distinct but unrelated developments in filmmaking: a modest revival of the Old Left, the disillusionment of the New Left, and the emergence of the blockbuster.

Revenge of the Blacklist

As the civil rights and anti-war movements culminated in the emergence of the New Left, the Old Left found itself rehabilitated. The activists who had been blacklisted and spurned in the fifties became the new heroes and heroines, and the old witch-hunt virtually reversed itself as HUAC's collaborators and friendly witnesses fell into disrepute. Lillian Hellman, Dalton Trumbo, Arthur Miller, and others who had been harassed became cultural icons, and the Old Left got its revenge in the movies, too.

In the grand Hollywood tradition, however, the first of these films, *The Way We Were* (1973), was more romantic than political. Star

The Front (1976)

casting and an eye toward prospective profits may have led to the toning down of the political content originally intended by director Sydney Pollack and writer Arthur Laurents, who adapted his own novel.

We learn early in the movie that Katie (Barbra Streisand) is politically combative as we hear her maniplating propaganda in a wartime radio script and then arguing with a "fascist rope-holder" at a nightclub. This established, we flashback to Katie's student activist days in the thirties. As president of the Young Communists League, she is serious and committed, even fanatical, and she works her way through college, too. The rich, handsome Hubbell (Robert Redford), however, is just out for a good time. Katie, who is Jewish, dismisses Hubbell as a rich WASP twit until one of his short stories is read aloud in class. "In a way he was like the country he lived in," the story begins. "Everything came too easily." From that moment, Katie is infatuated. During the war, she and Hubbell meet again and fall in love, but his WASP complacency and her activism keep the relationship tense.

When Hubbell accepts a job as a Hollywood scriptwriter, Katie is reduced to a busybody housewife, and the two of them begin to drift apart, apparently doomed by their differences. Politics precipitates a crisis when the Hollywood investigations begin and Katie publicly protests HUAC's persecution. This is the breaking point in their relationship. Hubbell and Katie separate, and the movie ends when they accidentally meet later in New York City. She's handing out ban-the-bomb literature, and he's taking his new WASP wife into the Plaza Hotel. Katie reports that she, too, has remarried, and they part somewhat nostalgically.

The romantic stars made *The Way We Were* a box office hit, but most reviewers criticized its soft politics, which reduced the movie to a melodrama of doomed love. In scenes that were cut from the movie at the last minute, Katie is called to testify before HUAC and must choose between naming names or refusing to do so and hurting Hubbell's career. She refuses and loses him for the sake of her politics. Had audiences seen this version, we might have wished the wimpy Hubbell good riddance, but instead we see Katie giving up Robert Redford just to stand on a street corner and hand out leaflets.

Nor surprisingly, the political theme of *The Way We Were* was lost on most audiences, but if its backers and makers played safe with their investment, those of *The Front* (1975) were more forthright. Of course, they were risking only $5 million, as compared to the $25 million that went into *The Way We Were*, and they had Woody Allen in the lead, so they could also count on some star power. Besides, several of the participants in the making of *The Front* had been blacklisted themselves: actors Zero Mostel, Herschel Bernardi, and Joshua Shelley;

writer Walter Bernstein; and director Martin Ritt. This fact was noted
in the end credits of *The Front*, adding to the film's credibility.

In this film, a blacklisted TV scriptwriter (Michael Murphy) asks his
friend Howard (Woody Allen) to "front" for him. This means that
Howard will put his name on the writer's scripts and deal with
producers in the writer's stead in return for a fee. Howard agrees
because he needs the money, and soon he is serving as a front for other
blacklisted writers as well. He enjoys the wealth and prestige of being
thought of as a writer. As fame and fortune go to his head, he begins to
criticize the scripts he has to front and to demand higher output from
the writers. The workings of the blacklist are seen not only through
Howard's dealings with the writers he fronts for, but also through
pressures on Hecky Brown (Zero Mostel), a comic. Called in to the
office of the enforcer of the blacklist, Hecky is accused of left-wing
activities, but he swears he only went to a few rallies and signed some
petitions in pursuit of a girl. Terrified of losing his job, he pleads that
he's "only an actor" and volunteers to say anything they want. They
order him to spy on Howard, but when Hecky loses his job anyway, he
kills himself.

The investigators then subpoena Howard. He has no politics and is
outraged at being wrongly accused, but he can't inform because to do
so would mean losing his stable of writers. The investigators demand
names – any names, even the dead, even Hecky Brown. One of the
writers Howard fronts for explains that all the persecuters really want is
to prove they can make Howard submit – a belief widely shared by
HUAC's critics. During the hearing, Howard balks at naming his dead
friend Hecky, declaring that he doesn't recognize the committee's right
to "ask those kind of questions and furthermore you can all go fuck
yourselves." He walks out, and the film ends with him being taken to
prison for contempt. A crowd cheers, his left-wing writers pat him on
the back, and he wins back his liberal girlfriend. The "front" is treated
like a hero as "Young at Heart" plays on the sound track ("Fairy tales
can come true, it can happen to you . . .").

The Front received mixed notices from critics, many of whom found
if unsatisfactory as either political analysis or comedy. The harshest
criticisms were from the left for taking the blacklisting too lightly,
particularly through the comic "intrusion . . . of the classic Woody
Allen character, the Jewish schlemiel."[1] Pauline Kael thought it was a
"slightly archaic" movie about a common man standing up for what
was right, "like the heroes of the forties wartime movies written by
those who were later blacklisted."[2] Audiences, however, liked *The
Front*, probably for the very reasons the critics didn't, and it was more
successful at the box office than a film with tougher politics might have
been.

The Front clearly described the workings of the blacklist and left no doubt that it was bad. If anything, the movie oversimplified this evil by making the investigators and enforcers gross caricatures with no credible motives. To the film's credit, however, not all of its blacklist victims were as innocent as Hecky and Howard. Still, *The Front* offered little real understanding of why the blacklist existed, and even its terrible impact on individuals was obscured by what most audiences took as a happy ending, despite the filmmakers' implication that it was fantasy. *The Front* was further weakened by the casting of Woody Allen in the lead, instantly making it "a Woody Allen movie." Howard learned, grew, and finally took action, yet because of Allen's presence the audience perceived the movie as a comedy, straining for laughs even when they weren't there.

In the end, *The Front* said blacklisting was wrong not for political reasons but because it hurt innocent people. Even the communists in this film were such nice guys that it was impossible to tell why anybody would be worried about them. *The Front* provided such a soft analysis of the blacklist that it disappointed many on both left and right.

The Way We Were and *The Front* illustrate how political messages can be subverted or obscured by Hollywood's imperative to find an audience and make money. Both films took on political subjects, then backed away, the former toward romance and the latter toward comedy. Both films would have been stronger if the motives of their main characters had been more clearly political, but the actions of Streisand's Katie were completely unfathomable and those of Allen's Howard were reduced to love and loyalty. On the other hand, the romance and comedy found audiences, which tougher politics might not have.

Although *Julia* (1977) wasn't explicitly about the blacklist, it must have been sweet revenge for HUAC critic Lillian Hellman, who wrote the book, *Pentimento*, on which this film was based. Directed by Fred Zinnemann, *Julia* starred Jane Fonda and Vanessa Redgrave, both of whom, like Hellman, had suffered career setbacks because of their politics.

Julia (Redgrave) is a student activist, an anti-fascist, and a committed revolutionary in Nazi Germany. She asks her friend Lillian (Fonda) to help her by doing something brave and dangerous. Lillian does so, out of personal loyalty rather than political commitment, and matures as a result. The politically conscious Julia is the moral center of the film and her commitment is strongly justified by her anti-fascism. Lillian, on the other hand, shows the naiveté of some people who associated with left-wing causes in the thirties, suggesting that HUAC exaggerated their subversiveness.

In most political films up to this time, women had been marginal if they were present at all, at best providing motivation. Julia and Lillian, however, were committed to their work and their friendship, both of which were treated with reverence. *Julia* had the courage to offer true heroines and to honor involvement, and feminists welcomed the strong women characters of this movie, even though Lillian's dependence on the approval of her lover and fellow writer, Dashiell Hammett (Jason Robards), qualified the film's feminism. By giving both women a firm basis for their actions and by letting us see Lillian's maturation, *Julia* provided a politically stronger condemnation of HUAC and the blacklist than either *The Way We Were* or *The Front*, even though those films were more politically explicit. Significantly, this film about friendship, bravery, and political commitment – which was not a romance and not a comedy – was a popular and critical success and won three Oscars.

Disillusionment

Whatever their shortcomings, *The Way We Were*, *The Front*, *Julia*, and *All the President's Men* acknowledged the potential for honorable individual action. *The Candidate* and the political thrillers of the seventies had argued that such action was futile against the over-powering corruption of the system, but their heroes were willing to join the struggle, and at least there was a central power that could be opposed, even if defeat was inevitable.

Other movies of the seventies were more deeply disillusioned, perhaps more accurately reflecting the spirit of the times. The most beloved political leaders had been killed. The movements of the sixties and seventies had fallen apart. Political action seemed useless to many liberals after the defeat of George McGovern and the reelection of Richard Nixon in 1972. Watergate, Nixon's resignation, and Gerald Ford's presidency only exacerbated the disillusionment, as did the evacuation of Saigon in 1975. Crime, violence, urban decay, and racial polarization were on the rise, and the environmental and sexual liberation movements seemed more personal than political. The country diffidently celebrated its bicentennial in 1976 as the little-known anti-politician Jimmy Carter was elected president. Not surprisingly, movies reflected the nation's disillusionment.

During this period, Warren Beatty, one of Hollywood's most politically active stars, produced, co-authored (with Robert Towne) and starred in *Shampoo* (1975), directed by Hal Ashby. Although this is not primarily a political movie, its climactic scene takes place at a political banquet and it uses constant television commentary on the 1968 election of Richard Nixon as a backdrop. Beatty said his movie was "about the intermingling of political and sexual hypocrisy,"[3] comparing Nixon's public behavior with our own private behavior.

Director Robert Altman showed similar disillusionment in *Nashville* (1975), using the country-and-western music capital as a microcosm of American society. Altman had taken on the military in *M*A*S*H* and had made corporate businessmen the villains in his "western," *McCabe and Mrs. Miller*. *Nashville* was more overtly political, although most viewers were unsure just what the message was. Like Altman's other films of the seventies, it destroyed all expectations with its multi-character structure and chaotic plot, yet it managed to remain profoundly humanist.

No less than twenty-four characters crisscross through *Nashville*. Their lives are a country-and-western version of Tom Wolfe's "Me Decade" as they dash around trying to attain or keep hold of stardom. Only two women and a black restaurant worker have integrity; all the other characters sell out, especially the white males. "The whole piece," scriptwriter Joan Tewkesbury said, "was about people who were trying to do the best job they could with the equipment they had in this dumb kind of social structure."[4]

As in *Shampoo*, politics provides a backdrop for the hustling in *Nashville*. Hal Philip Walker is the unseen "Replacement party" candidate for president. A roving sound truck constantly announces his vaguely populist proposals, including a new national anthem "that people can sing." An advance man (Michael Murphy), reminiscent of the campaign manager in *The Candidate*, is in Nashville lining up stars to support Walker at a big concert – a type of political rally that became common after *Nashville* was released. All twenty-four characters come together at the rally, and the movie climaxes when one of them, a country megastar, is murdered by an assassin who apparently panics while waiting to kill Hal Philip Walker. The film ends as an aspiring country music star picks up the microphone and sing "It Don't Worry Me," an anti-political song that says we'll all survive no matter what.

Audiences were mystified by *Nashville*, probably because of its chaotic structure, and its box office was mediocre, but the film was nominated for five Academy Awards, and critics raved about it. Some complained about its ending, however, and Tewksbury admitted that the assassination was added at Altman's request.[5] Such occurrences were on Americans' minds at the time, and this one pointed up the randomness of violence in our society, but as an ending, it may have been more convenient than political. The basic mood of *Nashville* was pessimistic, the film had no political answers, and only a few honorable characters offered hope for the future.

Martin Scorcese's *Taxi Driver* (1976) was even bleaker. This film's protagonist, Travis Bickle (Robert De Niro), is an unstable Vietnam vet who is drawn to politics by his infatuation with a campaign worker (Cybill Shepherd), who ignores him. To get attention or revenge, he plans to assassinate her candidate, but he is diverted by his obsession with a child prostitute (Jodie Foster) and ends up wreaking bloody havoc on her pimp (Harvey Keitel). Politics is viewed as a separate world in this movie, a world that is irrelevant to the hell Travis lives in. Like the beautiful campaign worker, politics is hypocritical and uncaring, incapable of providing salvation. Travis wreaks his crazy vengeance not on the politician, however, but on the pimp, a target many regarded as deserving. This grim, anti-political movie was allegedly an inspiration to John Hinckley, who attempted to assassinate President Ronald Reagan to gain the attention of Jodie Foster.

Network (1976) featured yet another crazy man and yet another assassination. Directed by Sidney Lumet and written by Paddy Chayefsky, *Network* was a huge popular and critical hit, with four Oscars and five more nominations, for although it was as cynical as *Nashville* and *Taxi Driver*, audiences found it more entertaining. "I've had enough and I'm not going to take it any more!" cries a TV anchorman (Peter Finch) when he's fired. He threatens to commit suicide on live television and becomes a cult hero. The network sees it has a good thing going and unscrupulously takes advantage of the newsman's insanity by giving him his own show. An old-style newsman (William Holden) disapproves, and in the end, he leaves the network. His traditional values are compromised by his affair with a programming executive (Faye Dunaway) who will broadcast anything that will get good ratings, including a sort of terrorist-of-the-week show. She's encouraged and rewarded by the vicious and unscrupulous network president (Robert Duvall), but even he is subordinate to the chairman of the board (Ned Beatty). Preaching like a revivalist converting sinners, the chairman warns the obsessed anchorman to contain his rabble-rousing because corporations like the one that owns the network have replaced nations and now rule the world.

Network's "I've had enough" slogan gave the film a populist tone, but its contempt for television audiences did not manifest faith in the public. In fact, *Network* offered no hope at all. Even the good liberal (Holden) was impotent and opted out. The film was most cynical about the entertainment industry itself, however.

Like other movies of the seventies, including both *Godfather* films, *Chinatown*, *The Parallax View*, and *Shampoo*, *Network* saw politics and politicians as less powerful than corporations, a more radical and distressing political analysis than that offered by earlier films. Even more distressing, these movies refused to offer even a glimmer of hope.

Blockbusting

Most other movies of the seventies, however, weren't at all worried about politics. This was the time of the new blockbusters and a new generation of film-makers like Francis Ford Coppola, Steven Spielberg, and George Lucas. They learned filmmaking in universities rather than in studios, they were committed to entertaining, and they seemed content to express themselves within traditional genres. These young men and others thrived in a Hollywood where producing a movie depended less on studios than on packaging a deal and putting together investors. They had spectacular early successes that gave them enormous freedom on later projects. Some say they saved the industry.

Coppola's *Godfather* successes were the beginning, but Spielberg's *Jaws* was the first real blockbuster, shooting to the top of *Variety*'s chart of box office champions. Although it was primarily a horror film, *Jaws* commented briefly on politics when the mayor of the shark-threatened resort forced the police chief to keep the beaches open so business wouldn't suffer. Spielberg went on to make *Close Encounters of the Third Kind*, *Raiders of the Lost Ark* and *E.T.*, all of which contained only minimal explicit political comment. Lucas started with *American Graffiti*, then went on to make *Star Wars* and its equally successful sequels.

All of these films were blockbusters, and all were intended purely as entertainment. Their lack of political content has been seen by some critics as a sort of conservatism, as has their reliance on individual heroes. One radical film journal even went so far as to condemn *Star Wars* as a fascist and militaristic movie, because of its hierarchies of sex, race, class, and species, complaining that only the humans, not the Wookies or the robots, got medals for their heroism.[6] Still, Lucas's humans did at least take action to overthrow the "evil empire" (a phrase later used by President Reagan) while the human beings in Spielberg's sci-fi films were brought together and given hope by friendly aliens rather than by their fellow human beings.

These movies were only mildly and probably unintentionally conservative, however, in comparison with other films of the time. Clint Eastwood played a cop in *Dirty Harry* (1971) and its sequels, all of which violently condemn permissiveness and liberalism. Charles Bronson got a vigilante's revenge on urban criminals in *Death Wish* (1974). In movies of this sort, danger and injustice were all around, often in the form of menacing minorities or poor people, but government was tied up by bleeding heart regulations, so the only solution was to go beyond the law. Meanwhile, horror movies made a comeback, often as "slashers," playing on fear and isolation. Disaster movies also fed paranoia, although sometimes in these films people worked together to rise above a crisis and save themselves. On a slightly more positive note, Sylvester Stallone's *Rocky* updated the American dream of the average guy winning out, a theme Stallone would reiterate with astounding success in seemingly endless sequels.

The conservative tendency of films like these was less in their content than in their eschewal of politics and analysis in favor of more superficial entertainment. James Monaco blames this propensity on the film-student generation, claiming that directors like Lucas, Spielberg, and Scorcese "had learned everything about film and nothing about life," resulting in "a cinema that is formally (technically) extraordinarily sophisticated at the same time that it is intellectually preadolescent." He laments that *The Graduate*, *Bonnie and Clyde*, *Easy Rider*, and *2001*, all of which had "a kind of political-cultural commitment and an analytical intelligence that had been lacking in the old Hollywood," turned out to be "anomalies" rather than models.[7]

If filmmakers were becoming "preadolescent," so were their audiences, 76 percent of whom were under the age of thirty by 1976, a figure that has declined only slightly since then. The number of theaters shrunk to 13,500, although multiscreen complexes would soon bring the number up again. The good news for Hollywood was that weekly attendance was creeping up, reaching 18.4 million in 1976 after having bottomed out at 17.7 million in 1970. Film production also increased in 1976, with 353 films released, the most since 1950, probably because of the rise in attendance, the movies of the film-student generation, and the blockbuster syndrome. The most lasting impact, however, was to be the persistent preponderance of young people in audiences, people who were far more interested in entertainment than in serious analytical or political films.

NOTES

1. Norman Markowitz, "*The Front*, Comic Revenge," *Jump Cut* no. 15.
2. Pauline Kael, *Reeling* (Boston: Little, Brown, 1976), p. 170.
3. *Film Review*, November 1975, p. 8.
4. *American Film*, March 1979.
5. Ibid.
6. *Jump Cut*, 18 August 1978.
7. James Monaco, *American Film Now* (New York: Oxford University Press, 1979), p. 51.

12

"God Bless America"
Hollywood Confronts Vietnam

As America grew more conservative, filmmakers and their audiences began to purge themselves of the pain of the recent past by confronting it and then coming to terms with it. Jimmy Carter was one response to this development; his ascent to the presidency reflected our willingness to acknowledge and accept our limitations through self-criticism and humility. It was appropriate that almost all of the early films about American involvement in Vietnam were made during Carter's term in office.

The Quiet American and *The Ugly American* had anticipated the Vietnam quagmire. Brian De Palma's *Greetings* was an anti-establishment comedy about draft dodging, and *Medium Cool* touched on the protest movement. Other films of the sixties and early seventies condemned the military and war without mentioning Vietnam. That war functioned only as background in *American Graffitti*, where it was seen as a part of growing up, and in *Nashville*, where an edgy Vietnam vet who could have been an assassin turned out to be a hero. The crazed veteran of *Taxi Driver* did explode into horrific violence. But for the most part, filmmakers avoided Vietnam, because war films had never been commercially successful and because public opinion on the war was deeply divided. Taking a position on a phenomenon still in progress is particularly risky because events may alter both the outcome and public attitudes about it. Besides, the news of the war satisfied the curiosity of most people and made fictional treatments look silly. As a consequence, Vietnam didn't get to Hollywood until the war was over — except in one movie, *The Green Berets*.

The Deer Hunter (1978)

Old and New Views of War

John Wayne beat the others to the Vietnamese battlefield by a decade when he co-directed an old-fashioned, patriotic pro-war film that could just as well have been about World War II. *The Green Berets* (1968) begins with a black officer's didactic lecture to trainees who are about to don the famous berets of the special forces. A white officer (Aldo Ray) explains that the Chinese and Russians are already involved in the conflict, but a visiting liberal journalist (David Janssen) asks skeptical questions. Their instructive exchanges occupy most of the first third of the movie. When the scene shifts to Vietnam, every trite convention of the old war movies is dragged out, including orphans, mascots, painful efforts at comedy, and a scrounger (Jim Hutton). But this middle third of the movie is even more like one of Wayne's westerns, with the Vietcong attacking the Green Beret base like Indians laying siege to a frontier fort. Portrayed as yellow savages, they strip white bodies and brutalize villagers, although a sympathetic South Vietnamese (George Takei) functions as the "good Indian." The liberal reporter (Janssen) is converted by all this, denouncing his biased publisher and proposing to quit his job to join the army's public relations team, but the Green Beret commander (John Wayne) insists that he has a higher duty. He must keep his job and take the truth to the American people. The final third of the movie is a *Mission Impossible*-style caper, with a team of Green Beret guerrillas infiltrating enemy territory to beat them at their own game. "You're what this is all about," Wayne tells the Vietnamese orphan-mascot as the movie ends with the sun setting, interestingly, in the east.

The Green Berets is a long, cliché-ridden lecture in defense of the war. It is the sort of movie in which you know which supporting actors will die as soon as you're introduced to them and in which even the violence is reassuringly old-fashioned. The box office pull of John Wayne and his film's cozy invocation of tradition were enough to generate a profit for the film despite bad reviews and the protests of anti-war activists. Wayne was sufficiently politically committed that he may not have cared as much about profits as about the message, however, which could account for the most transparently propagandistic American movie since the pro-Russian films of the forties. At any rate, the message was too late to matter, coming just as the Tet offensive showed the strength of the enemy. Public opinion turned against the war, and Lyndon Johnson decided not to run for reelection.

Only when the war was over did movies seriously begin to contemplate Vietnam. The first of these efforts, *Twilight's Last Gleaming* (1977), was as much a film of the seventies as *The Green*

Berets seemed a film of the forties. A thriller along the lines of *Fail Safe*, this movie offers a left-wing explanation of the war rather than a right-wing justification like *The Green Berets*. Director Robert Aldrich, one of Hollywood's most consistent leftists, had previously made the pro-Indian *Apache* and the anti-war, anti-class *Attack*.[1]

Lawrence Dell (Burt Lancaster), the protagonist in *Twilight's Last Gleaming*, is a renegade general but contrary to convention, he's a liberal rather than a fascist, and he wants the American people to know the truth about U.S. involvement in Vietnam. Drummed out of the air force and railroaded into prison for his fanaticism, he escapes with two other inmates, seizes a SAC missile silo in Montana, and threatens to launch the missiles unless the president makes public the minutes of a National Security Council meeting that will tell all.

Dell's request seems resonable to the president (Charles Durning), but his advisers are opposed to revealing the truth. The U.S. commitment in Vietnam is "blood over the dam," according to the secretary of state (Joseph Cotton). The president overrules his advisers and journeys to Montana to accompany his blackmailers to freedom and tell the people the truth. This truth, as it turns out, is that the war was fought for the "doctrine of credibility." In other words, it was waged with no expectation of winning, merely to demonstrate to the Russians America's "willingness to fight limited wars to prevent nuclear wars," and "to prove we were capable of inhuman acts." Unlike the calm presidents played by Henry Fonda and Fredric March, this one is "scared shitless," as nervous about his aides as he is about the renegades. He brings Dell and his accomplices out of the silo, but they are immediately gunned down by sharpshooters under the command of an air force general (Richard Widmark). With his dying breath, the president seeks reassurance from the secretary of defense (Melvyn Douglas) that he'll keep his promise to reveal the truth to the people, but the secretary says nothing and we suspect that he has known all along that the president would be shot. In the words of Dell's black associate, the men who control the system would sacrifice even the president rather than "blow their gig."

The film's chilling conclusion gains nuance and a certain ambiguity from good casting and fine acting, but audiences and critics were unenthusiastic. Perhaps the issues raised by the movie were too abstract or even ideological, as it debated the merits of democracy and open government versus the rule of a wise elite, although most of this was deleted when the film was first released. Even in the full version, any connection between economic interests and the movie's secretive elite was ignored. Dell and the president, however, act as they do for clear, unambiguous reasons: they are good men, and they want the people to know the truth. In the earlier days of Hollywood, the good guys usually won when the people learned the truth. Here the truth never comes out and the good guys lose, but at least the movie tells us such heroes do exist.

Catching Up

A few years after the fall of Saigon, Hollywood finally caught up with Vietnam, and movies about the war appeared more often. *Rolling Thunder* (1977) featured a Vietnam vet using skills acquired in the war to wreak vengeance at home. *Big Wednesday* (1978) was about three surfers who were drafted and sent to Vietnam. The effects of the war were taken up in *Who'll Stop the Rain* (1978), which suggested that America had corrupted itself through its involvement in Vietnam, as a disillusioned journalist, criminals, crooked federal agents, and relatively innocent bystanders fight over the spoils – drugs, in this case.

Go Tell the Spartans (1978) and *The Boys in Company C* (1978) were the first combat films about Vietnam since *The Green Berets*, although neither was as old-fashioned as that film. *Go Tell the Spartans* takes place in the early days when Americans are just advisers in Vietnam, but one of them (Burt Lancaster) begins to doubt the worthiness of the cause. Sidney J. Furie's *The Boys in Company C*, however, was a combat film with a difference.

Like a World War II movie, *The Boys in Company C* follows a cross section of American men – including a black, a big-city Italian, a hippie, and a good ole country boy – through training and their first month in Vietnam, but we soon learn that this is like no other movie war. Within a day of arriving in Vietnam, one takes heroin, another deals drugs, and a third blows up a general's trailer. Their officers are tyrants interested only in body counts, the enemy is an unseen terror, and the South Vietnamese officers are corrupt. The movie, however, makes a point of including some good Vietnamese civilians who are befriended by the streetwise black soldier who reluctantly becomes leader of the group, pulling them together and making the men loyal to one another.

The men are ordered to lose a soccer match to a Vietnamese team in order to boost the morale of their allies. In return, Company C will be taken off combat duty and sent on a soccer tour. The catch is that they have to keep losing. They refuse and return to the front, preferring to take their chances rather than become part of the all-pervasive corruption. *The Boys in Company C* does not, however, say that fighting to win is the best alternative. Rather, it honors those who refuse to sell out, whether they fight or desert, and especially if they are loyal to their peers.

The Boys in Company C adopted some of the conventions of the old World War II movies in order to make itself easily accessible to audiences, but it still managed to stay a long way from *The Green Berets*. It did only about half as well at the box office, however. Unfortunately, this fine little movie was overshadowed by Hollywood's first big star-studded productions on Vietnam. *The Deer Hunter* and *Coming Home* swept the 1978 Oscars and cleaned up at the box office. These two films were also widely, if somewhat unfairly, perceived as representing the right- and left-wing perspectives on the war.

The Deer Hunter, written by Deric Washburn and directed by Michael Cimino, is about a group of working-class men who leave their industrial hometown to go to war. They do so out of a sense of duty, without questioning why and with no particular prejudices either for or against the war. The cameraderie of their life at home gives way to the brutality, chaos, confusion, and pervasive evil of the war. Everything centers on their struggle for survival when they are taken prisoner. Before they escape, the men are forced to play a brutal game of Russian roulette by their evil Vietcong captors. Having lived through incredible degradation, some of the young men return to their community, but they are ineradicably altered by what they've gone through, and they have difficulty adjusting.

Michael (Robert De Niro), the leader of the group and the most avid deer hunter, no longer takes pleasure in hunting. He returns to Saigon just before its fall to try to save Nick (Christopher Walken), who has become obsessed with the game of Russian roulette he learned from the Vietcong and now plays before an audience for money. The game becomes a symbol of American involvement in Vietnam, and it also reveals that its South Vietnamese audience and gamblers are just as vile and bloodthirsty as the Vietcong. Nick finally loses and Michael returns to their home town where the film ends with the surviving buddies sadly singing "God Bless America."

Although *The Deer Hunter* was a popular and critical hit, many people perceived it as a right-wing film because of its failure to question the war and its uniformly racist portrait of Asians. The film is oblivious to the impact of the war on the Vietnamese, in effect blaming them and absolving Americans of any responsibility. The game of Russian roulette, which has an important symbolic function in the film, is an effective dramatic device, but it also serves as a symbol of the Asians' contempt for human life. Director Cimino claimed that this was an anti-war film, because "any good picture about war is an anti-war picture,"[2] From this point of view, the Russian roulette was a symbol of the pointlessness of war and the whole movie was about how war destroyed individuals and communities. Even the singing of "God Bless America" could have been ironic, as the singers try to convince themselves that they still believe the lyric. Finally, Michael's inability to hunt deer when he returns from the war could have been because the war had taken the pleasure out of killing – or merely because the buddy-structure was gone. But while a case can probably be made for Cimino's claim, that *The Deer Hunter* was anti-war, his denials of racism are less convincing. His film blames the war on the Vietnamese. The war was bad because they were bad – so bad that they ruined innocent Americans like Cimino's working-class heroes. His film absolved them and America from responsibility for the war.

Although Cimino deserves commendation for making a movie about the men who really fought the war, he treated his working-class heroes condescendingly, making them incapable of articulating their thoughts and oblivious to the politics of the war. In fact, *The Deer Hunter* might have been a far more right-wing film if Cimino had shown authentic working-class men with authentic attitudes about the war.

In contrast to Cimino's epic of working-class men, *Coming Home* (1978) focuses on the middle-class wife of an officer. Initiated by Jane Fonda and Bruce Gilbert, *Coming Home* was directed by Hal Ashby, photographed by Haskell Wexler, and written by Waldo Salt, Robert C. Jones, and Nancy Dowd. The message these liberals put together was very different form Cimino's but almost as muddled.

Jane Fonda plays Sally, whose officer husband (Bruce Dern) is sent to Vietnam. Sally at first dreads being left alone, but after a while she feels liberated. She gets a sports car and a house on the beach and starts working with paraplegics. Soon she meets and falls in love with Luke (Jon Voight), a veteran who is opposed to the war. Like many Fonda characters, Sally is naive in the beginning, but she grows and learns and, as Gilbert Adair has written, "turns into Jane fonda."[3] Despite his disabilities, Luke furthers the cause by helping her achieve her first orgasm. They have happy times and play at the beach. Sally's husband, Bob, is mentally unbalanced when he comes back from Vietnam, and although she tries to be nice to him, he's too far gone. When the meddlesome FBI tells Bob that Sally has been involved with an anti-war activist, he confronts them menacingly but in the end swims out to sea to kill himself.

Like *The Best Years of Our Lives*, *Coming Home* was about adapting, although the earlier film never suggested that joining an anti-war movement could be a form of salvation. Luke was the model, coming to terms with a bad war by opposing it. In so doing, he became a complete, caring human being, and helped Sally to adjust. Bob, on the other hand, was unable to adapt his traditional military values to new circumstances. Too rigid to change, he had to die. He was, however, allowed to choose his own end and die with some dignity, an act said to have been copied by at least one person who saw the film. It could have been worse for Bob; an earlier draft of the script had him sniping at freeway traffic.

As an anti-war movie, *Coming Home* could have convinced only those who had already been converted. Apparently the filmmakers thought they could make their point most effectively by fudging the politics and playing up the romance. Perhaps they were right, for although some critics disdained this film as superficial, it did well at the box office and won Academy Awards for best actress, actor, and screenplay.

Having finally confronted Vietnam, Hollywood waited with bated breath for the definitive film on the subject from Francis Ford Coppola, America's hottest contemporary director after his *Godfather* successes. The anticipation was heightened when Coppola was nearly bankrupted by prodigious production problems in the Philippines, for unlike *The Deer Hunter* and *Coming Home*, all of *Apocalypse Now* was to be set in Vietnam.

Based on Joseph Conrad's novel, *Heart of Darkness*, Coppola's movie follows Willard (Martin Sheen) on his mission to find and kill Kurtz (Marlon Brando), an American officer who has become a renegade and is now fighting the enemy on their own terms. During his journey Willard runs into a cavalry officer addicted to surfing who leads a helicopter raid on an innocent village in search of the perfect wave. Later, Willard's crew panics and slaughters a boatload of Vietnamese who also turn out to be innocent. As their adventures continue, Willard and his men witness American troops going berserk over a *Playboy* show imported for their entertainment, reiterating the uniqueness of this war and sending up Bob Hope's renowned troop shows. After all this, when Willard finally arrives at Kurtz's bizarre encampment, the arguments of the renegade leader and his admirers in favor of their mad methods seem relatively persuasive. In the end, Willard has to decide whether to eliminate Kurtz, join him, or replace him. Within the insane reality of the film, all these alternatives seem credible.

Critics and audiences were stunned by *Apocalypse Now*, for Coppola's nightmare of Vietnam was more surrealistic than realistic. Reviews of the movie were mixed, as both left and right took pot shots at the confusing (or confused) politics of the film, and despite eight Academy Award nominations, *Apocalypse Now* won only for cinematography and sound. Coppola's film nevertheless did well at the box office, surpassing the other war movies to join *Variety*'s top 100 box office champions.

Despite their reservations, the critics generally agreed that *Apocalypse Now* successfully communicated the horror of the war. Better than other films, it suggested the war's other-worldliness, its confusion of good and evil, and its contagious, destructive madness. Yet *Apocalypse*

Now could also be read as a defense of that destructiveness because of Kurtz's claim that he was driven to extreme action by the atrocities of the Vietcong. In fact, Kurtz's justification of his behavior seemed to be the point of *Apocalypse Now*, not only because the role of Kurtz was played by a superstar but also because the character was the subject of the quest that took up two hours of the film.[4] This interpretation was undercut, however, by Kurtz's apparent madness, Brando's low-key performance, and the obvious innocence of the Vietnamese civilians in the earlier scenes. Besides, Kurtz seemed ready, even eager, for death, which would end "the horror." Actually, the weakest sequence in *Apocalypse Now* was the meeting with Kurtz, which was more pretentious that portentous. If the events leading up to that meeting are intended to explain Kurtz's actions rather than endorse them, the film and its image of Vietnam as a quagmire make sense, and the movie does make clear the reasons for deeper and deeper U.S. involvement and excess.

Losing Interest

All of the films about Vietnam made money and some were very big hits, but Hollywood soon turned away from the war. Bad reviews and box office worries played a part in this disenchantment, but the nature of the war seemed the primary reason. The complexity of the situation in Vietnam made it difficult to catch in fiction films, especially when so much of it had been seen in news footage on TV. The Vietnam War also remained a very painful subject, not only because America lost, but because the reasons for involvement had never been clear.

Hollywood liked simpler wars, like World War II, in which our reasons for fighting were clear, but in the brief cycle of movies about Vietnam, only *Twilight's Last Gleaming* offered an explanation – "the doctrine of credibility." *Apocalypse Now* honorably contemplated the deepening American involvement and its increasing irrationality, but on the whole these films focused safely on the direct impact of the war on the individuals who fought it and on its effect on American society. Except for a handful of characters in *The Boys in Company C* and *Coming Home* who survived with their honor and their sanity intact, these movies unanimously concluded that the war screwed everybody up, a message that was basically anti-war. In this at least, the Vietnam movies were well within the Hollywood tradition: most war films made during peacetime are anti-war. But even the anti-war message was obscured by the films' focus on individuals, a sure way to defuse political content, since every issue is personalized and therefore not necessarily applicable to American society as a whole. Whatever the reasons for Hollywood's quick loss of interest in Vietnam, other issues soon absorbed the film industry's limited political attention, although quite a different view of Vietnam would appear on America's movie screens in just a few years.

NOTES

1. See Peter Biskind, *Seeing Is Believing* (London: Pluto Press, 1983).
2. Michael Cimino, Guardian Lecture, National Film Theatre, London, 11 August 1983.
3. Gilbert Adair, *Hollywood's Vietnam* (London: Proteus, 1981), p. 106.
4. Ibid., p. 165.

13

"What Makes You Think They're Looking for a Scapegoat?"

Workers, Unions, and Nuclear Power

America sank deeper into disillusionment and apathy through the seventies, but even as the nation as a whole turned away from politics, Hollywood continued in one of its most political periods, taking on not only Vietnam, but a wide variety of other issues. The films that resulted were generally liberal, giving few hints of the emerging conservatism that would sweep one of Hollywood's own into the White House in 1980. That election did not deflect filmmakers from politics, however, and only after Ronald Reagan's landslide reelection in 1984 did America's shift to the right show up on film.

Hollywood's politicization in the late seventies was partly due to the coming of age of filmmakers whose political consciousness had been shaped by the sixties, but changes in the corporate structure of the film industry were also a factor. Most of the big studios were absorbed by larger corporations in the seventies. The last to retain its independence was Columbia, which fell to Coca-Cola in 1982. Initially, fewer films were made by the corporate studios, but as the size of audiences and the number of cinemas increased, so did the number of movies.

The nature of production had changed, however. Making a movie increasingly depended on packaging writers, directors, actors, and others into a "deal." Such deals were still initiated by studios, but independent producers, agents, directors, actors and writers also put together deals and took them to studios, which then acted as investors or distributors. Independent funding eventually became easier with the evolution of cable television and videocassettes as sources of revenue. In short, the role of the studios had changed: movies could now be made without them. Both *Coming Home* and *Apocalypse Now*, for example, were independent productions, as were many other films of the era. Among them were *Norma Rae*, *The China Syndrome*, and *Silkwood*.

Norma Rae (1979)

Workers and Unions

Hollywood has never shown sustained interest in the working class. Movies have always been more likely to center on lawyers, architects, teachers, doctors, or even the idle rich. Workers appeared more frequently in the early silent movies, and Warner Bros. featured them often enough to earn the label "the workingman's studio" in the thirties. But by the fifites and sixties, working-class people had become an endangered species in the movies, despite an occasional *Marty* or *Joe*.

Union members fared even worse because the studios fought a long battle against the unionization of their own workers. Even after that battle ended, unions were rarely favorably treated in American movies. *The Grapes of Wrath* sided with the workers, but stopped short of the enthusiastic unionism of Steinbeck's novel. Outright pro-union films like the suppressed *Salt of the Earth* were rare. The corrupt and subversive unions of *Big Jim McLain* and *On the Waterfront* were more common.

Given Hollywood history, the number of films about workers and unions that appeared in the late seventies and early eighties was remarkable. The increasing independence of filmmakers may ·have contributed to this phenomenon, or perhaps these movies were a legacy of the sixties or a belated recognition of the widespread support for the struggle of the farmworkers to unionize. It is interesting that Hollywood took up this topic at a time when union membership was in decline and labor conflict was becoming a thing of the past. Like Vietnam, it was a safe subject by the time the movies got around to it.

Director Hal Ashby's *Bound For Glory* (1976) was about real-life folk singer Woodie Guthrie's travels with migrant farmworkers in 1936, but the treatment and the casting of David Carradine in the lead reduced the movie's hero to a moody agitator who didn't seem to care much about the people he stirred up. Factory workers took center stage in *Blue Collar* (1978) and *F.I.S.T.* (1978), although neither film had anything good to say about unions. Paul Schrader's *Blue Collar* powerfully conveys the alienation and frustration of assembly-line workers, but it soon turns into a grim caper movie as a trio of auto workers rob their corrupt union and then turn against one another. Norman Jewison directed *F.I.S.T.*, but the movie seems to have been more heavily influenced by Sylvester Stallone, its co-author and star, who plays the Hoffa-style leader of the union whose initials give the film its title. *F.I.S.T.* begins with a righteous strike that effectively makes the case for unions. The idealistic young hero joins up, grows more involved, and rises to leadership, but he ultimately betrays both his workers and his union as *F.I.S.T.* reiterates one of Hollywood's favorite political themes: power corrupts.

Despite movies like these and public antagonism to unions, one of the big hits of 1979 was the pro-union *Norma Rae*, independently produced and directed by one of Hollywood's most consistent liberals, Martin Ritt. *Norma Rae* did well at the box office, picked up two Academy Awards, and was praised by most critics. Based on the true story of a woman textile worker and union organizer, *Norma Rae* was released just as the effort to unionize the southern textile mills came to a head, helping to publicize the workers' call for a national boycott against J. P. Stevens, one of the biggest companies. Both the boycott and the movie had happy endings.

Norma Rae (Sally Field), a naive and apathetic single parent who works in one of the mills, is recruited by Reuben Warshovsky (Ron Liebman), a northern union organizer whom the other workers shun. Under his guidance, she develops into an effective grass-roots organizer and leader. This is no Pygmalion or *My Fair Lady*, however; these two learn from each other. He introduces her to literature; she tells him not to use so many big words in his leaflets. Their relationship is at the center of the film, but although movie tradition leads us to expect them to have an affair, they do not. Their cultural and class differences are driven home by the difficulties she faces as she grows and becomes more deeply involved in the fight for unionization. He's on his own, free to leave when he likes, but her roots are in the community and the personal pressures on her are enormous. Her family turns on her, and the factory managers try to isolate her as a troublemaker. In the end, however, the workers vote to join the union and she is triumphant. Reuben packs up his files and moves on to his next project, leaving Norma Rae in charge.

The upbeat ending ignored the tough battles to negotiate a contract and control the union that lay ahead, but the strengths of *Norma Rae* outweighed this weakness. Better than most films *Norma Rae* communicated the need for unions and the personal and political difficulties of organizing them. The fear that made other workers reluctant to support the union was sympathetically portrayed, and even the bosses were not caricatured too grossly. *Norma Rae* gave too much credit to two individuals, a shortcoming it had in common with most American political films, but unlike most, it said that by working together and taking action, average people could take care of themselves.

The Fonda Syndrome

Nine to Five (1980) may have meant to say the same thing as *Norma Rae*, but its point was smothered in farce. Jane Fonda, Lily Tomlin, and Dolly Parton star as office workers who kidnap their boss and, in his absence introduce humanistic reforms that increase productivity. Their reforms are validated, however, only when the male chairman of the board gives his blessings. When *Nine to Five* was released, Fonda toured the country campaigning for the unionization of secretaries, but her rhetoric was stronger than the movie, which hardly mentioned unions and never offered them as a solution. This well-intentioned movie was a box office smash, but its comedy was so broad that few workers or bosses could have identified with the situation.

Like *Nine to Five*, *The China Syndrome* was independently made by IPC, the Bruce Gilbert-Jane Fonda production company, and it also suffered from what might be called the Fonda syndrome, in that it committed itself to an important issue but then delivered an unnecessarily timid message. Although the film was inspired by the death of nuclear power worker Karen Silkwood, director and co-author James Bridges changed the story line so as to emphasize TV news as much as nuclear energy. Instead of playing blue-collar worker Karen Silkwood, Fonda played a glamorous TV reporter.

Kimberly Wells (Fonda) covers light stories but longs to do hard news, apparently more out of ambition than political or journalistic commitment. She's given a chance to do a series on nuclear energy, although initially it looks more like promotion than news. Then, by chance, she and her crew are present at a power plant during an "incident," and her aggressive free-lance cameraman (Michael Douglas) films the event surreptitiously. They rush back to the station with their scoop, but when the power company denies that anything unusual happened, the station manager (Peter Donat) refuses to let Kimberly air the story. The hot-tempered cameraman steals the film, confident that the TV station won't air anything detrimental to its capitalist partner.

Kimberly goes looking for the photographer and the film so she can give it back to the station manager and save her job. In a bar near the nuclear power plant, she meets Godell (Jack Lemmon), the engineer who was in charge at the time of the accident. He's nervous about talking to her, but he's also attracted to her, and she uses her good looks to get him to open up. Gradually, his doubts about what happened and his worries about a company cover-up come out. Kimberly's journalistic instincts take over, and she becomes more interested in getting a good story than in getting the film back.

Godell starts out as a true believer who is totally committed to nuclear power and to his company. When his co-worker, an uneducated twenty-five-year company man (Wilfred Brindley) says he's afraid the investigators will attribute the accident to human error and make him the scapegoat, Godell is incredulous. "What makes you think they're looking for a scapegoat?" he asks. "Tradition," answers the company man. When the shallow investigation concludes with a cover-up, the appalled Godell begins poking around and soon discovers falsified safety checks that prove the accident was more serious than the company has admitted. More worried about profits than safety, "California Gas and Electric" rejects Godell's charges, having already done a whitewash and had Kimberly's report suppressed with the collusion of her station. New safety checks would cost $15 million, they say, and the truth might delay the licensing of a new plant at a cost of half a million dollars a day. Godell contacts Kimberly and with the help of her activist cameraman she arranges for him to give evidence at hearings on the licensing of the new plant. When the engineer is harassed by company thugs, the reporters arrange for their Hispanic sound man (Daniel Valdez) to deliver the evidence, but he, like Karen Silkwood, is killed in an auto accident. Desperate, Godell seizes the control room of his plant and sends for Kimberly and her cameraman to broadcast his statement. Above them in a glass booth, a company executive oozes evil as he watches their preparations. By the time they go on the air, Godell is so nervous that he comes off as a nut. The police anti-terrorist squad breaks in and kills him, and at that very moment another nuclear accident begins.

Even as the power plant shakes and rattles, the company mounts a new cover-up, blaming it all on the dead Godell. Kimberly asks Godell's co-worker, the company man, whether management's allegations about his friend are true. He pauses, then says the company is wrong, that Godell was a good man. As the film ends, we assume the truth has come out, although a note of ambiguity is introduced when the movie takes us back to the television studio and the news broadcast is interrupted by an advertisement for microwave ovens.

Predictably, the nuclear power industry tried to discredit *The China Syndrome* even before it was released, but two weeks after it opened, an accident at Pennsylvania's Three Mile Island nuclear plant spectacularly gave the movie both credibility and publicity. Although the film was advertised as a thriller and most people responded to it on that level, the coincidence of Three Mile Island gave emphasis to what would otherwise have seemed a timid message. Thanks to the free publicity, heavy advertising, generally good reviews, three Oscar nominations, and many public appearances by Fonda, Douglas, and Lemmon, all of whom agreed with the movie's message, *The China Syndrome* did well at the box office.

In addition to foreseeable criticism from the nuclear power industry, the harshest reviews of this film came from the left, which flayed *The China Syndrome* for choosing entertainment over political substance, trivializing the opposition to nuclear energy, ignoring the problems of blue-collar workers, showing too much faith in the media, and substituting individual for collective action.[2] Certainly the movie oversimplifies the complex problems of nuclear energy, reducing them to a matter of adequate safety checks, which makes the movie not so much anti-nuclear as pro-quality. Also, the film's heroes and heroine are not against nuclear power; they just want to tell the public the truth. The actual opponents of nuclear energy are portrayed as cranks, but the proponents come off even worse, as men who are interested only in profits. A handful of good people stand up and tell the truth, however, another reassuring conclusion along the lines of *Mr. Smith Goes to Washington* and *All the President's Men*.

On another level, *The China Syndrome* is not so much anti-nuclear as it is anti-capitalist. The bad guys are the businessmen who run the power company and the TV station, an unsophisticated criticism of capitalism, but one shared by an increasing number of movies from *Network* to *Being There*. The good people are media and engineering professionals, but others share the credit, including the Chicano sound man and the blue-collar workers in the control room at the power plant. Big business is a powerful enemy, the movie says, but it can be beaten by ordinary people if they can overcome fear and if they are willing to risk their careers and their lives in courageous action.

The weakest point in *The China Syndrome* is the implication in the last scene that telling the truth about the accidents will be enough to mobilize the public and precipitate government action. And yet in a way it was. This popular and entertaining movie, considerably aided by the coincidence of Three Mile Island, added impetus to the long years of organizing, demonstrating and lobbying that ended the construction of nuclear power plants in America.

Although based on the same events that had inspired *The China Syndrome*, *Silkwood* (1983) came too late to have much influence on public opinion. Rejecting the unambiguous approach of the earlier movie, director Mike Nichols and writers Nora Ephron and Alice Arlen produced a more profound if less satisfying film. Both movies are about the dangers of nuclear power, but *Silkwood*, like *Norma Rae* is also about women, workers, and unions. On all these issues, *Silkwood* was stronger than the earlier films, but far less comfortable.

Karen Silkwood (Meryl Streep) is a blue-collar worker and single parent, like Norma Rae, but her awakening is far slower than either Norma Rae's or Kimberly's. Karen and her co-workers are ignorant and confused about their personal lives as well as the dangers they're exposed to at work. They begin to awaken, but except for Karen, they value their jobs too much to speak out. When she finally becomes active, we can't quite tell whether her commitment is genuine or she just likes stirring things up. Her union helps, but the locals are as dumb and helpless as she is, and the national organizers are so culturally and geographically distant that we can't tell whether they really care about her or are just using her. Karen continues to agitate, but she and her house are found to be thoroughly contaminated with radioactive material, apparently planted by the company. Then, while on her way to give evidence of falsified safety records to *The New York Times*, she dies in an auto wreck. Here the movie hedges: ominous headlights behind her suggest murder, but a postscript to the film notes that there were drugs in her blood, implying that she might have died accidentally.

Silkwood was nominated for four Academy Awards, but did less well at the box office than *Norma Rae* and *The China Syndrome*. Historical accuracy became a key issue in otherwise mostly good reviews, with *The New York Times* criticizing the movie in an editorial and *The Village Voice* persuasively denouncing the film as a slur on Karen Silkwood.[3] The filmmakers asked for such criticism by using a true story about a woman who had become a folk hero of the left, although as the *Voice* pointed out, they also had the advantage of five years of free publicity, including stories of the massive damage suit against Silkwood's employers.

Silkwood also made itself vulnerable to criticism by its refusal to take sides. It was ambiguous about Karen's character and motivations, the good faith of the union, the culpability of the company, and even her death. The movie kept its focus on working-class characters who did not blossom like Norma Rae but remained minimally articulate and self-aware and therefore less sympathetic than the white-collar professionals of *The China Syndrome*. *Silkwood* bravely let the audience decide about the characters, allowing Karen Silkwood to be more human then heroine. For some, particularly the partisans of the real-life Silkwood, that made for an unsatisfying film with no point of view.

Although tougher than *Norma Rae* or *The China Syndrome*, *Silkwood* refused to make its characters easy to like or understand, and it was satisfying neither as entertainment or advocacy. Without knowing whether Karen's death was murder or a drug-induced accident, audiences couldn't be angry at the culprits or sad at the tragedy. *Silkwood*'s politics were obscured by the film's extraordinary restraint toward its characters. Presumably this was an artistic choice, although fear of a lawsuit may have entered into it.

Farmers and Fishermen

In 1984, the movies shifted their focus from blue-collar laborers to rural workers in what came to be known as "the farm trilogy." *Places in the Heart, The River,* and *Country* all featured beleagured small farmers fighting the elements and the banks, and they all featured strong women. The three movies and their heroines also bore an uncanny resemblance to *Norma Rae, The China Syndrome,* and *Silkwood.*

Places in the Heart was the *Norma Rae* of the farm trilogy, with Sally Field playing another plucky heroine who overcomes adversity, this time with the help of a child, a blind lodger, and an itinerant black. *Places in the Heart* was less political than *Norma Rae* and the other two farm movies, however, because it was safely set in the past and because it was mainly about brave human beings triumphing over adversity by determination and hard work. The most popular of the farm movies, it won Oscars for Sally Field and scriptwriter Robert Benton.

Director Mark Rydell said *The River* was also about "a determined individual,"[4] but although Tom Garvey (Mel Gibson) is determined, he's unable to save his farm by himself. His wife Mae (Cissy Spacek) is the real backbone of the family, working the farm on her own when Tom goes to the city to scab in a steel mill, a moving sequence that manages to communicate both why scabbing is bad and why people do it. This film is unlike *Places in the Heart* in that hard work is not enough to save the family from flood, foreclosure, and the machinations of a greedy agribusinessman. He pressures a state senator to build a dam to irrigate his massive holdings, and he hires down-and-out farmers to break up the levee Tom has built to protect his land, but in the end the farmers turn on the agribusinessman and help the small farmer in a scene reminiscent of the ditch sequence in *Our Daily Bread.* The loser is unperturbed, however. "We'll win in the end," he says, "because we can outlast you." Nominated for four Academy Awards, *The River* was a modest success, despite criticism of its sentimentality. It was more political than *Places in the Heart,* yet it was still satisfying entertainment.

If *The River* is *The China Syndrome* of the farm trilogy, *Country* is its *Silkwood,* the slowest and least sentimental of the three movies. Its small farmers, in fact, are even more reserved and inarticulate than Karen Silkwood and her friends. Director Richard Pearce distanced them from us with few close-ups and little sentimentality. Just as we suspect that Karen Silkwood might be a troublemaker rather than a true believer, here we wonder if the farmers' difficulties are their own fault.

And again, a strong woman, Jewel Ivy (Jessica Lange), holds her farm family together as her husband (Sam Shepard) crumbles when their government loan is called in. They win at least a stay of execution, however, when Jewel organizes the small farmers to resist the government. As in *The River*, collective action saves the day, although we're not sure for how long. Like Field and Spacek, Jessica Lange was nominated for an Academy Award for her performance, but *Country's* unsentimental restraint appealed less to audiences than did the other farm movies.

Although far from radical, all three of these movies were critical of American farm policy. Inspired by foreclosures on small farms that were much in the news in the early eighties, these movies may have taken on the subject after it was too late to affect the policy, just as the movies about Vietnam had come too late to affect the war. *Places in the Heart* was the least political, with its nostalgic setting and self-help solution, while in *The River* little capitalists banded together to beat big capital aided by government (the water project). Only *Country* seemed to take on government directly, but its makers were nervous enough about its politics in the year of Reagan's reelection that they refused benefit showings for political causes to avoid "politicizing the film" and insisted that its "villain [was] not the Reagan administration," but monolithic bureaucracy and "government apathy."[5]

Shang Pierce (Ed Harris) also thinks government apathy is the problem in *Alamo Bay* (1985), directed by Louis Malle and written by Alice Arlen, co-author of *Silkwood*. "We defend everybody all over the world, but there ain't no protection for any American, and that ain't right," Pierce declares when hardworking Vietnamese immigrants drive him and his fellow white shrimp fishermen out of business in the recession-struck Gulf of Mexico. Glory (Amy Madigan) tries to save her small business by trading with the Vietnamese, but a Ku Klux Klan organizer takes advantage of the white fishermen's frustration to foment violence. The rich sail by in their yachts, glared at by the hardworking Pierce, and the middle-class teacher and minister offer only platitudes to resolve the conflict. Thanks to the resolve of Malle and Arlen, we sympathize with the immigrants while at the same time we understand the frustration of the white fishermen.

Movies and Workers in the Age of Reagan

Alamo Bay is a perceptive study of the situation confronted by the people at the bottom of America's economic heap. It has much in common with the equally reserved *Silkwood* and *Country*, but it rejects easy solutions even more resolutely than those films. Together, these three films constitute an indictment of American capitalism, a message audiences did not want to hear in the age of Reagan. The liberalism of these movies was shared by *Norma Rae, Nine to Five, The China Syndrome*, and *The River*, although these films, along with *Places in the Heart*, were far more affirmative about the possibility of taking action. All of these films focused on workers, whether on farms and shrimp boats or in mills and power plants, at a time when Yuppies were capturing the nation's attention. All of these films also featured strong women, making them feminist in varying degrees, even as the Equal Rights Amendment failed to win ratification.

The appearance of these movies in such times was largely due to the new independence of filmmakers. Only *The River* was produced by one of the old studios (Columbia), although big studios were involved to some degree in most of the others. But the reception of these films suggested that the country was not as deeply conservative as its enthusiasm for Ronald Reagan seemed to indicate. Most of these movies were favorably reviewed, and all but *Alamo Bay* were honored with Academy Awards or nominations. Some were box office hits as well.

NOTES

1. See Henry A. Giroux, "*Norma Rae*, Character, Culture and Class." *Jump Cut* 22, May 1980.
2. Doug Zwick, "The Genre Syndrome," and Michael Gallantz, "Meltdown in Hollywood," both in *Jump Cut*, 22, May 1980.
3. *Village Voice*, 21 February 1984.
4. *Films*, Volume 5, No. 5, May 1985.
5. *The New York Times*, 20 August 1984.

The Seduction of Joe Tynan (1979)

14

"When Were You Going to Tell Me You Were Running for President?"

The Reel Political Process

The issue movies of the late seventies and early eighties were political in varying degrees, but while they probed issues like the Vietnam War, unionization, nuclear power, and the plight of small farmers, they rarely looked at the political process itself. A few other movies of this era did put politics and politicians at the center stage, however. Some reiterated Hollywood's oldest themes about politics, and a few added new variations.

Mr. Alda Goes to Washington

"What do we do now?" asked Bill McKay (Robert Redford) when he won the election at the end of *The Candidate*. In 1979, *The Seduction of Joe Tynan* answered McKay's question. Alan Alda, who wrote the script, is Senator Joe Tynan, a good New York liberal with a warm heart and a sense of humor. To make sure we know this, the film plays up a busload of black kids in an opening montage of Washington monuments otherwise straight out of *Mr. Smith*. We next see Tynan alone in the Senate speaking about hunger, a scene that tells us he cares while others do not. At home that night, he romps in bed with his wife, Ellie (Barbara Harris), as they gleefully celebrate his success: "I got the works bill passed! I've got clout!"

The realities of politics are introduced in the next scene, when Senator Birney (Melvyn Douglas), a conservative from Louisiana, asks a favor of Tynan. The president has nominated a racist from Birney's state to fill a vacancy on the Supreme Court, and the nominee must now be approved by the Senate. Birney wants the nomination approved so as to eliminate the man as a potential opponent. His constituents are turning against him because of his age, he says, and we can see why when he has a senile lapse into French during the conversation. He's cogent enough, however, to try to neutralize Tynan's opposition. "Vote against him if you like," he says, "just don't start a crusade." Tynan agrees as a personal favor, and we support this mild compromise because, thanks to the fine acting of Melvyn Douglas, we share Tynan's sympathy for the old man.

When Tynan later takes a phone call, his aide quickly reminds him to ask solicitously about the caller's wife, letting us know that Tynan is practical, a little hypocritical, and very dependent on his aide. Like *The Candidate*, this film is full of such moments, giving us insights into Tynan's character, but also accurately reflecting the way real politicians operate, for it is minor compromises like these that please people and advance careers.

The Supreme Court nominee comes up again when Joe meets Karen Traynor (Meryl Streep), a southern labor lawyer, counsel for a black group, and daughter of a powerful politician. Karen wants Joe to lead the opposition to the judicial nomination, and she seduces him into it with an enticing description of what this move could mean to his career. All he has to do is use some film footage of the nominee making a racist speech. "When I think of the splash you could make with this piece of film, I get weak in the knees," she gushes, quickly adding that "of course it's the right thing to do." The seduction is soon sexual as well as political. She's excited by his power, and he likes talking about his political maneuvers with a woman who is interested in them, because his wife Ellie is not. She's got her own career as a psychiatrist, we're told, although we never see her work.

Karen and Joe obtain the incriminating film of the judicial nominee saying, "In my heart I have never accepted integration and I never will." Senator Birney threatens Joe when he learns he's broken his promise, but the old man is shattered. He slips into senility and speaks French again, this time in public. In the end, the president withdraws the nomination, and the media report a victory for Joe Tynan. His staff prepares to press his advantage, hiring a speech and video coach to polish up his act, planning visits to newspaper editorial boards, and preparing a direct mail campaign.

By this time Joe and Karen have gone their separate ways, but Ellie is increasingly repelled by her husband's unrelenting absorption in politics, or perhaps she just feels left out. "When were you going to tell me you were running for president?" she asks. "At the inaugural ball?" But for the moment, Joe is only positioning himself for a candidacy, angling to give a crucial speech at a party convention. He attains this modest goal, but Ellie seems about to leave him even as the convention crowd chants, "We want Joe!" He gazes at Ellie from the convention podium. Her mouth quivers. Is it a smile? Will she stay? The ending is ambiguous, but most viewers think she will.

Karen seduces Joe sexually, and with the help of his Iago-like aide she also plays on his ego and ambition, thus seducing him with prospect of success as well. Joe is not a victim, however. He is an active and enthusiastic participant in both seductions, and he has few qualms about breaking his word to Senator Birney and destroying a nice old man. The treachery of the hero is mitigated, of course, by the racism of the judicial nominee, who doesn't belong on the Court, and by the senility of the old man, who doesn't belong in the Senate. Besides, we like Tynan-Alda.

Remarkably, *The Seduction of Joe Tynan* raises the issues of compromise and ambition and makes audiences understand Tynan's position and even feel sympathy for him. Joe's future remains unclear, however. "After a while," warns a colleague who has decided not to run for another term, "you forget why you're here. You just try to hang on to clout." The senile Senator Birney has forgotten why he's there, although other politicians – like the lecherous cynic played with relish by Rip Torn – may never have known. Joe will not walk away from politics like his honorable colleague or like the candidates in *State of the Union* and *The Best Man*, but can he stay and still retain his integrity? That question is left unanswered.

The Seduction of Joe Tynan won mixed reviews, but did fairly well at the box office, thanks at least in part to Alda's popularity. *The New Yorker* derided the movie's "have a nice day" politics and called the film "overwrought, airless and pious."[1] *Time* thought the film, had a fifties look and remarked that the absence of the press was odd, but it praised Alda for taking "the sanctimoniousness out of heroism."[2] Feminists approved of the presence of strong women with careers, but expressed disappointment that their ultimate function was to support the male.

Despite its shortcomings, however, *Joe Tynan* reflects political reality. More than most films about politics, it rings true on the personal costs of political life, its small compromises, and its corruptions. The process is convincingly portrayed without resorting to dirty little secrets like *Advise and Consent* and *The Best Man* and thus keeping the melodrama within the relam of credibility. *Joe Tynan*'s great strength, like that of *The Candidate*, is its feel for politics and politicians. Bill McKay and Joe Tynan face the horrors and carry on. They may sell out, but we understand why because the movies make sure we continue to like them. However cynical these movies are, they are more realistic than other movies about politics because they keep their politicians human. Their view may be less than reassuring, but their truthfulness is an advance for political movies.

We're All the Same Corporation Now

A different kind of seduction takes place in *Being There* (1979), written by Jerzy Kosinski from his novel and directed by Hal Ashby. Chance Gardener, played with brilliant reserve by Peter Sellers, is a retarded illiterate who has lived all his life on the estate of a wealthy benefactor, watching television and tending the garden. When his protector dies, Chance is turned out on the streets, but he is unable to discern fully the difference between television and reality. When some street toughs harass him, he tries to make them go away by changing the channel on the TV remove control he carries. He walks into the street and is hit by a limousine. Its passenger, Eve Rand (Shirley MacLaine), takes him to her mansion for treatment, apparently worried about a lawsuit.

Eve's husband, Benjamin (Melvyn Douglas yet again and even better), is a dying mega-industrialist and one of the men who run the country. The tycoon is impressed by his guest, whose rare comments are either noncommittal, and so taken as agreement, or refer to gardening, in which case they are taken metaphorically. The Rands introduce Chance to their circle, and he comes to be seen as some kind of authority. His cool reserve and his gardening comments, which seem to be metaphors, make him an instant celebrity when he appears on a television talk show. "It's a white man's world in America," mutters the black housekeeper of Chance's original benefactor when she sees him on TV. She alone knows he's a fool while the wealthy and powerful men who rule America appear to be taken in.

Rand introduces Chance to his protégé, the president of the United States (Jack Warden), who suspects he's a crackpot and has him investigated. No records or identification can be found, but the president forgets his worries when Chance delights him with what he takes to be optimistic advice about the economy: "As long as the roots are not severed, all will be well in the garden. . . . There will be growth in the spring." When Rand dies, his fellow corporate power brokers come together as his pallbearers. "Life is a state of mind," the president eulogizes ridiculously, even as the power elite chooses the imbecilic Chance as their next presidential candidate. Meanwhile, Chance wanders into the wintery garden. The film ends as he crosses a pond, walking on the water.

Sellers was nominated for an Academy Award for his fine portrayal of Chance, and Melvyn Douglas won a well-deserved Oscar for his supporting role, but although the movie was a box office success, some critics were put off by the absurdity of *Being There*. Intended as devastating satire, the film came across as ominous rather than funny. People were unsure about its message and some even took Chance's final walk on water literally rather than ironically.

Like *Network*, *Being There* was a condemnation of television, which numbs people's minds and creates instant celebrities who do not deserve respect. Both films also insisted that America was run by businessmen, not politicians, although it could be argued that the rulers in *Being There* were duped by Chance like everyone else except the black housekeeper.

Being There was only one of many movies of the late seventies and early eighties that featured the pervasive influence of business, perhaps reflecting Hollywood's greater independence as well as its anxiety about its own corporate status. Jane Fonda starred in a whole string of anti-business movies during this period, from *Dick and Jane*, *Comes A Horseman*, *The Electric Horseman*, and *The China Syndrome*, to *Nine to Five*. *Winter Kills* (1979), a complex and confusing movie praised by some critics but ignored by the public because of limited distribution, was a political thriller about a Kennedyesque president put in office by his father's money and later assassinated by a conspiracy of behind-the-scenes powers. In a variation on the anti-business theme, Fonda and Kris Kristofferson starred as good business people saving the nation from an Arab-instigated economic crisis in *Rollover* (1981), an unsuccessful thriller centering on the energy crisis. *The Formula* (1980), directed by John Avildsen, also took up the energy crisis. The plot centers on the efforts of a cartel of oil companies to suppress a formula for synthetic fuel, but despite a cast that included Marlon Brando, George C. Scott, and John Gielgud, this muddled movie failed with audiences and critics alike. In this movie, individuals and even nations no longer matter because, as one of the characters observes, "we're all the same corporation now."

Michael Cimino's anti-capitalist film, *Heaven's Gate* (1980), was an even bigger disaster than *The Formula*, though less deservedly so. *Heaven's Gate* is about the nineteenth-century range wars in Wyoming, during which the land barons, aided by hired thugs and the army, brutally crush immigrant settlers. Cimino's dazzling technique directs our sympathy to the heroic immigrants, whose community is movingly portrayed, but a dearth of dialogue and an obscurely motivated hero (Kris Kristofferson) make *Heaven's Gate* too dependent on images for success. The critics panned it even before it was released for being boring, pretentious, and overlong, and distributors withdrew the film before the public got a proper chance to see it. The movie, which cost $44 million, brought in less than $2 million. It deserved better, not only because of its visual beauty, but also because of its revisionist view of the history of the West. Its anti-capitalism also suggested that the interpretation of Cimino's earlier work, *The Deer Hunter*, as right wing was unfair.

The few defenders of *Heaven's Gate* argued that the film bombed because the American people were not prepared to see the truth about their history. Perhaps *Rollover* and *The Formula* failed because their messages were too frighteningly anti-capitalist. And yet, *Network*, *Being There*, and most of Jane Fonda's films had already proved that audiences were perfectly willing to see business portrayed as evil. More likely, *Rollover*, *The Formula*, and *Heaven's Gate* flopped because they just weren't very good.

Judging Judges

Another social issue of interest to filmmakers of the late seventies and early eighties was the criminal justice system, perhaps because of the public's fascination with the Watergate hearings. One worthy but disregarded political film of this type was *The Private Files of J. Edgar Hoover* (1978), directed by Larry Cohen and starring Broderick Crawford. This film argued that Hoover stayed in power because he kept secret files on America's leaders, including John F. Kennedy and Martin Luther King. Although he was brutal and power hungry, the film made it clear that Hoover believed he was acting in the national interest, "holding back" the excesses of politicians like Kennedy and Nixon. Cohen's view of politics and justice as conspiratorial was seen by few people, however, because his low budget showed and the awkward, stagy film was not widely distributed.

The legal system was more righteously condemned in Norman Jewison's *And Justice for All*, and Sidney Lumet examined pervasive police corruption in *Serpico* and *Prince of the City*, both of which featured informers as heroes. *The Verdict* reiterated Lumet's faith in the jury system as a desperate attorney (Paul Newman) defeated corrupt judges, lawyers, doctors, and hospital administrators.

Robert Redford played a reforming prison warden in *Brubaker* (1980), directed by Stuart Rosenberg, but the movie's central political theme had to do with compromise. The liberal governor's aide (Jane Alexander) supports Brubaker but urges him to make concessions to the conservative powers-that-be. He refuses and ultimately loses. Since Brubaker is played by Robert Redford, we take his side and accept the movie's condemnation of compromises. Another virtuous man walks away from politics, although Jane Alexander's powerful presence makes us wonder whether a case for compromise could have been made.

The U.S. Supreme Court takes center stage in Ronald Neame's considerably lighter *First Monday in October* (1981), which also raises the issue of compromise. Here Jill Clayburgh is somewhat improbably cast as the first woman member of the Court, a conservative anti-pornography campaigner from California's Orange County. Walter Matthau is her liberal antagonist, a justice committed to free speech even if it's smutty. The workings of the Court are instructively presented, and the antagonists debate the meaning of the First Amendment credibly if simplistically. A crisis arises when the woman justice's integrity is impugned by the revelation that her late husband helped cover up the secrets of an ominous corporation. She prepares to resign, but her liberal colleague talks her out of it, despite their ideological disagreements.

First Monday was reminiscent of a Tracy-Hepburn movie, but it barely touches on romance. The deological rivalry of the Clayburgh and Matthau characters develops instead into a good working relationship, as the movie lauds honorable debate among honorable people, almost reverting to the consensus of the fifties. Both characters are treated respectfully, although the Clayburgh character seems weaker, and it is Matthau's white liberal male who legitimizes her continuing presence on the Court. Although *First Monday* reiterates the big-bad-business theme, its main message is that decent men and women can have differing views and that these views need not be based on self-interest of corruption. Above all, the movie respects Court politics and tells us that the system works. Given the public antagonism to liberal judges dating back to the civil and criminal rights decisions of the sixties, the movie seemed a virtual defense of the courts. *First Monday in October* was innocuous, but unlike most American political films, it respected politics and the people who participate in it. The critics were unenthusiastic, but the movie had respectable box office thanks to its optimism, its cast, and its good timing: *First Monday* was released just as President Ronald Reagan appointed Sandra Day O'Connor, an Arizona conservative, as the first woman justice of the U.S. Supreme Court.

Less optimistic but more in keeping with popular prejudice was Peter Hyams's *The Star Chamber* (1983), with Michael Douglas as a young liberal judge frustrated by the legal loopholes used by attorneys to get their guilty clients off. Another judge (Hal Holbrook) introduces him to the Star Chamber, a group of renegade judges who take the law into their own hands by hiring hit men to murder criminals who have avoided punishment through legal niceties. After unleashing the Star Chamber on an innocent man, the young liberal has second thoughts, however, and betrays the vigilante judges. Frequently irrelevant action sequences calculated to hold audience interest overwhelmed *The Star Chamber*'s politics, and its message is ambivalent at best. First it says that protecting defendants subverts justice, giving approval to the Star Chamber's punishment of wrongdoers, all of whom happen to be members of minority groups or of the lower class and who also happen to be such repulsive scum that they seem to deserve what they get. Perhaps to minimize offense, the filmmakers include a woman and a black in the avenging Star Chamber. In the end, however, this judicial elite gets its comeuppance, too. Only the young judge and the black cop who break up the Star Chamber come off well. All things considered, this is a law-and-order movie, covering its exploitation of social prejudice and lust for vengeance with a liberal gloss, condemning and then upholding the system, but never resolving the question of whether the law gives too much or too little protection to those accused of crime. The critics saw through *The Star Chamber*, but audiences primed on the exploits of Clint Eastwood and Charles Bronson didn't seem to mind its inconsistencies at all.

Not Quite the Right Stuff

Unlike most political movies, *The Right Stuff* (1983) was expected to make a big splash in real-life politics. Adapted from Tom Wolfe's best-seller and directed by Philip Kaufman, *The Right Stuff* was about America's first astronauts, one of whom, Senator John Glenn, was a serious contender for the Democratic presidential nomination in 1984. Reagan and Glenn's Democratic opponents feared that *The Right Stuff* would provide the astronaut's candidacy with a powerful send-off, but both the movie and the campaign flopped.

The Right Stuff contrasts the men who became astronauts with test pilot Chuck Yeager (Sam Shepard), who did not, making it clear that he is too much of an individual to jump through hoops and conform, as the others willingly do. Yeager is an old-fashioned Hollywood-style hero while John Glenn (Ed Harris) comes off as a fairly obnoxious straight arrow. At first the film keeps its distance from the astronauts and seems to make fun of them, but in the end we like them all, including Glenn. President Lyndon Johnson throws a crass barbecue in their honor, and as Sally Rand does a fan dance, the astronauts look quietly at one another. They've attained success by compromise and conformity, like Joe Tynan, but we know they've kept their integrity. They've got the right stuff, especially in contrast with the crude reporters, foolish politicians, and offensive hangers-on with whom the movie surrounds its heroes.

Although John Glenn ultimately came off well in *The Right Stuff*, the movie wasn't enough to save his dull and inept presidential campaign. Some film industry people thought association with the politician jinxed the film, because "no one would pay to see a movie they thought was a political polemic."[3] Unenthusiastic reviews and the movie's reluctance to play the astronauts as either buffoons or heroes didn't help, either, and the movie failed financially.

In a way, *The Right Stuff* was the first film to reflect the spirit of the Reagan era, but its revival of individualism and heroism was too cautious to catch the emerging national mood. As we have seen, most filmmakers lagged behind public opinion, generally expressing liberal sentiments if they dealt with politics at all. In fact, after Reagan's first victory, moviemakers seemed to move even further to the left. Only after he was reelected in 1984 did Hollywood truly begin to reflect and exploit the national shift to the right.

NOTES

1. *The New Yorker*, 20 August 1979.
2. *Time*, 20 August 1979.
3. *The New York Times*, 20 August 1984.

Reds (1981)

15

"I'd Forgotten All About Them – Were They Socialists?"

Nostalgia in the Age of Reagan

After Watergate, the Iranian hostage crisis was the most traumatic event in America's recent history. It was also the most important factor in Ronald Reagan's defeat of Jimmy Carter in the 1980 presidential election, as Carter's inabilty to resolve the crisis came to symbolize his general ineptitude. The modest, self-questioning attitudes that made him refreshing in 1976 worked against him in 1980. He seemed to be apologizing for America and selling it short. He tried to accommodate the nation to its limitations in resources and international influence, but Americans didn't want to hear such messages.

They turned instead to Ronald Reagan. In doing so, the people were protesting the hostage crisis, rejecting the Carter style, demanding less government, and moving to the right, but they were also looking nostalgically back toward their own past. Reagan himself was part of that past, having appeared on movie and television screens since 1937, first as an actor and thirty years later as a politician. His familiarity, his likable personality, and his very presence were reassuring. So was his rhetoric as he called up traditional values and revived patriotism. Reagan had simple, old-fashioned answers and the kind of unflinching faith in America that people longed for.

This nostalgia was also evident in the popular movies of the late seventies and early eighties. The *Rocky* movies, for example, were old-fashioned stories based on traditional values. So were the *Star Wars* and *Superman* movies. *On Golden Pond* featured Katharine Hepburn and Henry Fonda, stars of Reagan's generation, with a message of family loyalty and reconciliation. *Raiders of the Lost Ark* and *E.T.* were slick, modern versions of old movies, with frequent references to classic films adding another layer of notalgia. Americans even gobbled up British nostalgia, making *Chariots of Fire* one of the big hits of 1981.

Ironically, some of this cinematic nostalgia was more radical than conservative. *Ragtime* (1981), for example, was based on E. L. Doctorow's panoramic historical novel of the turn-of-the-century America, with a variety of characters and political themes in elaborately interwoven stories. Director Milos Forman and writer Michael Weller chose to focus on a mild-mannered young black man, Coalhouse (Howard E. Rollins, Jr.), who is driven to radical revenge by the actions of white racists. With no recourse in the law, he resorts to violence. A black attorney refuses to help Coalhouse on the persuasive grounds that other clients have greater needs, and Booker T. Washington (Moses Gunn) makes a strong case for his own pacifist tactics, but *Ragtime* stays resolutely on the side of Coalhouse as well as its other nonconformist, anti-authoritarian characters.

To its credit, *Ragtime* was one of the few films of the eighties that dealt with race, and its treatment of the subject was very different from that of Sidney Poitier's movies of the 1960s. Despite the film's historical setting, Coalhouse was an up-to-date character, proud and stubborn, with a chip on his shoulder, insistent on his rights, unwilling to placate whites on any terms. Unfortunately, whatever message *Ragtime* meant to send was lost in obscure motivations and a confusion of subplots. From Coalhouse's extreme actions to his shooting on the order of a seemingly decent police commissioner (James Cagney), *Ragtime* provided few clues as to the reasons for his actions or those of its other characters. Despite fine performances, this distancing kept audiences from identifying with the characters, and *Ragtime*'s rich and beautiful evocation of the American past was not enough to sustain it. Critics and audiences were unenthusiastic, and although the movie was nominated for five Academy Awards, it won none.

Comrades

Warren Beatty's *Reds* (1981) did a little better than *Ragtime*. Long one of Hollywood's most politically active stars, Beatty took advantage of his potency at the box office and his success as a producer to make one of America's most important political films. Beatty was not only the film's star but also its director, producer, and co-author, with Trevor Griffiths.

The subject of *Reds* is John Reed, the left-wing journalist whose books about his experiences in the Mexican and Russian Revolutions were classics and who was the only American ever to be honored by burial in the Kremlin Wall. Beatty had been interested in Reed since a visit to Russia in the sixties, when aging revolutionaries told him he looked like the writer.

We meet John Reed as he offends a social gathering in Portland, Oregon, with his left-wing views. He then meets Louise Bryant (Diane Keaton), a married woman who feels stifled by provincial society. She wants to write and shows Reed her work. He invites her to return to New York with him. "What as?" she asks, fearing she'll still be trapped in a subordinate role when independence is what she most desires. She goes with him, however, and joins an exciting society of left-wing artists and intellectuals in Greenwich Village. "I write," she says when asked what she does, but most of the time she doesn't.

Reed is driven by commitment, constantly dashing off somewhere to write about and sometimes to participate in political events. Bryant complains, impatiently condemning his need for "another shot of limelight." When she has an affair, Reed sets aside his principles to marry her. They settle down in a cozy cottage with a puppy dog, but he's still peripatetic and she's still discontented. Finally, she leaves him to go to France, where she writes, with little success, about World War I. Reed follows and persuades her to join him in Russia where the Revolution is under way. Caught up in the spirit of events, they work well together, criticizing each other's writings respectfully and sharing the excitement of the Revolution, of which they eventually become a part. *Reds* effectively evokes the chaos of that conflict as well as the intoxicating meetings of workers, so we're with Reed when he rises to speak at a turbulent rally. "We'll join you in revolution!" he proclaims on behalf of American workers. At the end of his speech, Reed and Bryant are separated by the crowd, but they struggle toward each other, and the film's intermission comes as they make love while outside a marching crowd sings the rousing "Internationale." Political, professional, and personal commitment come together in one glorious – or ludicrous – moment.

Reed and Bryant return to America, she to lecture and he to write his classic *Ten Days That Shook the World*. Reed joins one of the contending communist factions and prepares to return to Russia to have it recognized as the official party in America. "You're not a politician," Louise protests. "You're a writer. . . . You're an artist." He goes anyway, and the party orders him to stay and work on propaganda. He finds that his old pal Emma Goldman (Maureen Stapleton) has grown disillusioned with the Revolution. "The dream is dying," she sighs. "The centralized state has all the power. They're putting anarchists like me in jail, exterminating all dissenters."

"What did you think, anyway?" Reed responds. "It was going to work right away?" The party sends him on a tour to speak on behalf of American workers in support of the Revolution. When a party official edits his speech, he is offended. "You don't rewrite what I write," he insists, repeating one of his catch-phrases and reminding us he's an artist.

We suspect that Reed is coming to share Goldman's disillusionment, but before further political developments can occur, we return to Louise, who is now determined to join him. Getting into revolutionary Russia is difficult, however, and she makes a Zhivago-like journey through the snowy wastes of Finland. The lovers rush toward each other in yet another crowd and are tearfully reunited just in time for Reed to fall ill. When he tells Louise they will go on together, she again asks, "What as?"

"Comrades," he says, and dies.

Beatty's decision to emphasize the personal life of his protagonists was a concession to Hollywood tradition that made his lavish epic more romantic than political. John and Louise could almost be Rhett and Scarlett. Unlike *Gone with the Wind*, however, *Reds* is true except for a few incidents like the lovers' reunion in France and Bryant's trek across Finland. Reed and Bryant were real American radicals, members of a group whose history, unlike that of the landed aristrocracy of antebellum South, had been ignored by Hollywood.

Reds is also distinguished by Beatty's innovative use of "witnesses" – real people, some of them famous, whose reminiscences about Reed are interspersed throughout the film, giving Beatty's epic resonance and credibility and making it more than a romance. Their disagreements and confusion warn that memory, and therefore history, is fallible. "I'd forgotten all about them," one witness says of Reed and Bryant. "Were they socialists?" The witnesses validate some parts of *Reds* and challenge others, but even their disagreements strengthen the movie by reminding us that the film itself is just one interpretation of history.

Beatty also gives his film a feminist subplot in the transformation of Louise Bryant. Reed himself changes only slightly in the course of the film, moving from journalist to activist, but Bryant grows from a whining wife to an equal and independent professional, winning the approval of even Emma Goldman. Unfortunately, the structure of the film and Diane Keaton's facile interpretation of Bryant's growth obscure Beatty's declared intent. She complains and moans so much in the first half of the film that we lose sympathy for her search for identity, and she spends most of the second half of the film following her man to the almost literal end of the earth.

Beatty is more successful at what he described as "reclaiming history" by making a film about the left when it was still a viable force in American politics, or as he put it, at the last historical moment before the America's ideology "hardened."[1] One critic dismissed his efforts as "nostalgia of the left,"[2] but nostalgia or not, *Reds* deals with a history that had been lost for most Americans. The anti-war movement of World War I, the American socialist and communist parties and their factions, the Wobblies, Eugene Debs, Emma Goldman, Max Eastman, Big Bill Haywood, and others were a part of our past, and we should know about them, whether we share their values or not. By making one of these "reds" a romantic hero in the grand Hollywood tradition, Beatty's movie went further than merely reclaiming history.

Reds is far from purely left-wing in its own point of view, however. The movie has it both ways, leaning "red" in its choice of heroes and heroines and its initial romantic view of the Revolution, but anti-"red" in its ultimate portrait of Soviet totalitarianism. The film witholds final judgement by implying rather than explicitly stating Reed's disillusionment. On another level, *Reds* has it both ways by emphasizing the individualism of people who advocate collective politics, not only by focusing on their personal lives, but in its insistence on artistic integrity ("You don't rewrite what I write").

Reds never makes the political values of its characters clear, nor does it define the class conflict on which real-life politics in both the United States and Russia then centered. It is a more personal than political film, although it is at its most trite when it dwells on the purely personal with its quaint cottage, cute puppy, and clumsy man in the kitchen. This was presumably a commercial choice made by Beatty; screenwriter Trevor Griffiths's original script was more political than romantic. But at least *Reds* respects politics as an important part of its characters lives, and unlike most American films, it also shows the importance of work in people's lives. Indeed, the greatest strength of *Reds* may be its presentation of the way personal lives blend with work, careers, and politics. And *Reds* is more complex and willing to question than most movies about politics. The witnesses and the positive picture of the Russian Revolution and America's radical past are also worthwhile contributions.

The reviews of *Reds* were generally good, although many pointed out that Beatty's politics were more cautious than radical. *The New York Times* called it old-fashioned American optimism, about "as ideological as the puppy."[3] Stanley Kauffman saw *Reds* as a biography about commitment rather than an exploration of political questions, excusing it with the observation that "film is an expensive art. Private or government subsidy is not often forthcoming for work intended to upset the status quo."[4] Andrew Sarris also liked *Reds*, but he was more enthusiastic about its politics, praising it as an "open-minded historical inquiry" with the "clang of paradox and contradiction."[5]

With twelve Academy Award nominations, *Reds* looked set to dominate the 1981 Oscars, but in the end *Chariots of Fire, On Golden Pond*, and *Raiders of the Lost Ark*, all as nostalgic in their own ways as

Reds was, did as well or better. Beatty won the award for best director, and his epic won for cinematography and supporting actress (Stapleton). On accepting his own award, Beatty summed up his message in *Reds* and his view of the movie business in a manner that suggested he was no more radical than his critics had argued:

I want to name Mr. Barry Diller, who runs Paramount, . . . and Mr. Charles Bluhdown, who runs Gulf & Western and God knows what else, and I want to say to you gentlemen that no matter how much we might have wanted to strangle each other from time to time, I think that your decision, taken in the great capitalist tower of Gulf & Western, to finance a three-and-a-half-hour romance which attempts to reveal for the first time just something of the beginnings of American socialism and American communism, reflects credit not only upon you; I think it reflects credit upon Hollywood and the movie business wherever that is, and I think it reflects more particular credit upon freedom of expression that we have in American society, and the lack of censorship we have from the government or the people who put up the money.

But the star and his studio must have been disappointed not to get the sweep of the Oscars they needed to boost *Reds* at the box office, for despite three Oscars and good reviews, however, Beatty's very expensive picture was a financial failure. Audiences didn't like the "witness" technique as much as critics did, and many found the film long, boring, and even silly.

Hard Left

Despite the financial disappointments of *Ragtime* and *Reds* and the disaster of *Heaven's Gate*, American filmmakers continued to make political movies, but they refrained from making them on such a grand scale and even the less ambitious political movies of the era had difficulty finding investors when they took on tough subjects. Sidney Lumet's *Daniel* (1983), a daring and difficult examination of left-wing history, was produced by the artists themselves with no studio assistance at all. Lumet had been directing political movies since 1957, when he did *Twelve Angry Men*. He had dealt with informers in *A View from the Bridge*, nuclear war in *Fail Safe*, feminism in *The Group*, police corruption in *Serpico* and *Prince of the City*, homosexuality in *Dog Day Afternoon*, and corporate control of television in *Network*. All these movies treated controversial issues in complex and interesting ways, rarely oversimplifying, resorting to clichés, or making their messages unnecessarily obvious. Lumet shuns the "political" label, however, perhaps because he believes the Hollywood myth about message movies. Even *Daniel*, he disingenuously claimed, was "about parents and children and the damage people do without meaning to."[6]

Daniel (Timothy Hutton) is the son of the Isaacsons, Jewish communists who, like the Rosenbergs, were executed as Soviet agents. The story of their death is told from their son's point of view, thus connecting the two generations and showing how one affects the other. Daniel is disillusioned, alienated, and apolitical, cruel to his young wife, harsh to his adoptive family, and impatient with his neurotic sister. While he retreats deeper and deeper into himself, his sister tries drugs and then political activism. He hates the memory of their parents while she venerates it, but in the end she goes insane and commits suicide whereas Daniel finally makes his peace with himself and his memories and takes a step toward political commitment by joining an anti-war demonstration.

Daniel, like *Reds*, restores a part of the history of the left by showing its rallies and concerts as well as its paranoia and persecution. The Isaacsons' guilt or innocence is never established in the film, although their apparent poverty and innocent activism made them unlikely spies. Whether they were innocent or merely complicit, however, their children were damaged, and Lumet claims that this is the subject of his movie. His point is that the parents' political commitment destroyed the children, so it doesn't matter whether the parents were artists or activists. But Lumet's gloomy statement of family psychology contradicts the affirmative ending of his movie. Daniel's wife and child are with him when he joins the anti-war demonstration, and this step toward political commitment is presented as Daniel's way of rejoining the human race. Commitment had separated Daniel from his parents, and it had failed to save his sister, yet for Daniel it is salvation, perhaps because he embraces it with his family and with more emotional maturity than his sister.

Like most of Lumet's other films, *Daniel* was dark and depressing, with complex characters, few of whom were likable. That hadn't kept audiences away from Lumet's earlier movies, but *Daniel* was more political, despite the director's denials. Like *Ragtime* and *Reds*, *Daniel* was a flop. Critics picked at its family neuroses and exploitation of the Rosenbergs. Some thought the family melodrama muddled its politics. Considering these critiques, Andrew Sarris pointed out that "political movies are damned if they do, and damned if they don't."[7] If they make their political point clear, people may dislike the message or its obviousness, but if the point isn't clear, people find the film muddled and confusing.

Soft Left

Nostalgia for the more recent past also showed up in a few movies. Milos Forman's *Hair*, a counterculture musical about the 1960s, was belatedly filmed in 1979, and several filmmakers took up the stories of sixties activists and idealists as they matured. Joan Micklin Silver's *Between the Lines* (1977), for example, is about a co-op newspaper that is bought by a counterculture capitalist, an occurrence that symbolizes the sellout of the hippie generation. The fates of three Harvard students of the sixties are assessed in *A Small Circle of Friends* (1980), but this movie attributes the past activism of the trio to personal relations rather than to politics, thus trivializing the political involvement of a whole generation.

The Return of the Secaucus Seven (1980) focuses on the reunion of a group of sixties activists who were once arrested in Secaucus, New Jersey, en route to an anti-war demonstration in Washington. Followers rather than leaders, the seven were marginal to the anti-war movement and yet were affected by it. Although writer-director John Sayles set his film in the late seventies, his characters' cultural roots are clearly in the sixties, and while Sayles makes the limits of their political involvement clear, he manages to do so without belittling sixties activism.

The Big Chill (1983), directed by Lawrence Kasdan, is a strikingly similar film about a weekend reunion of sixties pals, but it reached a much larger audience. This group is brought together by the suicide of Alex, its dominant member. These idealists of the sixties have sold out, however, to become career-oriented professionals, and their friend's death symbolizes the death of the values of the sixties.

Between the Lines, *A Small Circle of Friends*, *The Return of the Secaucus Seven*, and *The Big Chill* all looked back nostalgically on the sixties, but it was Kasdan's popular and entertaining film that most clearly defined today's attitude toward that generation. These movies were about shattered dreams and aging, however, not about politics. Their characters represent the attitudes of much of their generation, and their stories should be told, but the film industry so far has not managed to treat the politics of the sixties with respect, accuracy, or understanding. The activism and social concern of the period have been derided, trivialized, and finally scorned in films about the sellouts of the Big Chill Generation.

Commitment

All of the movies that look to previous political eras nevertheless share a respect for political commitment. *Ragtime* treats it with dignity. *Reds* makes commitment seem exciting and rewarding while admitting its costs. The psychological price of involvement is higher in *Daniel*, but in the end it is seen as a means of salvation. Even the films that look back to the sixties mourn the loss of commitment. It seems that in the early eighties, people missed commitment even though they were too fearful, cynical, or self-absorbed to believe in it anymore. They didn't flock to these films, however. *Between the Lines* and *The Return of the Secaucus Seven* fared well on the art-house and university circuit, and *Reds* was a critical success, but only *The Big Chill* was a box office hit. Perhaps its portrait of sold-out radicals made it more in tune with its times than the other movies.

NOTES

1. *Film Quarterly*, vol. XXXV, Spring 1982, pp. 43–47.
2. Morris Dickstein, "Time Bandits," *American Film*, Vol. VII, October 1982, p. 42.
3. *New York Times*, 4 December 1981.
4. *New Republic*, 16 December 1981.
5. *Village Voice*, 14 December 1981.
6. Lecture, London Film Festival, 3 December 1983.
7. *Village Voice*, 6 September 1983.

Missing (1982)

16

"See You in Thailand"
America and the Third World

After Vietnam, America grew cautious about its international role, grappling with the limits of power and struggling toward a foreign policy that emphasized detente, human rights, and a new respect for the Third World. Under President Jimmy Carter, the nation turned briefly inward, almost isolationist.

Because of Vietnam jitters, neo-isolationism, and Carter's support of human rights and noninterventionism, the United States stood by as two of its authoritarian allies, the Shah of Iran and President Somoza of Nicaragua, were overthrown. A guerrilla war started in El Salvador, near enough to Nicaragua to increase worries about all of Central America. Another war was under way in Angola, and unrest was increasing in South Africa. Then, in 1980, the Soviet Union invaded Afghanistan. Within a few years other friendly right-wing leaders were challenged in the Philippines and Haiti, but still, the United States took no action.

When Ronald Reagan became president in 1980, however, he immediately turned the nation's foreign policy around. Friendly authoritarian – as distinguished from totalitarian – regimes were to be supported. Human rights were given a low priority, and interventionism was back, although the Reagan administration showed flexibility when necessary, withdrawing from Lebanon and refusing to sustain Philippine president Marcos in office, for example. On the whole, however, the Reagan foreign policy was one of speaking loudly and carrying a big stick, an almost complete turnabout from that of Jimmy Carter.

Inevitably, this change in foreign policy showed up in the movies, but the first filmmakers to join the debate firmly opposed Reagan's foreign policy, most specifically as it was applied in Latin America. Their movies were among the most critical ever made about America and its foreign policy, yet some were popular and critical successes.

The Sleeping Giant

Hollywood, like the nation, ignored Latin America for a long time, venturing south of the border only occasionally for a big movie like *Juarez* or *Viva Zapata!*, and using Latin American settings for costume epics and musicals. The movies also ignored Hispanic Americans, except for occasional appearances as stereotypical bandits, whores, maids, venal generals, and bureaucrats. Then the revolution in Nicaragua and El Salvador and the growing assertiveness of America's huge Hispanic population pushed Latin America back into the national consciousness.

Not surprisingly, Hispanics started showing up more in the movies. *The Candidate*, *The China Syndrome*, and *Nine to Five*, for example, featured Hispanic characters, albeit minor ones. *Boulevard Nights* (1979) was a sort of Hispanic version of *Saturday Night Fever*, with L.A. lowriders replacing New York disco dancers and a Chicano youth trying unsuccessfully to break away from street gangs. *Zoot Suit* (1981) was more political, telling the story of the Sleepy Lagoon murders and the anti-Mexican riots in Los Angeles during World War II.

The Border (1981), co-authored by Deric Washburn (*The Deer Hunter*) and director Tony Richardson, shifted the focus to an Anglo immigration officer (Jack Nicholson) on the Mexican border. The exploitation and corruption of the border are seen through his tired and cynical eyes, but he at least tries to help a Mexican girl (Elpidia Carillo).

By contrast, *El Norte* (1984), was a low-budget production filmed in Spanish and featuring unknown actors. Told from the point of view of two young Guatamalan immigrants to the United States, according to director and co-author Gregory Nava, the film focused on their personal story because "an overtly political film . . . would have put off too many people. As it is, left, right, and center seem to like it and political people can easily make the connections."[1] *El Norte* left little doubt that the immigrants were refugees from an oppressive system or that they were exploited once they arrived in this country, but by not overstating their case, Nava and co-author Anna Thomas directed the viewers' sympathy toward the immigrants without giving offense. They rejected suggestions to cast stars like Robbie Benson and Brooke Shields in the leads and to make the protagonists lovers rather than brother and sister, because although such compromises would have made it easier for them to raise money for their independent production, they felt they would blur the film's focus. Their judgment proved valid. *El Norte* won good reviews and was a small-scale hit.

American Interests

Movies about politics in Central America itself were more popular than border stories, however, especially when they featured big stars and plenty of action. *Missing* (1982) was the first of these and also Costa-Gavras's first American production in English. A Greek-born citizen of France and one of the world's finest and most political directors, Costa-Gavras first examined American involvement in Latin America in *State of Siege* (1972), the story of the kidnapping of a CIA agent (Yves Montand) by Uruguay's Tupamaro guerrillas, but *Missing* was a more accessible and traditional film that reached a much bigger audience.

In *Missing* Charlie Horman (John Shea), a nice young American living in Chile with his wife Beth (Cissy Spacek), disappears in the aftermath of the coup that brought down the popularly elected Marxist government of Salvador Allende. When Beth and the American embassy can't find him, Charlie's father Ed (Jack Lemmon), an all-American conservative, arrives, suspecting that his son got himself into trouble with his political dabbling. This alienates Ed from Beth, but he gradually comes to share her belief that the American bureaucrats are duplicitous and that Charlie has disappeared not because of anything he did, but because he was with a tourist friend in the town that was the base for American involvement in the coup and he saw too much.

After visiting a stadium full of political prisoners and a morgue full of bodies, including the corpse of Charlie's friend who, according to the embassy, had left the country, Ed confronts the American officials with information he's come across on his own. They confirm that Charlie has been killed by the Chilean military. Ed is outraged. "I do not think that they would dare do a thing like that unless an American official co-signed the kill order," he says.

"Why would we want him dead?" the ambassador asks.

"Probably because he knew of our involvement in the coup," Ed answers, calling the ambassador's denial "a bald-faced lie."

The embassy's CIA man effectively admits complicity in Charlie's death, telling Ed that his "kid . . . was a snoop" and deserved what he got.

"What is your role here besides endorsing a regime that murders thousands of human beings?" Ed demands of the ambassador.

"If you hadn't been personally involved," the ambassador explains, "you'd have been sitting at home, complacent and more or less oblivious to all this. This mission is pledged to protect American interests. *Our* interests, Mr. Horman. . . . There are over three thousand U.S. firms doing business down here. Those are American interests. In other words, *your* interests. I'm concerned with the preservation of a way of life."

Until this didactic scene, Costa-Gavras exercises uncharacteristic restraint in making his political points. Charlie was clearly a harmless do-gooder caught up in the violence of Latin American politics. Ed is a skeptical father who gradually learns about the brutality of the coup and becomes aware of American complicity. As we follow Ed through the learning process, we finally come to share his rage. U.S. officials, the film tells us, have helped overthrow a foreign government, lied to their own citizens, and possibly approved of the death of one innocent American. We learn virtually nothing about the deposed government or the internal reasons for the coup, but Costa-Gavras, after all, was making a movie for Americans. He focused on American victims and American perpetrators, and his movie reached its intended audience.

Missing was a box office hit and was nominated for several Academy Awards, although it won only for best script. Mixed reviews praised the film's pacing and performances, but some thought the movie's politics were too blatant, and others objected to its conclusions. Like *Silkwood*, this film was based on a true story, and also like the earlier movie, it was attacked for distorting the record. The State Department denied the movie's allegations while from the left, one critic condemned Costa-Gavras for focusing on individuals, saying it was odd "to see a European filmmaker falling into . . . one of the ways Americans hide from the concrete realities of the rest of the world."[2]

Missing would have been strengthened by the presence of one or two strong Chilean characters to point out the more devastating impact of the coup on them, but Costa-Gavras chose characters with whom he was sure Americans would identify. Focusing on Chileans would have diverted attention at least to some extent from Costa-Gavras's primary concern, American involvement. It could also have reduced the characters to Chilean good guys and American bad guys, which would have been neither as palatable or as persuasive to American audiences as the all-American confrontation he chose instead. Through these characters and dramatic devices, Costa-Gavras conveyed the extent of American involvement in the coup, which came as a shock not only to Ed Horman, but to his liberal son Charlie and to the American public. *Missing* did what a political movie should do: it entertained people and it made a point. The controversy over the film's interpretation of historical fact only confirmed its power.

Critics raised some of the same objections to *Under Fire* (1983), another film about U.S. involvement in Latin America seen through the eyes of Americans. Photographer Russell Price (Nick Nolte) joins his friends, Alex (Gene Hackman) and Claire (Joanne Cassidy), in Nicaragua, where the Sandinistas are about to overthrow Somoza. After Alex leaves to become a networkanchorman, Russell and Claire become lovers and develop a sympathy with the revolution, which the film tells us is totally justifiable. When the rebels need to persuade the media and the people that their recently deceased leader is alive, they ask the photographer to fake a picture. He resists, considering it a violation of his journalistic integrity, but finally gives in, sure that the revolution is a higher cause. Then he discovers that some photos he shot while at the rebel camp have fallen into the hands of the CIA, which is using them to identify and kill rebel activists. As the Somoza regime collapses, Alex returns to Nicaragua and demands that the photographer arrange an interview with the (dead) rebel leader. Before the request can be dealt with, however, Alex is shot by the national guard. Russell photographs the killing, and we are led to believe that the anchorman's death outrages the American public, thus precipitating the fall of Somoza and affecting the war as the photographer had hoped his fake picture would do.

In *Under Fire*, the rebels are good and Somoza's national guard is bad, but while the movie sides with the rebels, the anti-revolutionary line is forcefully if unsympathetically put forth by a CIA agent (Jean-Louis Trintignant) and a mercenary (Ed Harris). All revolutions turn to dictatorships, they tell the idealistic journalists, so what difference do they make? More insultingly, the mercenary tells them that they're paid to do their jobs, just like him. "See you in Thailand," he says as the film ends.

Under Fire, like *Missing*, is about Americans, not Latinos. None of its central characters are Nicaraguan, just as none of *Missing*'s were Chilean. *Under Fire* also insults the genuinely collective leadership of the Sandinistas with its fable of a single heroic leader without whom the revolution could not prevail. There was no such person. The movie is better as a treatise on journalists under pressure, trying to come to terms with their own power and to use it for good rather than have it used by malefactors (like the CIA agent). This power may have been exaggerated, but at least the film and its characters are aware of it. *Under Fire* presents a moral choice between professional ethics and good politics (helping the revolutionaries). Russell chooses politics, but the film refuses to make his choice so obvious as to obscure its difficulty or to stifle argument about it, a respectable accomplishment for a political film. *Under Fire* should also be praised for providing a strong, independent woman character. Claire makes her own choices and functions as an equal in her relationships with the two men, rather like the person Louise Bryant wanted to be. Although it is individualistic and ethnocentric, *Under Fire* is about adults and raises important issues.

Under Fire was a success in Europe, but flopped in the United States. Some critics thought its subject was too much in the news at the moment. Others thought the movie failed because it was anti-American. "The film may be the only American movie in recent decades to side with a foreign government against which the United States has aligned itself," said *The New York Times*. Roger Spottiswoode, the British director of *Under Fire*, insisted that the film was "not anti-American," however. "It is a film against American policy in Central America," he explained, "and it's made with the hope that the United States doesn't get involved in a conflict there that it cannot win. In that sense it's got political content," but "it's an exciting story and it has lots of different levels other than the political one."[3] Supporters of American foreign policy nevertheless condemned *Under Fire*'s bias while critics on the left denounced its portrait of a "one-dimensional Third World where the natives pull liberal heartstrings – until they get reckless."[4]

If being about a contemporary issue and opposing U.S. policy were the first two strikes against *Under Fire*, its treatment of journalists may have been the third. The press was highly critical of the film for justifying the fakery of the photograph. Labeling Russell's ruse "Rambo-think in reverse," Enrique Fernandez condemned the movie for saying "it's okay to lie for the left."[5] Vincent Canby called *Under Fire* "absolutely absurd" for oversimplifying the success of a revolution and for adding to public mistrust of the press.[6] Pauline Kael, however, said other journalists unconsciously do the same sort of thing Russell did,[7] but with few defenders and so much antagonism, *Under Fire* was doomed.

Made in Britain

Some of the issues raised in *Missing* and *Under Fire* were dealt with more successfully in *The Killing Fields* (1984), produced by David Puttnam and directed by Roland Joffe. Although it is a British production, *The Killing Fields* was made for America, and Warner Bros. had an interest in it.

Set in Cambodia at the time of the Khmer Rouge takeover, *The Killing Fields* is the true story of *New York Times* reporter Sidney Schanberg (Sam Waterston) and his friend and assistant, Dith Pran (Haing S. Ngor). Pran worries that his association with Americans will damn him if Cambodia falls to the communists, but the self-confident

Schanberg assures him that he will be evacuated when the Americans go. In the event, however, Pran is left behind and imprisoned. Schanberg suffers guiltily until Pran's escape. Their reunion provides a happy conclusion, although the movie ends with a reminder of the tragedy in Cambodia.

The Killing Fields was a box office and critical success, winning three Oscars, including best supporting actor for Haing S. Ngor. Perhaps it pleased audiences more than *Missing* or *Under Fire* because its politics were more complex and because few could disagree with its contention that the Khmer Rouge was bad. The film also escaped at least one of the major criticisms of the other films, since it revolved around an Asian, Dith Pran, rather than an American.

The Killing Fields was widely praised for its treatment of journalists. Schanberg was sometimes cocky, obnoxious, and dangerously over-confident, but the film respected him as a hardworking reporter. "Unlike Clark Kent," Vincent Canby wrote, Schanberg had to "overcome all sorts of bureaucratic and physical difficulties, including boredom, to get the story."[8]

The Killing Fields further distinguished itself from *Missing* and *Under Fire* by criticizing U.S. policy without appearing anti-American, although Bruce Robinson's original script for the movie was toned down by producer Puttnam and his company's U.S. partner, Warner Bros. The Americans in *The Killing Fields* were brash and arrogant, but they were not oversimplified bad guys. Some criticism of American policy emerged in scenes where Schanberg watched TV reports on the aftermath of U.S. withdrawal from Southeast Asia and it became apparent that the U.S. had abandoned its allies just as Schanberg had abandoned Dith Pran. But *The Killing Fields* showed that films could "go against the grain of mainstream American sensitivities" and still succeed, according to critic James Park. "The film was not there to hector people," director Joffe told Park. "Neither was it meant to wrap everything up in a neat package of anger and discontent. What I wanted to do was to bring people close to the emotional color of the events, from which they are free to draw off ideas."[9] Because the film worried more about the Cambodian victims than whom to blame, some viewers may have missed its criticism of U.S. policy, or even seen it as primarily anti-Khmer Rouge.

Another international production that presented a Latin American perspective on revolutionary politics, if not U.S. policy, was *Kiss of the Spider Woman* (1985), also a popular and critical success. Brazilian Hector Babenco directed this adaptation of Manuel Puig's novel in English with an American cast, clearly aiming at an American audience. The story takes place in a South American prison, where a homosexual, Luis Molina (William Hurt), befriends a revolutionary, Valentin

Arregui (Raul Julia). Molina is an apolitical romantic, who survives prison by retelling the stories of the movies he loves, among them a fascist melodrama that appalls Valentin. When Molina is freed, he carries out a political act on the instructions of his cell mate. His motive is romantic rather than political, however, and he is used by both the police and the revolutionaries. Nevertheless, for Molina to act at all is redemptive. Meanwhile, Valentin, still in prison, has learned to dream. Romance and politics have changed places. One character has learned romance to survive, the other has learned to act to fulfill himself. In a way, *Spider Woman* is cynical about politics, yet the love and pride of the self-sacrificing homosexual make a superficially meaningless act heroic.

Hollywood Contras

Two other films released during the Reagan years criticized U.S. support of the reactionary government of El Salvador and the counter-revolutionary Contras of Nicaragua. Both films were from Hollywood veterans, and both were low-budget independent productions.

In *Latino* (1985), directed by Haskell Wexler (*Medium Cool*), Eddie Guerrero (Robert Beltran) is a Green Beret who is sent to train Nicaraguan counterrevolutionaries, a job he likes less and less. His Nicaraguan lover adds to his doubts about the U.S. stance in Central America, and the sweet but determined farmers of a Sandinista co-op provide a sharp contrast to the crude Contras. Eddie becomes so disillusioned that he allows himself to be taken captive on a raid. The army sends Chicanos like Eddie to Central America precisely because they can pass as natives if they are captured, but he violates orders, keeping the dog tag that will identify him as an American and reveal U.S. involvement in the conflict.

Although *Latino* was well-meaning, it was too obvious. The movie lost money, and even critics who were sympathetic with its politics panned it. "I guess I'm damning it," David Edelstein wrote, "for not stirring people up the way a hack right-wing action flick does – for forgetting that, in American movies, it's not enough to tell the truth."[10] More advice – or money – from George Lucas (*Star Wars*), one of *Latino*'s backers, might have helped.

Salvador (1986) did at least some of what Edelstein seemed to want from *Latino*: it vividly communicated the chaos and horror of revolution. In fact, *Salvador* looked more like a right-wing movie than the left-wing movie it was. Oliver Stone, the Academy Award-winning writer of *Midnight Express*, directed and co-authored this low-budget production with Richard Boyle, the gonzo journalist whose story it tells. Boyle (James Wood) seems to have been present at every highly publicized atrocity of the long war in El Salvador, including the assassination of an archbishop and the murder of three nuns. Through it all, he drinks, takes drugs, mistreats women, abuses his responsibility, and disappoints those who trust him. He's such an offensive character, in fact, that his conversion to the revolutionary cause lessens its credibility, but he also prevents the politics of *Salvador* from seeming pious. The film's reverential treatment of the rebels in their quiet camps strains belief, however, as does Boyle's one speech explicitly denouncing U.S. policy. Boyle's disgust when the rebels kill some prisoners is an attempt to provide balance, as is his admission that his sympathy for the Khmer Rouge had been wrong, but *Salvador* is still less balanced than even *Missing* or *Under Fire*. It ends with Boyle and his Salvadoran lover being led off in handcuffs – by U.S. immigration officers. "The man who made this movie is no gentle persuader hoping to cast a wide net out in the mainstream," wrote one offended critic.[11] *Salvador* is sometimes crude and simple-minded, but Stone's no-holds-barred political filmmaking leaves a powerful impression. Like *Latino*, this film bombed with the reviewers, but it did better at the box office.

The failures of these movies might have discouraged the making of others on the subject, but with U.S. policy toward Nicaragua and other Latin American countries still a hot issue as the Reagan era ended, more films would follow.

NOTES

1. *The Guardian*, 19 July 1984.
2. *American Film*, March 1982, p. 79.
3. *The New York Times*, cited in *The Sunday Times* London *Magazine*, 22 January 1984.
4. John Powers, "Saints and Savages," *American Film*, January-February 1984, p. 38.
5. *Village Voice*, 2 December 1986.
6. *New York Times*, 2 December 1984.
7. *New Yorker*, 31 October 1983.
8. *New York Times*, 2 December 1984.
9. *Sight and Sound*, Winter 1984–1985, pp. 15–16.
10. *Village Voice*, 11 March 1986.
11. *California*, June 1986.

Platoon (1986)

17

"Do We Get to Win This Time?"

The New Patriotism

Movies critical of American foreign policy were made throughout the Reagan years and some were popular successes, but the era will be remembered for a very different sort of film. Like President Reagan himself, these movies called up traditional values, emphasizing individualism, self-sufficiency, competition, courage, pride, and patriotism in a conveniently simplified world. The American voters expressed their longing for a return to these vlaues when they elected Ronald Reagan in 1980. They wanted a president who was sure of himself and his nation, unbothered by doubt, and unfazed by the complexities of the nation, the world, or human behavior.

People liked Reagan himself even more than they liked his policies. They were often willing to overlook his political shortcomings because of his congeniality and his communication skills. Worries about his lack of experience in foreign affairs were soon swept away by an almost unprecedented wave of patriotic fervor. The joyous return of the Iranian hostages on the day of Reagan's inauguration launched the revival of American pride and patriotism.

Reagan called for a renewal of American power and boosted the nation's military might with massive increases in defense spending. Suddenly the Cold War was back, and so was interventionism. Reagan bombed Beirut, sent troops into Lebanon, and loosed the U.S. Marines on the tiny island of Grenada. He intervened cautiously but decisively in El Salvador, propping up a right-wing regime, then pushing it to elections and modest reform. It was too late for such action in Nicaragua, so Reagan isolated that nation economically and backed the Contra counterrevolutionaries. Later on, Reagan sent U.S. jets to raid Libya, which he claimed was the headquarters of world terrorism. Much of America loved every bit of it. Nearly six years of self-congratulation culminated in the 1986 rededication of the Statue of Liberty, an orgy of patriotism produced in the lavish style of a Hollywood movie. And much of this patriotic frenzy is reflected in a group of films produced during Reagan's presidency.

A New Cold War and New Patriotism

Reaganite movies didn't come into their own until after the 1984 reelection, but the trend started in 1982 with Sylvester Stallone's *First Blood*, for which the *Rocky* movies and *F.I.S.T.* had paved the way. John Rambo (Stallone), a former Green Beret and winner of the Congressional Medal of Honor, is an alienated and itinerant Vietnam vet searching for a buddy who survived the war. After learning that his friend has died of Agent Orange-induced cancer, the distraught Rambo wanders around, looking like a cross between a hippie and a Hell's Angel. Not surprisingly, a small town sheriff (Brian Dennehy) orders him to move on and drives him to the outskirts of town. Rambo, who does not like being told what to do, starts back into town. The two men fight, and Rambo is arrested. In jail, he becomes a victim of police brutality. With visions of Vietnam in his head, Rambo goes berserk and breaks out, fleeing to the woods.

A posse pursues Rambo. The most brutal deputy dies when he goes too far, but Rambo only wounds the rest, declaring, "Out here I'm the law!" Supplemented by the National Guard and state police, the posse traps Rambo. The pursuers think he's dead, but he's only angry. Resurrected, he chases the nasty sheriff to his headquarters and kills him. His old Green Beret commander (Richard Crenna) tries to talk the surrounded Rambo into surrendering. "Do you want a war you can't win?" he asks.

"They drew first blood," Rambo replies, "not me," at long last explaining himself. "It wasn't my war. You asked me, I didn't ask you. And I did what I had to do to win, but somebody wouldn't let us win. And I come back to the world, and I see all those maggots at the airport, protesting me, calling me a baby-killer and all kinds of vile crap. Who are they to protest me, huh? Back there I could fly a gunship, I could drive a tank. I was in charge of million dollar equipment. Back here I can't even hold a job."

First Blood condemned the maltreatment of Vietnam vets, a message with which few would disagree, but the real point of this film was action. Although critics laughed at the movie, Stallone laughed last: *First Blood* was a box office smash, and he followed it with a dumber movie that was an even bigger hit.

The next Reaganite movie was *Red Dawn*, directed by John Milius, the author of *Apocalypse Now*. It is the story of a small Colorado town that is invaded by Russian, Cuban, and Nicaraguan communists. The Wolverines, a group of teenagers who resemble the partisans in World War II movies, resist the attackers. Politicians are represented by the mayor of the town, who collaborates with the communists. The teenagers run rings around the occupying army for a while, but in the end they sacrifice themselves in a kamikaze-style mission. The movie closes with a shot of "Partisan Rock", a monument to the heroes of the resistance.

"Movies like *Red Dawn* are rapidly preparing America for World War III," said the chairman of the National Coalition on Television Violence, denouncing its 134 acts of violence per hour and labelling it "the most violent film ever seen."[1] Dismissed by critics as a mediocre action movie, *Red Dawn* was nevertheless a box office hit: it made $10 million in its first five days in release. "The ferocity of the American people," director John Milius smugly observed, "has always been underestimated."[2] Certainly the popularity of his film was due to its action rather than its politics. *Red Dawn* was anti-communist, but only because communists were convenient enemies; the bad guys had no perceivable political ideology and could just as easily have been from outer space. The inclusion of Latinos among the invaders distinguished *Red Dawn* from the anti-communist movies of the 1950s, but otherwise it was no more politically sophisticated. Indeed, it was more rabidly individualistic than anti-communist.

Although it was hard to take the politics of *Red Dawn* seriously, the movie did set precedents that other films would soon follow. It revived communists as convenient enemies, and it proved the marketability of posturing patriots as heroes. Few movies had fallen back on these old stereotypes since the fifties. After the Cuban missile confrontation in the early sixties, America and the Soviet Union moved toward detente, and so did the movies. Superpatriot heroes and communist villains went out of style and stayed out during the cynical sixties and seventies, when movies like *The Spy Who Came in from the Cold* and *Dr. Strangelove* were more common than films like *The Green Berets*. But in the eighties, the public response to Ronald Reagan made patriotism and anti-communism okay again, and *Red Dawn* proved they were good box office.

Once unleashed, Reaganite cinema became even cruder. *First Blood* and *Red Dawn* looked sophisticated compared to what followed. *Missing in Action* (1984) and *Invasion U.S.A.* (1985) were crude action flicks starring Chuck Norris, a wooden actor whose gift for stunt work presumably accounts for his great popularity. In *Missing in Action*, Norris plays an escaped prisoner of war who returns to Vietnam with an American senator who is investigating allegations about American soldiers "missing in action" (MIAs). Discredited by the evil Vietnamese and disowned by the American politician, the hero wreaks havoc on various enemy encampments, prisons, and convoys, saves the MIAs, and brings them back to Ho Chi Minh City to repudiate the Vietnamese liars. "You guys are going home," he assures the MIAs. Quite rightly, critics didn't take *Missing in Action* seriously. Like other Chuck Norris movies, however, it did well at the box office, despite its lack of tension, credibility, and excitement.

In Norris's other box office hit, *Invasion U.S.A.*, he plays an ex-CIA agent who comes out of retirement to stop a Russian "invasion" of Florida. This invasion might more accurately have been called a terrorist infiltration, but that wouldn't have made as good a title. Diabolical communists in various disguises slaughter Cuban refugees, ghetto dwellers, Christmas shoppers, and families in suburban homes, stirring up distrust and unrest and turning people against one another. "America has not been invaded by a foreign enemy in nearly two hundred years," the communist villain sneers. "Look at them . . . soft, spineless, decadent. They don't even understand the nature of their own freedom or how we will use it against them. They are their own worst enemies, but they don't know it." The movie confirms this analysis when cowardly FBI agents phone in sick and spoiled citizens whine about rationing. The "tide of terror" turns into a "threat to democracy," with demands for martial law and the suspension of the Constitution, but happily, the hero stops the invaders single-handedly. Thanks in part to a larger budget, *Invasion U.S.A.* was better than *Missing in Action*, although neither of Norris's popular movies had much to say about politics. International tensions were merely an excuse for violent action, feeding Reaganite anti-communism. More seriously, *Missing in Action* cheaply exploited a subject that genuinely worried some Americans.

Rambo's return was almost as crude, but *Rambo: First Blood Part II* (1985), written by Sylvester Stallone, was even more popular than the Reaganite movies that preceded it. John Rambo (Stallone again) wins a pardon for his earlier rampage in the woods when he accepts an assignment to find American MIAs in Vietnam. "Do we get to win this time?" Rambo asks his former Green Beret commander (Richard Crenna). He's only supposed to photograph the MIAs for evidence, but he tries to bring one back. The helicopter sent to pick him up abandons them, and the Vietnamese and their Russian advisers capture and torture Rambo. He escapes, slaughters the enemy, frees the MIAs, and leads – or drags – them to safety. He trashes the headquarters of the U.S. mission when he gets back and warns its bureaucratic chief to find the rest of the MIAs or risk the wrath of Rambo. This movie places the blame for the MIAs' continued captivity squarely on the U.S. government, which first declined to win the war and then refused to pay war reparations to Vietnam in exchange for the MIAs.

In a promotion video for *Rambo*, Stallone, unlike most filmmakers, was forthright in declaring his movie political. "I hope to establish a character that can represent a certain section of the American consciousness," he said, "and through the entertainment [I also hope to] be educational. . . . More than being just a fighting man, [Rambo] represents the entire fighting force." Stallone also claimed his movie was part of the "pre-stages of a true historical event" in which the existence of the MIAs would be verified. "It's no big secret," he declared. "Vietnam wants reparations from us. We don't want to pay all those billions," possibly because "our officials are being paid off." Movies like *Rambo* were popular, Stallone asserted, "because the people are on to something. There's a thirst for verification."[3]

Despite derisive reviews and Stallone's pretensions, *Rambo* was a big hit, even though the action was facile and without tension. *First Blood* was a better action film because of more skillful direction and because Rambo's white antagonists were not reduced to racist stereotypes, which may also be why *Invasion U.S.A.* had more tension than *Missing in Action*. David Morell, the author of the novel on which *First Blood* was based, dismissed *Rambo* as "a cartoon. On military bases," Morell said, "they show it as a comedy."[4] Others took it more seriously, though few critics liked it. David Halberstram labeled Stallone "a cinematic Joseph McCarthy" for his assertions about the existence of the MIAs and for conveying the "exact reverse of the real message of the Vietnam War."[5] President Ronald Reagan, on the other hand, admired Stallone's message. "After seeing *Rambo* last night," he joked during a terrorist crisis, "I know what to do next time this happens." He failed to comment on *Rambo*'s contention of U.S. government complacency in freeing the MIAs, however.

Anti-communism was also the theme of three other movies released in 1985: *Rocky IV*, *Eleni*, and *White Nights*. Stallone wrapped himself in the flag for his fourth Rocky film, in which the boxing hero comes out of retirement to defeat a Soviet fighter produced by biochemical engineering rather than old-fashioned hard work. The fight takes place in Moscow, where a hostile crowd of communists ends up cheering Rocky and he calls for international understanding in a concluding speech that attempts to mitigate the anti-communism of the rest of the film. *Eleni*, the true story of journalist Nicholas Sage's search for the communists who killed his mother in the Greek civil war, made no such gesture. "It is cartoon time even for the supposedly political cinema," wrote critic Andrew Sarris, "but *Eleni*, alas, doesn't work even as a cartoon."[6] It was the only one of the new cold war films to fail at the box office. *White Nights* was more successful thanks to the presence of Mikhail Baryshnikov and the direction of Taylor Hackford (*An Officer and a Gentleman*). An airliner makes an emergency landing in Soviet territory and a Russian ballet dancer (Baryshnikov) who has defected to the United States is taken captive. He escapes with a black American tap-dancer (Gregory Hines) who has defected to the Soviets. Director Hackford played down his movie's politics, claiming it was "only realistic about artistic freedom," but Baryshnikov was more accurate when he said that "this film is politically right wing and patriotic."[7]

Iron Eagle, *Heartbreak Ridge*, and *Top Gun* (all 1986) soon added to what the Soviet press labeled "war-nography." In *Iron Eagle*, an American teenager flies to the rescue of his father, whose plane has been shot down over North Africa. The movie praises President Reagan as "this guy who don't take no shit from no gimpy country," but Reagan's government fails to save the captive pilot, forcing the teenager to do the job himself. *Heartbreak Ridge* featured a tough career soldier (Clint Eastwood) making men of his trainees, who are ultimately tested in the triumphant, if fanciful, invasion of Grenada.

Top Gun topped them both, though, at least at the box office, becoming the biggest ticket seller of 1986. Maverick (Tom Cruise), the young pilot who must become "top gun," is obsessed by the memory of his father, who was shot down under mysterious circumstances over Southeast Asia. It turns out that Dad was a hero, but details of his death have been kept secret for political reasons. Maverick ultimately proves himself in a skirmish with an unnamed enemy whose pilots fly MIGs. *Top Gun* takes such confrontations for granted, beginning with U.S. and enemy jets playing tag, and ending in real combat. Lest the audience worry that this incident might trigger World War III, we are told that "the other side denied the incident." The implication that this sort of thing is a daily occurrence is terrifying – all the more so because the U.S. Navy wholeheartedly endorsed and cooperated in the making of this picture. *Top Gun* is a throwback to old-fashioned war movies, no longer calling for calm vigilance, as did *Strategic Air Command* in 1955, but advocating confrontational machismo instead. Slick and shallow, it was the essence of Reaganite cinema.

This same strutting self-confidence ran through all the patriotic movies of the Reagan years, but as in other Hollywood eras, this was not the only vision.

Other Visions

John Badham's *WarGames* (1983) and *Short Circuit* (1986) and Marshall Brickman's *The Manhattan Project* (1986) played to youthful audiences by focusing on teenage heroes, but unlike the confrontational and patriotic *Top Gun* and *Iron Eagle*, these films expressed traditional liberal concern about nuclear apocalypse. The threat in all three films came from uncontrollable technology and in all three, disaster was averted by teenage intellectuals or nerds – considerably more credible heroes than the beefcakes of the other movies. These films also raised the issue of accidental nuclear war, a subject that had been largely ignored since the sixties, although they did so mainly as a premise for action and entertainment. Critics were unimpressed, but *WarGames* was a major box office hit.

Adults claimed center stage in three far less popular political films. *The Little Drummer Girl* (1984), directed by George Roy Hill and adapted from John Le Carré's novel, took up the subjects of terrorism and Middle Eastern politics slightly before the nation was ready for them. An actress (Diane Keaton) who is sympathetic to the Palestinian Liberation Front is recruited by the Israelis to infiltrate the terrorist organization. With typical Le Carré cynicism, both the Israelis and the PLO are portrayed as brutal and ruthless, an ambiguity that left audiences and critics dissatisfied. John Schlesinger's *The Falcon and the Snowman* (1985) told the true story of two young Americans who bumbled their way into spying for the Soviet Union. Schlesinger attributed their actions to alienation rather than ideology, and his turncoats were neither fully sympathetic nor roundly condemned. As in *Drummer Girl*, ambiguity seems to have been the reason why the public rejected this film. But ambiguity wasn't the problem in Robert Altman's *Secret Honor* (1984), a bravura one-man show in which Richard Nixon (Philip Baker Hall) tells all to a tape recorder. He refuses to accept responsibility for his own downfall, insisting that he was controlled by an economic elite which forced him out of office when he refused to carry on the war in Southeast Asia to facilitate their heroin trade. The thesis strained credibility, but *Secret Honor* was a unique, if bizarre, attempt to understand Nixon. It was also one of the few films to assert a radical analysis of American politics.

Protocol, directed by Herbert Ross and written by Buck Henry, was more popular and more orthodox than the other political films of the day. Almost a Ms. Smith Goes to Washington, it centers on Sunny Ann Davis (Goldie Hawn), a Washington cocktail waitress who accidentally foils an assassin. The Arab potentate she saves takes a fancy to her, and the State Department cynically offers her as a pawn in negotiations for a military base. Sunny, who has never voted, becomes a protocol officer and does a fast study of American government, which is presented in a montage of Washington reminiscent of Mr. Smith's arrival or our introduction to Joe Tynan. But then Sunny travels to the Middle East, and her visit precipitates a coup d'état and a scandal. Testifying before a congressional committee investigating "Sunnygate," the heroine refuses to blame the bureaucrats who set her up. "I'm responsible," she declares. When Congress acts, "it has a direct effect on we the people's lives, so if we don't – I mean if *I* don't – know what you're up to, and if I don't holler and scream when I think you're doing it wrong, and if I just mind my own business and don't vote or care, then I just get what I deserve, so now that I'm Sunny Davis, a private citizen, again, you're going to have to watch out for me, 'cause I'm gonna be watching all of you ... like a hawk." Sunny gets the guy and is elected to Congress, too. The critics derided *Protocol*, but audiences liked the comedy, and they may also have liked the movie's trite but positive message of individual responsibility. As familiar from old movies as the president himself, the message fits almost as well with Reaganite philosophy as did *Rambo* or *Top Gun*. It was even anti-government in the same way Reagan was, mistrusting bureaucrats and Congress in particular.

Roger Donaldson's *Marie* (1985) was a sort of real-life *Protocol* or *Mr. Smith*, with Cissy Spacek as a spunky woman who uncovers corruption in a southern state. Discredited, she loses her job, but fights back and wins in court. Although *Marie* was an inspiring true story, the movie suggested only some of the pressures on the single mother who took on the system. Marie was strong enough never to question whether what she was doing was right; her strength and her politics, which seemed to consist entirely of personal integrity, were taken for granted rather than developed. Her struggle remained individual throughout, and she received little help from anyone but her attorney. The real-life Marie was a heroine, but the movie was too predictable to please audiences or critics.

Marie could have taken some lessons from *Rocky*, but Irwin Winkler, who produced *Rocky IV*, seemed to have forgotten the secrets of his own success when he made *Revolution* (1985) – or maybe he needed Sylvester Stallone instead of Al Pacino in the lead. *Revolution* was produced in Britain and directed by Hugh Hudson (*Chariots of Fire*). The movie follows one man and his son through the American Revolution, but it was a dull movie without much to say about politics or anything else. To its credit, *Revolution* attempted to look at the war from the bottom, but unfortunately it did so through inarticulate and unsympathetic characters who act for personal rather than political reasons. Even just wars are horrible and exploitative, *Revolution* argued, but the point was ineptly made and in the era of Reagan, badly timed. Producer Winkler compared *Revolution* and *Rocky*, pointing out that "both are films about the common man and how they make good against the establishment," but he admitted that in *Revolution* he and writer Robert Dillon had gone "against the tide" of "people looking for heroes."[8]

Sidney Lumet's *Power* (1986) was an even bigger disaster. Here Pete St. John (Richard Gere) is a political media wizard who tells clients, "My job is to get you in. Then you do whatever your conscience tells you to do." Using opinion polls and clever TV ads St. John cynically packages candidates to fit what the public wants. He's finally disillusioned, however, when he discovers he's being used by Arab oil sheiks seeking to block solar energy legislation. Confronting an idealistic young candidate being managed by a rival media man, St. John denounces his own profession and tells the budding politican to say what he really believes. He does, and he gets more votes than expected, although he still doesn't win. The film ends with "The Stars and Stripes Forever" playing as the camera pans over video equipment and computers.

Like Lumet's *Network*, *Power* was over-the-top, but while *Network* succeeded as black comedy, *Power* was merely ludicrous melodrama. Lumet could have used the help of *Network*'s author, the late Paddy Chayevsky. The villains of *Power* are neither funny nor credible, and the good guys are terrifyingly naive. Director Lumet and writer David Himmelstein ignore the fact that politicians have always manipulated voters, blaming the sad state of the nation almost entirely on the new technology. The voters are suckers for it, though, and all of the politicians in the film are willing dupes, except for Michael Learned's female governor. *Power*'s insights into the techniques used by media consultants were instructive, but the movie grossly exaggerated their influence.

Movies like *Power* and *Marie* offered an alternative to the conservative superpatriot films, and they were slightly more sophisticated than the purely Reaganite movies, but they were also considerably less popular. Oliver Stone's *Platoon* (1986) was the astounding exception. Less overtly political than *Salvador*, Stone's earlier film, *Platoon* is a tough, gritty movie about American soldiers in Vietnam. Based on Stone's own experiences, the film is filled with powerful images of the horror of that war. Compared to *Apocalypse Now* and *The Deer Hunter*, *Platoon* is unpretentious and down-to-earth. It deals with the ways in which the war affected a small group of men, rather than attempting to communicate a profound or symbolic message.

"You volunteered for this shit, man?" declares a black soldier on discovering that Chris Taylor (Charlie Sheen) is in Vietnam because he felt the fighting shouldn't be left to "poor kids." "You got to be rich in the first place to think like that!" the soldier scoffs. In a series of terrifying patrols and battles, two sergeants struggle for "possession" of young Taylor's soul. Barnes (Tom Berenger) is a scarred, gung-ho soldier driven to win at any cost and furious at the constraints imposed on the fighters by the politicians. "Our captain Ahab," Taylor calls him.

Elias (Willem Dafoe) is a mellow, dope-smoking progressive. When Taylor asks if he believes in what he's doing, Elias says he did in 1965, but "now.... No.... We're gonna lose this war.... We been kickin' other people's asses for so long I figure it's time we got ours kicked."

Throughout his harrowing film, Stone focuses relentlessly and respectfully on the men who actually fought the war, the grunts. "They're poor, they're the unwanted, yet they're fighting for our society and our freedom," Chris observes at the beginning, but by the end, he's saying "we did not fight the enemy, we fought ourselves and the enemy was in us." Like most of the earlier movies about Vietnam, *Platoon* pays little attention to what we did to the Vietnamese and makes no effort to analyze the reasons for the war. Such restraint is somewhat surprising from the maker of *Salvador*, but by focusing on the real horrors of fighting the war rather than its politics, Stone broadened his audience and, perhaps ironically, helped drive his point home. Dedicating his film to "the men who fought and died in Vietnam," Stone said "I'd like (Vietnam vets) to see it and feel it and walk out and say never again."[9]

Many vets and other viewers seem to have done so, but the film does not make clear whether they are saying never again to limited war or to interventionism. Considered in the context of *Salvador*, Stone's earlier film, it is difficult to deny the anti-war message of *Platoon*, however. "We didn't set out to make an anti-war film," producer Arnold Kopelson said, but "if, through *Platoon*, the public perceive Vietnam as a war America shouldn't have got involved in, then it may raise their consciousness about what's going on in Nicaragua."[10]

Praised by Steven Spielberg, Jane Fonda, Gary Hart, David Halberstram, and a wide range of critics, *Platoon* was a big box office hit and won four Academy Awards, including best picture and best direction. The success of *Platoon* came as a surprise to many, who found its politics dramatically out-of-sync with the patriotic conservatism of the Reagan era. Among the most surprised were the Hollywood studios that had refused to finance *Platoon*, forcing Stone to turn to Britain's Hemdale, as he had for *Salvador*.

Movies like *Rambo* and *Top Gun* had seemed to dominate the era – and they definitely dominated box office grosses – but other films, with other points of view, had been offered. Some, like *Missing*, *WarGames*, and *The Killing Fields*, had been highly successful. *Platoon* was even more successful, perhaps because it avoided political comment. The most remarkable thing about this film, though, is that it seemed to defeat the Stallone-Norris-Eastwood movies at their own game. Unlike those movies, *Platoon* demonstrated that the American public was willing to contemplate the harsh realities of Vietnam rather than simply to fantasize about some sort of revenge victory.

Into the Future

Politically and cinematically, *Platoon* may have signified the end of an era. The movie was released just as the aging president had begun to lose his hold on the American imagination following the "Iranamok" scandal, and the forces of Reaganism were in retreat. Reaganite films had dominated the cinema in the mid-1980s, but movies from *Reds* to *Silkwood*, *Salvador*, and *Power* had examined politics from another perspective. Many had addressed tough issues, presented complex characters, and refused to offer facile solutions. Political commitment, these movies asserted, was difficult but worthwhile. Some films, of course, continued to manifest naive faith in the system, the people, or the press, but these movies were fewer in number than they had been in earlier eras. Most motion pictures leaned to the left, and favored activism even while the country as a whole lurched to the right and grew apathetic. Although the great box office triumphs of the era were movies like *Rambo* and *Red Dawn*, the eighties saw the return of political movies with varied subjects, presented from different points of view. Even the increasingly youthful audience and rising production costs − averaging $16 million in 1986 with half again as much for promotion − did not discourage the making of serious films about politics. As cable television, videocassettes, and an increasing number of movie theaters provided new outlets, revenues, and investors for filmmakers, and independent production increased, the eighties may yet rank with the thirties as one of the most fertile eras for political films.

NOTES

1. *Stills*, 13 October 1984, p. 15.
2. Ibid.
3. *The Guardian*, 20 July 1985.
4. *Time Out*, 23–29 April 1986.
5. *California*, July 1986.
6. *Village Voice*, 5 November 1985.
7. Quoted in *People*, 16 December 1985.
8. *The Guardian*, 6 February 1986.
9. *Nightline*, ABC-TV, 19 December 1986.
10. *The Guardian*, 14 February 1987.

Afterword
Reel Politics

"I want this picture to be a commentary on modern conditions, stark realism, the problems that confront the average man," says Joel McCrea in *Sullivan's Travels* (1941). Tired of making movies with titles like *Ants in the Pants*, the rich and famous Hollywood director disguises himself as a hobo and goes out to research his magnum opus, *Brother, Wherefore Art Thou?* His life on the road is funny at first, but it turns serious when he's mugged, loses his money and his memory, and finds himself truly down and out. After a scuffle in a freight yard, he's convicted of assault and sent to a grim prison farm where life is lightened only by occasional movies shown by a local black church. When he manages to get back to Hollywood, he wants to make only comedies. "There's a lot to be said for making people laugh," Sullivan declares. "Did you know that's all some people have? It isn't much, but it's better than nothing."

With his usual flair, Preston Sturges, the writer and director of *Sullivan's Travels* (1941), was sending up the social conscience films of the Depression. Films, his itinerant director asserted, are supposed to amuse people and take their minds off their troubles. Although Sturges portrayed America's underclass with sympathy, he refused to accept responsibility to help other than by providing momentary diversion. Sturges chose entertainment over educating, helping people understand their society, or providing inspiration or instruction as to how to change it. Entertainment is itself a worthy goal, and *Sullivan's Travels* proves that movies about serious subjects can be entertaining. But *Sullivan's Travels* also sums up Hollywood's attitudes about politics and political movies. American filmmakers are cynical, not only about whether movies should deal with politics, but about politics itself.

Repeated Messages

Political movies have debated the great issues of the day as the nation debated them, sometimes ahead of the public and sometimes lagging behind, sometimes dissenting and sometimes reinforcing. Regardless of the state of the union, however, some ideas about politics are constantly reiterated by movies. If audiences absorb these repeated messages, their cumulative effect must surely be cynicism and apathy.

Above all, American political films tell us that politics is corrupt. From the Victorian villains of the silent melodramas to the corporate or bureaucratic monsters of latter-day thrillers, politicians and power-holders have been portrayed as greedy, self-interested shysters. Usually, lust for power or personal ambition is their motivation but sometimes ambition is supplemented or even subsumed by greed, as in the case of the bosses and "interests" of the thirties movies. Ever since the silents, bad men have used politics for their own economic benefit, although corporations replace individual villains in many of the later movies. This is a more radical analysis, but it usually stops with the single guilty corporation instead of examining the system as a whole. Sometimes, especially in thrillers, an ominous presence lurks "out there," more terrifying because it is not defined. It could be a communist conspiracy or a corporate cabal, but usually it is more obscure than that, and too big for individuals or even governments to struggle against. Perhaps it is the filmmakers' metaphor for "the system" against which individuals are impotent, yet it seems more specific. Whatever it is, it's pretty scary. And whether the source of corruption in a movie is an individual, a group, or a system, the cinematic view of politics is grim, and getting grimmer.

Perhaps corruption is just a convenient source of tension and drama. Perhaps moviemakers are gloomy pessimists or mocking cynics, too self-obsessed, paranoid, or even idealistic to understand or accept the reality of politics. Or maybe politics is as corrupt as they say. But whether they're brainwashing us with fantasy or instructing us in reality, their negative view of politics is unlikely to be empowering. After all, if it takes Warren Beatty, Jane Fonda, or Robert Redford to beat the system, what chance do the rest of us have? And if even they can't beat it, how can we? Ironically, the most pessimistic movies are often the most radical in that they condemn the system as a whole, yet they help entrench it by discouraging action. Not all movies are fatalistic, however. A few optimistic films show that problems can be solved by great leaders, scrappy individuals, or by appeals to "the people."

From the twenties through the fifties, the great leader solution was common. Abraham Lincoln was a favorite, but Franklin Roosevelt and others like him also became part of the pantheon. Their pronouncements were treated like the word of God, never questioned or doubted. But even if Lincoln and Roosevelt were as great as the movies portray them, waiting for a leader isn't a realistic political strategy, and movies started giving up hope of such saviors as early as 1948 when *State of the Union* told us that good guys couldn't win. Either they had to walk away from politics to preserve their integrity, or they were destroyed by it. Later, Bill McKay and Joe Tynan couldn't even walk away from it. They were seduced, but the possibility that they could do some good remained. Like the knowledgeable pols of *Advise and Consent*, they would stay and play – a less certain but more realistic view of politics, and probably a healthier one.

These movies are still cynical about politicians, however, and there would have been a shortage of heroes if it hadn't been for the cinematic tradition of the common man rising to meet a challenge. From *Mr. Smith* and *The Grapes of Wrath* to *Norma Rae* and *Red Dawn*, ordinary people who stumble onto evil and corruption, overcome their fear and fight the system single-handedly and successfully. These heroes and heroines suggest that action by ordianry people can make a difference; surely this is a more positive message than the one delivered by the fatalistic thrillers or the movies that rely on great leaders.

Such heroes and heroines may be inspiring, but the message of these movies is limited by their tendency to confine problems to a single person, group, or circumstance. But what if the problem is more pervasive? What if a courageous person isn't around to take up the cause? Movies rarely present problems with the political system as a whole and they almost never raise issues that aren't self-contained. This reduces politics to a need for occasional individual action to regulate an essentially good, smoothly functioning process by pointing out flaws in the form of bad individuals and sometimes bad organizations like gangs, machines, and corporations. Only *Dr. Strangelove* and the paranoid thrillers of the seventies seriously doubted that the system would work in the end.

Some movies insist that "the people" must be called upon. Once they know the truth, all will be well. Mr. Smith rallied the people, and the journalists of *All the President's Men* and *The China Syndrome* told them the truth about Watergate and nuclear meltdown, although the people didn't actually take action in these later movies. This faith in "the people" is as mass-oriented as American movies get. Action is virtually always individual and rarely collective. Despite our democratic ideals, when people get together in American movies, they are more likely to be condemned as a lynch mob than to be praised for their cooperative endeavor. The exceptions are few and far between. *Our Daily Bread*, *Norma Rae*, *Reds* and a few other movies attempt to validate the idea of people working and organizing together. *The Grapes of Wrath* features the family and "the people"; *The Last Hurrah* centers on the good old boys of the machine. Other movies show friends or co-workers sticking together, as in *The Boys in Company C*, *Nine to Five* and *The Right Stuff*. Most of these movies don't go much beyond a stand-by-your-pals message, but at least they aren't waiting for Abraham Lincoln or John Wayne to come along.

But whether action is taken by great leaders, individuals, or groups, the motivation in American movies is almost always negative: the bad guys act out of greed or ambition, and the good guys act to stop the bad guys. Except when Abe Lincoln frees the slaves or Woodrow Wilson makes the world safe for democracy, higher motives are rarely expressed. In fact, Lincoln and Wilson acted for a variety of reasons, some of which were not particularly lofty, and by the same token, ordinary people and real-life politicians sometimes act for positive good rather than just to save the nation from bad guys.

This fear of higher motives is partly political and partly artistic. Getting beyond individual motives and issues means getting into ideas – or ideology. Artistically, it's hard to create genuine characters and write credible dialogue that reflect and articulate ideas without seeming to pound in the message with a sledge-hammer. Furthermore, any discussion of political ideas beyond accepted democratic values may offend some segment of the audience. Americans are uneasy with ideology, especially any ideology other than their own; most movies respect this by remaining resolutely centrist and issue-oriented.

The exclusion of ideology reduces all motives to self-interest and thus trivializes politics, which ultimately means that politics and politicians are held in contempt. It also means that few American political movies deal with class or with ideas that are out of the mainstream. The right and left usually appear only as caricatures when Hollywood campaigns against fascists, communists, or the KKK. American political movies support the status quo through this narrowing of the political spectrum and by their insistence that the political process works. When problems arise, heroic individuals take action and usually succeed.

There are exceptions to this avoidance of ideology, of course, although few American movies stray far from the center. Some lean to the right, stressing individualism and traditional values like self help, hard work, family, and patriotism, often criticizing moral decline, bureaucracy, and big government, and especially concerned about external threats to the nation. Others lean left, emphasizing tolerance and co-operation, criticizing discrimination, conformity, greed, and sometimes capitalism, and they worry about domestic fascism and authoritarianism. Most notable among these are the honorable group of movies that crusaded for racial and sexual equality. Even these are cautious, however, usually preaching that we should be nice to one another, and that minorities and women should behave like white males. Almost invariably, these films individualize and over-simplify. But even though the moderation of movies like *Guess Who's Coming to Dinner* or *Nine to Five* disappointed many, they did push us gently in the right direction.

Innumerable critics have pointed out that political films sometimes seem liberal or even radical because they raise an issue (nuclear peril, racism, corruption) and get us all worked up only to reassure us that heroic individuals, "the people," or the political process itself will make all well in the end. Certainly we ourselves won't have to do anything. Despite the liberal or even radical intent of these films, their net effect is conservative because they reinforce faith in the system, ultimately endorsing rather than criticizing. If blind faith in the system isn't enough to keep us passive, the hope that a hero will come along may do just that. Furthermore, by raising up heroes or letting the system right itself, movies fail to try to explain larger forces, especially economic ones. Movies that do address these forces are even more despairing, however. They warn us that politics is mean and evil, that it is best avoided because there's not a lot we can do about it, and that if we try to beat these forces, they'll smash us. Such films communicate a futility that inspires apathy as effectively as those that reassure us that the system works.

The end results are not encouraging. American political films grapple with problems only to solve them too easily or to predict apocalypse. We end up with "dramas of reassurance"[1] or pessimistic pictures of utter hopelessness, with too few movies suggesting that we can do anything about politics. The gap between the bland happy ending and the bleak tragedy is too great. We need more films somewhere in the middle and more that help us understand our world. Most of all, we need more movies that respect politics as a constructive activity.

Reasons to Be Cautious

The cautious messages of American political films are the result of a variety of factors. Like Preston Sturges and his fictional director, American filmmakers are primarily committed to entertaining. When they try to make political points as well, the conflict between the two goals often results in compromises that weaken one or the other, or in some cases, both. But economics, audiences and nature of movies as an art form also influence the making of political movies and what they have to say.

Movies are produced to make money and their content is strongly influenced by economics. U.S. filmmakers receive no government subsidies, so movies are business ventures and expensive ones at that. The cost of a feature film averaged just $400,000 in 1941; by 1985 it was over $12 million. That means high finance. The big studios used to provide this money, and often still do, but banks, insurance companies, and individual investors are now more prominent. These institutions and people tend to be conservative, both olitically and economically. They invest accordingly.

Films that criticize the political system are still made, but often they have to be toned down or laced with stars to get the funding in the first place, like *Grapes of Wrath* or *Reds*. Less compromised films such as *Our Daily Bread*, *Salt of the Earth*, *Daniel* and *El Norte* are made, but rarely. These movies were financed cooperatively and with difficulty, and all had distribution problems once made.

The conservative orientation of investors is widely believed to have increased as the corporate money men took over and the power of the studios declined, but in fact, the collapse of the studio system made it easier for independent filmmakers to develop political projects. They still need lots of money, which means finding investors. Some artists solve this problem by starting their own production companies and investing themselves. Small investors have also become more important, and cable television and videocassettes have provided new outlets and new investors. Independent filmmakers still need the studios at least to some extent for both investment and distribution, but even the studios have changed. Would any of the old studios except perhaps Warner Bros. have laid out $52 million for *Reds*? Paramount did – under the corporate ownership of Gulf and Western. The conglomerate thought the film would make money, so it was willing to invest, even if it didn't endorse the film's politics, just as other studios invested in *Missing* and *The Killing Fields*. "Hollywood has nothing against message films as long as they make money," says John Frankenheimer. "You could get *The Manchurian Candidate* made today – provided you had Jack Nicholson in the Sinatra role and Rob Lowe playing Raymond Shaw."[2]

Audiences – or filmmakers' perceptions of audiences – also influence politics in the movies, not only because decades of boycotts and protests have made filmmakers cautious about political subjects, but also because the box office has become the ultimate measure of a movie's success. To sell tickets, filmmakers try to please us. We in turn expect to be entertained, perhaps because movies have trained us to. We seem to prefer to be terrified by slasher movies rather than forced to think by social or political commentary. Many political filmmakers therefore refrain from making us think by muting their films' political content or rejecting politics altogether. The political message of a movie may be played down in order to avoid offending any major segment of the diverse American audience, or it may be moderated so that as many people as possible will agree with it, and buy tickets.

The political content of Jane Fonda's movies, for example, is less radical than her own politics because she wants to reach the largest possible audience. "The public doesn't want to see films that they think are good for them," says Fonda's producer, Bruce Gilbert. "The first question they ask themselves is, are they going to be entertained and have a good time."[3]

Unfortunately, audiences have been changing in ways that can only increase the difficulties political filmmakers face in reaching them. "The audience today is dumber than it was," says Sidney Lumet. "They're morons. They don't know how to behave in theaters – they can't even be quiet. . . . They're totally corrupted by the television experience. And they expect the same television emotional results: sentimentality instead of emotion, tactile sensation and shock instead of thrill."[4] Accustomed to TV, we grow impatient with wordy movies or slow, subtle films that take time to build characters and approach their points. Our impatience impels filmmakers to over-simplify, goose up their movies with action, or avoid talk. Films today must grab us and take us for a fast ride, not only because of our TV orientation but also and significantly because movie audiences are young; a majority is under twenty-four, and this is the only segment of the audience that's growing. The bigger this part of the audience gets, the more moviemakers go after it and the less articulate their movies become.

Audience expectations of glitz, gloss, and special effects also frustrate political filmmakers. *Latino* had more to say than *Top Gun*, but *Top Gun* was closer to what contemporary audiences expect of a movie, and it did far better at the box office, thanks at least in part to lavish production values and a slick advertising campaign. Audiences have come to expect not only entertainment, but slick entertainment.

The nature of movies as an art form may also moderate their politics. Directors are usually credited with definitively shaping movies, as they have been in this book, but this emphasis is vigorously disputed by writers and other collaborators in filmmaking. "It sure as shit isn't true in Hollywood," declares screenwriter William Goldman. "Movies," he insists, "are a group endeavor."[5] Directors may be central figures, but many creative people contribute to the final shape of a film, including writers, producers, cinematographers, editors, designers, and actors. The politics of these individuals may differ, and their perception of what audiences want to see, need to be told, or will accept may also vary. Out of the conflict of these differing biases and perceptions comes the movie.

The written script is probably the most important component, but it may be altered or given different emphasis in the process of filming. However forthright the politics of a project is at its inception, it is often muted by the time the concept becomes a movie. Profit-minded filmmakers will seek to please the largest possible audience by de-emphasizing the political message. This can be done in all sorts of ways – by revising or deleting dialogue, by cutting political scenes, by emphasizing romance, or by camera placement and casting.

The choice of actors, as we have seen, can radically alter the message of a movie. Known actors and especially stars bring their own personae to parts. *The Front* would have been a different movie without Woody Allen in the lead, as would *Reds* without Warren Beatty or *All the President's Men* without Redford and Hoffman. But while the presence of a star can give tone and resonance to a character, it can also shift the emphasis of a movie. Scripts may be re-written to suit stars and their images. An actor can also reshape a movie by giving an extraordinary performance that shifts the focus from one character to another and thus alters the balance of the film. Melvyn Douglas and Meryl Streep, for example, accomplish this even in supporting roles.

Casting is just one element of the collaborative art of filmmaking. But casting isn't only an artistic choice, it's also a commercial one. Stars bring in audiences and therefore money. Casting a big star may mean compromising the politics of a film in order to ensure ticket sales. Other elements of filmmaking require similar trade-offs and compromises that can affect the political impact of a movie.

One of these other elements is cinematography, the creation of that series of photographic frames which, together, will constitute a motion picture. Here, too, filmmakers make crucial choices – a close-up of Jane Fonda's face, for example, instead of a long shot of the nuclear reactor room – and in doing so they subtly influence the moviegoer's perception of the situation. The use of close-ups serves a number of purposes, political and otherwise, in a film. Among them is the crucial function of drawing the audience more deeply into the action. "We are held to films by the human face," Leo Braudy has written. "Faces hold us more than plot, direction, photography."[6] Close-ups are artistically and emotion-ally satisfying, but by focusing our attention on one person at a time, they may cause us to lose sight of the shared experiences of the characters or the historical and political context of events. All is reduced to the one person we see; everything is individualized. Movies don't have to do this, however, and directors from Griffith to Capra, Altman, Ritt, Lumet, and Pakula have found ways to let us see their central characters in larger contexts.

Other conventions of American movies also contribute to their individualism. Most focus on heroes, for example, partly because of the star system and partly because of the requirements of melodrama, the standard form of American movies. Melodramas revolve around conflict that must be solved, usually happily and almost always by a hero. That's what we expect and that's what most movies deliver, but these conventions and expectations raise special problems for political filmmakers.

The requirement to entertain, the focus on individuals and the need to solve problems by the end of the movie can result in over-simplification which is why American political films almost invariably deal with only one problem at a time. Even this single issue may be simplified so much that the outcome is obvious. In *Guess Who's Coming to Dinner*, for example, the solution is so readily apparent that our own racist attitudes aren't really challenged: of course our daughters could marry nice black doctors like Sidney Poitier. *Red Dawn* and *Rambo* leave us no options either. The villains of such movies – whether they're racists, communists, bureaucrats, or businessmen – are so broadly caricatured that we have no choice but to reject them, and we certainly can't identify with them.

This tendency to simplify and caricature is further encouraged by a fear of words in political movies. Too much dialogue can result in a static movie, so filmmakers emphasize the visual over the verbal, which limits the expression of ideas in movies. We grow bored with too much explanatory dialogue, or worse, we are offended because the filmmakers seem to be driving their points in with a sledgehammer. If they use too little dialogue, however, we may miss the point altogether.

In short, the very nature of the film medium complicates the task of political filmmakers. Add to this the limits placed on films by audience expectations and the need to make a profit and it's easy to see why the messages of political films are muted.

These factors might be sufficient to explain the political caution of filmmakers if movies were made in a vacuum, but they are not. In America even more than elsewhere, politics itself has had an impact on the movies. Besides public protests and demands for censorship, politicians also pay close attention to movies and frequently offer criticism, not to mention dire warnings. A few, including Woodrow Wilson, Franklin Roosevelt, John Kennedy, and above all Ronald Reagan, have enjoyed movies and even given active support to filmmakers. Other politicians worry about foreign reaction to the movie image of America, and many complain about the way the movies caricature their profession – and what the voters must think of them as a result. A few, like the HUAC investigators, and the Justice Department, have done more than criticize and complain.

Reasons to Proceed

Between complaining politicians, protesting audiences, anti-trust suits, HUAC, the Production Code, and the requirements of melodrama, profit, and entertainment, it shouldn't be surprising that American political films are timid. It's more surprising that they're made at all. But even though American filmmakers fear that political content will mean box office poison, they continue to make straightforward political movies. Either they can't resist the poison or they've developed an immunity.

Many political filmmakers have at one time or another felt strongly enough about a political project to work on it even without studio support. Why do filmmakers take such risks? Many are quite simply and genuinely interested in politics. Some are politically committed; one even became president. But in addition to interest and commitment, and often quite separately from either, many filmmakers are or wish to be serious artists. They are not content to make family melodramas or comedy, science fiction, horror, and action movies, although these genres can be serious and do not preclude political content. Indeed, many political films are best described as comedies or action movies and may be intended as little more. But for many filmmakers, serious art requires a serious subject like politics.

Filmmakers are further encouraged to make political movies by the recognition they receive from their colleagues, the critics and even the public. Political movies make the film industry look serious, even intellectual, so Hollywood takes them seriously and often rewards them with Oscars. Almost half of the films discussed in this book have been nominated for Academy Awards, and many, from *All Quiet on the Western Front* to *Platoon*, have won major awards. Oscars do not prove a film's artistic, intellectual, or political merit, but they do give it Hollywood's stamp of approval, improve its box office performance, and provide its makers with clout and credibility for their next project.

Similarly, critics pay special attention to political movies because they deal with "important" themes, or because they want a chance to say something about politics themselves. Although political movies are often given rough treatment because of their content, the reviews are by no means always bad. *The New York Times'* annual "Ten Best" movies, for example, has included at least one overtly political film every year since *The Dramatic Life of Abraham Lincoln* appeared on the first list in 1924. Critical praise has been heaped on political movies from *The Birth of a Nation* to *Platoon*.

Perhaps more surprisingly, the public also takes political films seriously. Far from box office poison, some political films have been popular hits. *The Big Parade* was the highest-earning silent film, followed closely by *The Birth of a Nation*. *Mr. Smith Goes to Washington* was a top box office draw in 1939, as was *The Best Years of Our Lives* in 1947. Stanley Kramer's didactic films almost always did well. *All the President's Men*, *The China Syndrome*, *Norma Rae*, *Missing*, and *Red Dawn* have been box office hits in recent years and even movies about the political process like *The Candidate* and *The Seduction of Joe Tynan* have fared well.

Few political films, however, were blockbusters. Only *M*A*S*H*, *All the President's Men*, *The Deer Hunter*, *Apocalypse Now*, *Rambo*, *WarGames*, *Top Gun*, and *Platoon* rank in *Variety*'s 100 highest earning films. Among these, only *All the President's Men* was seen by audiences as primarily political. Still, about 25 percent of the films discussed in this book qualify as "all time box office champions," according to *Variety*.[7]

A specialized segment of the audience has even learned to look beyond the mainstream of American commercial cinema to documentaries and foreign films in search of strong political content. Documentaries can make stronger political statements than fictional movies, but American audiences tend to avoid them, and so do exhibitors. People may watch documentaries on TV, but when they go to the cinema, they demand slick entertainment.

Foreign films are another alternative, although their reputation for being stronger and more forthright in their treatment of politics than American movies is exaggerated. Only the best films of other countries reach us; in fact, the tradition of social criticism is no stronger abroad than in the United States. In most countries, it is weaker. "Whether a film like *I Am a Fugitive from a Chain Gang* could be made in any other country," says British film scholar I. C. Jarvie, "is much to be doubted."[8]

Strong political films are a tradition, however, in Italy and France. Both countries have produced movies with broader and more penetrating social criticism than almost any American films. Bernardo Bertolucci's *The Conformist* and *1900*, Francesco Rossi's *Christ Stopped at Eboli*, *Three Brothers* and *Investigation of a Citizen above Suspicion*, Gilo Pontecorvo's *Burn!* and *Battle of Algiers*, Jean Luc Goddard's *La Chinoise* and *Weekend*, Costa-Gavras' *Z* and *State of Siege*, and Louis Malle's *Lacombe, Lucien*, make American political films seem pretty weak. The list could go on and filmmakers from other countries, especially Germany and Cuba, could be added, but it is unlikely that proportionately more political films are produced in other nations than in the United States unless the countries are totalitarian and the movies are propaganda.

Europeans may make superior political films in part because their audiences are more sophisticated about politics and their politics is more ideological and analytical than ours. We tolerate views that stray only slightly to the right or left of center, but opinion in Italy and France runs across the whole ideological spectrum, giving filmmakers greater freedom of expression and also providing at least a specialized audience interest. Perhaps because of this diversity of opinion, Europeans argue about politics more than we do and vote in greater numbers than we do, even though they are far more cynical than Americans. Their ideological politics prepares them for newspapers that do not pretend to objectivity, as ours do, and for tendentious movies as well. European filmmakers have also been content to make smaller, cheaper films and to reach smaller audiences. Blockbuster fever hasn't hit most of Europe yet.

Italian and French movies are not infinitely superior to ours, however, and audiences there can be just as enthusiastic about American blockbusters as we are, although they are also more likely to admire films like *Heaven's Gate*, *Under Fire*, or *Salvador*. European political filmmakers, in fact, voice some of the same complaints as their American counterparts. "Nobody likes political films," says Costa-Gavras, claiming that even when he features big stars he has trouble raising money for his films. He also complains about having to draw in the supposedly sophisticated French audience by promoting his works as thrillers rather than political movies.[9]

The success of a fair number of American political films as well as the specialized audience that has developed for foreign films, and to a lesser extent documentaries, suggests that critics like Pauline Kael and James Monaco are correct in their belief that the film industry has too little faith in audiences. The American tradition of political films is respectable, but the movies could be better. They could be less cautious and superficial. They could be stronger, more complex, and more profound. They could offer a wider variety of political perspectives and analyses. Perhaps most importantly in a democratic political system, they could be more positive about participation and involvement.

Filmmakers and audiences need not give up entertainment to have better political films. Entertainment is the reason we love the movies, but being entertained does not preclude being encouraged to think, or even educated. In fact, political and social points can often be most effectively made in traditional entertainment movies because all of us grasp issues better when we see how they affect actual people, even in the movies. Filmmakers should have more faith in their audiences and take more chances with movies about politics. Investors and distributors should support them. The film industry needs to accept, however, that good movies about politics may reach only a segment of the audience, even a subculture. That segment or subculture could be large enough to make a movie profitable, although even good movies about politics are unlikely ever to be blockbusters. If filmmakers and their backers can accept this limitation, they can escape from the compulsion to make consensus movies that offend few and say little. The ideology of entertainment and profit are too deeply entrenched in the American film industry to expect our movies to become politically profound, much less to transform our political system, but brave filmmakers can make more and better movies, and critics and audiences should support them.

"Movies can't change a country," Costa-Gavras says, and "it's just as well that it's not that easy."[10] They make a contribution, however. They inform and educate. They provide catharsis, helping us come to terms with our worries and fantasies by acting them out. Sometimes they make us feel less alone. Despite their mildness and reassurance, their constant social criticism has helped keep us self-conscious as a nation. They have particularly and rightly condemned injustice, intolerance and corruption. Less creditably, they have also told us to rely on leaders and heroes for salvation, ignored the alternative of collective action, and neglected or condemned opinions that stray from the mainstream. Worse, they have disparaged politics in general, presenting it as evil and corrupting, best avoided by decent people. This image of politics reflects and reinforces popular prejudice, but it also helps to entrench alienation and apathy. Movies that reinforce, reassure or warn us to stay away from politics keep us passive even more effectively than entertainment as pure opiate. No wonder critics on the left see movies as a tool through which those who run the country control the rest of us.

Perhaps unfortunately, we seem content to let ourselves be controlled. We love movies. But precisely because we love them, we should take a close look at what they teach us and demand more from them. We can't expect too much of movies, but they can and should at least keep us thinking and talking.

NOTES

1. James Linton, "But it's only a Movie," *Jump Cut*, no. 17, April 1978.
2. *San Jose Mercury*, 16 November 1986.
3. "Hollywood's Progressive Producer," *Cineaste*, vol. IX, no. 4, Summer 1979, p. 4.
4. *San Jose Mercury*, 17 August 1986.
5. William Goldman, *Adventures in the Screen Trade* (London: Futura, 1983), pp. 100, 102.
6. Leo Braudy, *The World in Frame* (New York: Doubleday, 1977), pp. 186–187.

7. "All Time Box Office Champions," *Variety*, 7 May 1986.
8. I. C. Jarvie, *Movies as Social Criticism* (London: Scarecrow, 1978), p. 153.
9. Costa-Gavras, Guardian Lecture, National Film Theatre, London, 16 March 1984.
10. Ibid.

Bibliography

BOOKS

Adair, Gilbert, *Hollywood's Vietnam* (London: Proteus, 1981).

Behlmer, Rudy, ed., *Inside Warner Bros.* (New York: Viking, 1986).

Bergman, Andrew, *We're in the Money* (New York: NYU Press, 1971).

Biskind, Peter, *Seeing is Believing* (London: Pluto Press, 1984).

Bluestone, George, *Novels into Film* (Baltimore: Johns Hopkins, 1957).

Bogle, Donald, *Toms, Coons, Mulattoes, Mammies, and Bucks* (New York: Bantam, 1974).

Braudy, Leo, *The World in Frame* (New York: Doubleday, 1977).

Brownlow, Kevin, *The Parade's Gone By* (Berkeley: University of California Press, 1968).

Cogley, John, ed., *Report on Blacklisting I: The Movies* (New York: Fund for the Republic, 1956).

Cook, David A., *A History of Narrative Film* (New York: Norton, 1981).

Coppola, Eleanor, *Notes* (New York: Pocket, 1979).

Cripps, Thomas, *Slow Fade to Black* (New York: Oxford, 1977).

Crowther, Bruce, *Hollywood Faction* (London: Columbus, 1984).

Culbert, David, ed., *Mission to Moscow* (Madison: University of Wisconsin, 1980).

Davies, Philip, and Brian Neves, ed., *Cinema, Politics and Society in America* (Manchester: Manchester University, 1981).

Dowdy, Andrew, *The Films of the Fifties* (New York: William Morrow, 1973).

Fitzgerald, F. Scott, *The Last Tycoon* (London: Penguin, 1941).

Goldman, William, *Adventures in the Screentrade* (London: Futura, 1983).

Halliwell, Leslie, *The Film Goers' Companion* (6th edn, London: Paladin, 1979).

Halliwell, Leslie, *Halliwell's Film Guide* (4th edn, New York: Scribner's, 1985).

Haskell, Molly, *From Reverence to Rape* (New York: Penguin, 1973).

Jacobs, Lewis, *The Rise of the American Film* (New York: Harcourt Brace, 1939).

Jarvie, I. C., *Movies as Social Criticism* (London: Scarecrow, 1978).

Jowett, Garth, *Film: The Democratic Art* (Boston: Little, Brown, 1976).

Jowett, Garth, and James M. Linton, *Movies as Mass Communication* (Beverly Hills: Sage, 1980).

Kael, Pauline, *5001 Nights at the Movies* (New York: Holt, Rinehart and Winston, 1982).

Kael, Pauline, *The Citizen Kane Book* (New York: Holt, Rinehart and Winston, 1971).

Kael, Pauline, *I Lost It at the Movies* (Boston: Little, Brown, 1965).

Kael, Pauline, *Kiss Kiss, Bang Bang* (New York: Bantam, 1969).

Kael, Pauline, *Reeling* (Boston: Little, Brown, 1976).

Katz, Ephraim, *Film Encyclopedia* (New York: Perigee, 1979).

Kracauer, Siegfried, *From Caligari to Hitler* (Princeton, New Jersey: Princeton University Press, 1974).

Lawson, John Howard, *Film in the Battle of Ideas* (New York: Masses and Mainstream, 1953).

Leab, Daniel, *From Sambo to Superspade* (London: Secker and Warburg, 1975).

MacCann, Richard Dyer, and Jack C. Ellis, eds., *Cinema Examined* (New York: Dutton, 1982).

McDonald, Ray, *SUFG Bulletin* (2nd Term, 1957).

Maland, Charles J., *American Visions* (New York: Arno Press, 1977).

Maltby, Richard, *Harmless Entertainment: Hollywood and the Ideology of Consensus* (London: Scarecrow, 1983).

Mellen, Joan, *The Big Bad Wolves* (New York: Pantheon, 1977.

Miller, Randall M., ed., *The Kaleidoscope Lens* (Englewood, New Jersey: Ozer, 1980).

Monaco, James, *American Film Now* (New York: Oxford, 1979).

Mordden, Ethan, *The Hollywood Musical* (London: David and Charles, 1981).

Navasky, Victor, *Naming Names* (New York: Penguin, 1983).

O'Connor, John E., *The Hollywood Indian* (Trenton: New Jersey State Museum, 1980).

O'Connor, John E., and Martin A. Jackson, eds., *American History/American Film* (New York: Frederick Ungar, 1979).

Quart, Leonard, and Albert Auster, *American Film and Society Since 1945* (New York: Praeger, 1984).

Ray, Robert B., *A Certain Tendency of the Hollywood Cinema* (Princeton: Princeton University Press, 1985).

Reader, Keith, *Cultures on Celluloid* (London: Quartet, 1981).

Roddick, Nick, *A New Deal in Entertainment* (London: British Film Institute, 1983).

Roffman, Peter, and Jim Purdy, *The Hollywood Social Problem Film*, Bloomington: Indiana University Press, 1981).

Rosen, Marjorie, *Popcorn Venus* (New York: Coward, McCann and Geoghegan, 1973).

Russo, Vito, *The Celluloid Closet* (New York: Harper and Row, 1981).

Sarris, Andrew, *Politics and Cinema* (New York: Columbia University Press, 1978).

Sayre, Nora, *Running Time* (New York: The Dial Press, 1982).
Shindler, Colin, *Hollywood Goes to War* (London: Routledge and Kegan Paul, 1979).
Sklar, Robert, *Movie-Made America* (New York: Random House, 1975).
Stein, Ben, *The View from Sunset Boulevard* (New York: Basic, 1979).
Thomas, Tony, *Hollywood and the American Image* (Westport: Arlington House, 1981).
Thomson, David, *America in the Dark* (New York: William Morrow, 1977).
Tyler, Parker, *Screening the Sexes* (New York: Anchor, 1973).
White, David Manning, and Richard Averson, *The Celluloid Weapon* (Boston: Beacon, 1972).
Wiley, Mason, and Damien Bona, *Inside Oscar* (London: Columbus, 1986).
Woll, Allen L., *The Latin Image in American Film* (Los Angeles: UCLA Press, 1978).
Wood, Michael, *America in the Movies* (New York: Basic Books, 1975).
Wright, Will, *Sixguns and Society* (Berkeley: University of California Press, 1975).

ARTICLES

Cohen, William S., and Gary Hart, "TV's Treatment of Washington – It's Capital Punishment," *TV Guide*, 24 August 1985.
Davis, John, "Notes on Warner Brothers Foreign Policy, 1918–1948," *Velvet Light Trap*, no. 17, Winter 1977.
Edelman, Rob, "The Politician in Films," *Films in Review*, vol. XXVIII, no. 9, November 1976, pp. 531–7.
Fell, J. L., "Darling This Is Bigger Than Both of Us," *Cinema Journal*, vol. xii, no. 2, spring 1973, pp. 56–64.
Flamini, Roland, "The Presidents and their Movies," *American Film*, vol. I, no. 10, September 1976.
Giroux, Henry A., "*Norma Rae*, Character, culture and class," *Jump Cut*, 22 May 1980.
Koper, Peter, "Can Movies Kill?" *American Film*, vol. 7, no. 9, July–August 1982, p. 46.
Linton, James, "But It's Only a Movie," *Jump Cut*, 17 April 1978.
Markowitz, Norman, "*The Front*, Comic Revenge," *Jump Cut*, 15 December 1977.
Rooney, Andy, "Anything you say, Senator Ewing," *San Francisco Chronicle*, 29 September 1985.
Ross, N. L., "Portraying Presidents," *Films in Review*, vol. XXIII, no. 8, October 1972, pp. 482–8.
Roth, Mark, "Some Warners Musicals and the Spirit of the New Deal," *The Velvet Light Trap*, 17, Winter 1977.
Sandy, Gary, and A. G. Block, "Hooray for Hollywood," *California Journal*, no. 16, 1985, pp. 445–7.
Tolchin, Martin, "How Reagan Always Gets the Best Lines," *The New York*

Times, 9 September 1985.
Zwick, Doug, "The Genre Syndrome," and Michael Gallantz, "Meltdown in Hollywood," *Jump Cut*, 22 May 1980.

Political Filmography

Film	Year	Director	Scriptwriter(s)
Abe Lincoln in Illinois	1940	John Cromwell	Grover Jones
Abraham Lincoln	1930	D. W. Griffith	D. W. Griffith
Abraham Lincoln (the Dramatic Life of)	1924	Phil Rosen	
Absence of Malice	1981	Sydney Pollack	Kurt Luedtke
Advise and Consent	1962	Otto Preminger	Wendell Mayes
Alamo Bay	1985	Louis Malle	Louis Malle
Alice Doesn't Live Here Anymore	1975	Martin Scorcese	Robert Getchell
All Quiet on the Western Front	1930	Lewis Milestone	Milestone, et al.
All the King's Men	1949	Robert Rossen	Robert Rossen Robert Penn Warren
All the President's Men	1976	Alan Pakula	William Goldman
America	1924	D. W. Griffith	D. W. Griffith
American Madness	1932	Frank Capra	Robert Riskin
The American Way	1986 (UK)	Maurice Phillips	Scott Roberts
And Justice For All	1979	Norman Jewison	Valerie Curtin Barry Levinson
Apocalypse Now	1979	Francis Coppola	Francis Coppola John Milius
Arrowsmith	1931	John Ford	Sidney Howard

Film	Year	Director	Scriptwriter(s)
Beau James	1957	Melville Shavelson	Melville Shavelson Jack Rose
Being There	1979	Hal Ashby	Hal Ashby
Between the Lines	1977	Joan Micklin Silver	Joan Micklin Silver
The Best Man	1964	Franklin Shaffner	Gore Vidal
The Best Years of Our Lives	1946	William Wyler	Robert Sherwood
The Big Chill	1983	Lawrence Kasdan	Lawrence Kasdan Barbara Benedeck
Big Jim McLain	1952	Edward Ludwig	James Edward Grant
The Big Parade	1925	King Vidor	Lawrence Stallings Harry Behn
Big Wednesday	1978	John Milius	John Milius Dennis Aberg
The Birth of a Nation	1915	D. W. Griffith	D. W. Griffith Frank E. Woods
Blockade	1938	William Dieterle	John Howard Lawson
Blow Out	1981	Brian de Palma	Brian de Palma
Blue Collar	1978	Paul Schraeder	Paul Schraeder Leonard Schraeder
The Border	1981	Tony Richardson	Deric Washburn Walon Green David Freeman
Born Yesterday	1950	George Cukor	Albert Mannheimer
Bound for Glory	1976	Hal Ashby	Robert Getchell
The Boys in Company C	1978	Sidney J. Furie	Sidney J. Furie Rick Natkin
Brubaker	1980	Stuart Rosenberg	W. D. Richter
The Candidate	1972	Michael Ritchie	Jeremy Larner
Casablanca	1942	Michael Curtiz	Howard Koch
Catch 22	1970	Mike Nichols	Buck Henry
Che!	1969	Richard Fleischner	Michael Wilson Sy Bartlett
Cheyenne Autumn	1964	John Ford	James R. Webb
The China Syndrome	1979	James Bridges	James Bridges T. S. Bridges Mike Gray

Film	Year	Director	Scriptwriter(s)
Chinatown	1974	Roman Polansky	Robert Towne
Citizen Kane	1941	Orson Welles	Herman Mankiewicz
Coming Home	1978	Hal Ashby	Waldo Salt Robert C. Jones
Confessions of a Nazi Spy	1939	Anatole Litvak	Milton Krims John Wexley
Country	1984	Richard Pearce	Richard Pearce
Crisis	1950	Richard Brooks	Richard Brooks
Crossfire	1947	Edward Dmytryk	John Paxton
Daniel	1983	Sidney Lumet	E. L. Doctorow
The Dark Horse	1932	Alfred E. Green	Joseph Jackson Wilson Mizner
Days of Glory	1944	Jacques Tourneur	Casey Robinson
Days of Heaven	1978	Terence Malick	Terence Malick
Dead Zone	1983	David Cronenberg	Jeffrey Boam
The Deer Hunter	1978	Michael Cimino	Deric Washburn
The Defiant Ones	1958	Stanley Kramer	Nathan E. Douglas H. J. Smith
Dr. Strangelove	1964	Stanley Kubrick	Stanley Kubrick Terry Sothern Peter George
Dr. Zhivago	1965	David Lean	Robert Bolt
Duck Soup	1933	Leo McCarey	Bert Kalmar, et al.
Easy Rider	1969	Dennis Hopper	Dennis Hopper Terry Sothern Peter Fonda
El Norte	1984	Gregory Nava	Gregory Nava Anna Thomas
Eleni	1985	Peter Yates	Steve Tesich
Endangered Species	1982	Alan Rudolph	Alan Rudolph John Binder
The Enforcer	1976	James Fargo	Stirling Silliphant Dean Riesner
Executive Action	1973	David Miller	Dalton Trumbo
Exodus	1960	Otto Preminger	Dalton Trumbo
A Face in the Crowd	1957	Elia Kazan	Budd Schulberg
Fail Safe	1964	Sidney Lumet	Walter Bernstein

Film	Year	Director	Scriptwriter(s)
The Falcon and the Snowman	1985	John Schlesinger	Steven Zaillian
The Farmer's Daughter	1947	H. C. Potter	Allen Rivkin Laura Kerr
First Blood	1982	Ted Kotcheff	Michael Kozoll, William Seckheim Sylvester Stallone
First Family	1980	Buck Henry	Buck Henry
First Lady	1937	Stanley Logan	Rowland Leigh
First Monday in October	1981	Ronald Neame	Jerome Lawrence Robert E. Lee
F.I.S.T.	1978	Norman Jewison	Joe Eszterhas Sylvester Stallone
For Whom the Bell Tolls	1943	Sam Wood	Dudley Nicholls
Forbidden	1932	Frank Capra	Frank Capra Jo Swerling
A Foreign Affair	1948	Billy Wilder	Billy Wilder Charles Brackett Richard Breen
The Formula	1980	John Avildsen	Steven Shagan
The Fountainhead	1949	King Vidor	Ayn Rand
The Front	1976	Martin Ritt	Walter Bernstein
Full Metal Jacket	1987	Stanley Kubrick	Stanley Kubrick Gustav Hasford Michael Herr
Gabriel Over the White House	1933	Gregory La Cava	Carey Wilson Bertram Bloch
Gandhi	1982 (UK)	Richard Attenborough	John Briley
Gardens of Stone	1987	Francis Coppola	Ron Bass
The General Died at Dawn	1936	Lewis Milestone	Clifford Odets
Gentleman's Agreement	1947	Elia Kazan	Moss Hart
Getting Straight	1970	Richard Rush	Robert Kaufman
Giant	1956	George Stevens	Fred Guiol Ivan Moffatt
The Glass Key	1942	Stuart Heisler	Jonathan Lattimer
The Godfather	1971	Francis Coppola	Francis Coppola

Film	Year	Director	Scriptwriter(s)
The Godfather, Part II	1974	Francis Coppola	Mario Puzo
Gone with the Wind	1939	Victor Fleming	Sidney Howard
Go Tell the Spartans	1978	Ted Post	Wendell Mayes
The Graduate	1967	Mike Nichols	Buck Henry Calder Willingham
The Grapes of Wrath	1940	John Ford	Nunnally Johnson
The Great Dictator	1940	Charles Chaplin	Charles Chaplin
The Great McGinty	1940	Preston Sturges	Preston Sturges
The Great White Hope	1970	Martin Ritt	Howard Sackler
Greed	1923	Erich von Stroheim	Erich von Stroheim
The Green Berets	1968	John Wayne Ray Kellog	James Lee Barrett
Greetings	1968	Brian de Palma	Brian de Palma
The Group	1966	Sidney Lumet	Sidney Buchman
Guess Who's Coming to Dinner	1967	Stanley Kramer	William Rose
Hail the Conquering Hero	1944	Preston Sturges	Preston Sturges
Hair	1979	Milos Forman	Michael Weller
Heartbreak Ridge	1986	Clint Eastwood	James Carbatsos
Heaven's Gate	1980	Michael Cimino	Michael Cimino
Her Honor the Governor	1926	Chet Withey	Doris Anderson
High Noon	1952	Fred Zinnemann	Carl Foreman
Hi Mom!	1969	Brian de Palma	Brian de Palma
Hitler's Children	1943	Edward Dmytryk	Emmett Lavery
The Hitler Gang	1944	John Farrow	Frances Goodrich Albert Hackett
Hitler's Madman	1943	Douglas Sirk Peretz Hershbein	Melvin Levy D. Molloy
Home of the Brave	1949	Mark Robson	Carl Foreman
The Honorary Consul	1983 (UK)	John MacKenzie	Christopher Hampton
I Am a Fugitive from a Chain Gang	1932	Mervyn Le Roy	Sheridan Gibney, et al.
Idiot's Delight	1939	Clarence Brown	Robert E. Sherwood

Film	Year	Director	Scriptwriter(s)
I Married a Communist	1949	Robert Stevenson	Charles Grayson Robert Hardy Andrews
The Informer	1935	John Ford	Dudley Nichols
Inherit the Wind	1960	Stanley Kramer	Nathan E. Douglas Harold J. Smith
In the Heat of the Night	1967	Norman Jewison	Sterling Silliphant
In This Our Life	1942	John Huston	Howard Koch
Intolerance	1916	D. W. Griffith	D. W. Griffith
Intruder in the Dust	1949	Clarence Brown	Bed Maddow
Invasion U.S.A.	1985	Joseph Zito	James Bruner Chuck Norris
Iron Curtain	1948	William Wellman	Milton Krims
Iron Eagle	1986	Sidney J. Furie	Sidney J. Furie Kevin Elders
I Was a Communist for the FBI	1951	Gordon Douglas	Crane Wilbur Matt Cvetic
Joe	1970	John G. Avildson	Norman Wexler
Johnny Got His Gun	1971	Dalton Trumbo	Dalton Trumbo
Juarez	1939	William Dieterle	John Huston, et al.
Judgment at Nuremberg	1962	Stanley Kramer	Abbey Mann
Julia	1977	Fred Zinnemann	Alvin Sargent
The Killing Fields	1984	Roland Joffe	Bruce Robinson
A King in New York	1956	Charles Chaplin	Charles Chaplin
Kiss of the Spider Woman	1985	Hector Babenco	Leonard Schrader
The Last Hurrah	1958	John Ford	Frank Nugent
Latino	1985	Haskel Wexler	Haskel Wexler
Lifeboat	1944	Alfred Hitchcock	John Steinbeck Jo Swerling
A Lion Is In the Streets	1953	Raoul Walsh	Luther Davis
Little Big Man	1970	Arthur Penn	Calder Willingham
The Little Drummer Girl	1984	George Roy Hill	Loring Madel
M*A*S*H	1970	Robert Altman	Ring Lardner, Jr

Film	Year	Director	Scriptwriter(s)
The Man	1972	Joseph Sargent	Joseph Sargent
The Manchurian Candidate	1962	John Frankenheimer	George Axelrod
The Manhattan Project	1986	Marshall Brickman	Marshall Brickman Thomas Baum
Man on a Tightrope	1953	Elia Kazan	Robert Sherwood
The Man with the Golden Arm	1955		
Marie	1985	Roger Donaldson	John Briley
M*A*S*H	1970	Robert Altman	Ring Lardner, Jr
Medium Cool	1969	Haskell Wexler	Haskell Wexler
Meet John Doe	1941	Frank Capra	Robert Riskin
The Milagro Beanfield War	1987	Robert Redford	John Nichols David Ward
Missing	1982	Costa-Gavras	Costa-Gavras Donald Stewart
Missing in Action	1984	Joseph Zito	Joseph Zito
The Mission	1986 (UK)	Roland Joffee	Robert Bolt
Mission to Moscow	1943	Michael Curtiz	Howard Koch
Monsieur Verdoux	1947	Charles Chaplin	Charles Chaplin
The Moon is Blue	1953		
Mr Deeds Goes to Town	1936	Frank Capra	Robert Riskin
Mr. Smith Goes to Washington	1939	Frank Capra	Sidney Buchman
My Man Godfrey	1936	Gregory La Cava	Gregory La Cava Morrie Riskind, et al.
My Son John	1952	Leo McCarey	Myles Connelly
Nashville	1975	Robert Altman	Joan Tewkesbury
Network	1976	Sidney Lumet	Paddy Chayefsky
Nine to Five	1980	Colin Higgins	Colin Higgins Patricia Resnick
Norma Rae	1979	Martin Ritt	Irving Ravetch Frank Harriet, Jr
The North Star	1943	Lewis Milestone	Lillian Hellman
One, Two, Three	1961	Billy Wilder	Billy Wilder I. A. L. Diamond

Film	Year	Director	Scriptwriter(s)
On the Beach	1959	Stanley Kramer	John Paxton James Lee Barrett
On the Waterfront	1954	Elia Kazan	Budd Schulberg
Orphans of the Storm	1921	D. W. Griffith	D. W. Griffith
Our Daily Bread	1934	King Vidor	King Vidor Elizabeth Hill
The Parallax View	1974	Alan J. Pakula	David Giler Lorenzo Semple, Jr
Paths of Glory	1957	Stanley Kubrick	Stanley Kubrick Calder Willingham Jim Thompson
Patton	1969	Franklin Schaffner	Francis Coppola Edmund H. North
The Pawnbroker	1965	Sidney Lumet	David Friedkin Morton Fine
The Phantom President	1932	Norman Taurog	Walter de Leon Harlan Thompson
Pinky	1949	Elia Kazan	Phillip Dunne Dudley Nichols
Places in the Heart	1984	Robert Benton	Robert Benton
The Plainsman	1936	Cecille B. De Mille	Waldemar Young, et al.
Platoon	1986	Oliver Stone	Oliver Stone
Politics	1931	Charles Reiner	Wells Root
Power	1986	Sidney Lumet	David Himmelstein
The President Vanishes	1934	William Wellman	Cary Wilson Cedric Worth
The Private Files of J. Edgar Hoover	1978	Larry Cohen	Larry Cohen
Protocol	1984	Herbert Ross	Buck Henry
P.T. 109	1963	Leslie Martinson	Richard L. Breen
The Quiet American	1957	Joseph L. Mankiewicz	Joseph L. Mankiewicz
Ragtime	1981	Milos Forman	Michael Weller
Rally Round the Flag Boys	1958	Leo McCarey	Leo McCarey Claude Binyon
Rambo	1985	George Pan Cosmatos	James Cameron Sylvester Stallone
Red Dawn	1984	John Milius	John Milius Kevin Reynolds

Film	Year	Director	Scriptwriter(s)
Reds	1981	Warren Beatty	Warren Beatty Trevor Griffiths
Return of the Secaucus Seven	1981	John Sayles	John Sayles
Revolution	1985 (UK)	Hugh Hudson	Hugh Hudson
The Right Stuff	1983	Phillip Kaufman	Phillip Kaufman
The River	1984	Mark Rydell	Robert Dillon Julian Barry
Rocky	1976	Sylvester Stallone	Sylvester Stallone
Rocky IV	1985	Sylvester Stallone	Sylvester Stallone
Rolling Thunder	1977	John Flynn	Paul Schrader Heywood Gould
Rollover	1981	Alan J. Pakula	David Shaber
The Russians are Coming! The Russians are Coming!	1966	Norman Jewison	William Rose
Salt of the Earth	1954	Herbert Biberman	Michael Wilson
Salvador	1986	Oliver Stone	Oliver Stone Richard Boyle
The Sea Hawk	1940	Michael Curtiz	Howard Koch Seton I. Miller
Secret Honor	1984	Robert Altman	Donald Freed Arnold Stone
The Seduction of Joe Tynan	1979	Jerry Schatzberg	Alan Alda
The Senator Was Indiscreet	1947	George Kaufman	Charles MacArthur
Sergeant York	1941	Howard Hawks	Aben Finkel Harry Chandler Howard Koch John Huston
Seven Days in May	1964	John Frankenheimer	Rod Serling
Shampoo	1975	Hal Ashby	Robert Towne Warren Beatty
Ship of Fools	1965	Stanley Kramer	Abby Mann
Short Circuit	1986	John Badham	S. S. Wilson Brent Maddock
Silkwood	1983	Mike Nichols	Nora Ephron Alice Arlen

Film	Year	Director	Scriptwriter(s)
Small Circle of Friends	1980	Rob Cohen	Ezra Sacks
Soul Man	1986	Steve Miner	Carol Black
The Spy Who Came in from the Cold	1966 (UK)	Martin Ritt	Paul Deh Guy Trosper
The Star Chamber	1983	Peter Hyams	Peter Hyams
State of the Union	1948	Frank Capra	Anthony Veiller Miles Connelly
Steelyard Blues	1972	Alan Myerson	David S. Ward
Strategic Air Command	1955	Anthony Mann	Valentine Davies Beirne Lay, Jr
The Strawberry Statement	1970	Stuart Hagmann	Israel Horovitz
Storm Center	1956	Daniel Taradash	Daniel Taradash
Storm Warning	1950	Stuart Heisler	Daniel Fuchs Richard Brooks
Sullivan's Travels	1941	Preston Sturges	Preston Sturges
Sunrise at Campobello	1960	Vincent J. Donohue	Dore Schary
Taxi Driver	1976	Martin Scorcese	Paul Schrader
Tell Them Willie Boy Is Here	1969	Abraham Polonsky	Abraham Polonsky
Tender Comrade	1943	Edward Dmytryk	Dalton Trumbo
Testament	1983	Lynne Littman	John Sacret Young
They Won't Forget	1937	Mervyn LeRoy	Robert Rossen Aben Kandel
Three Days of the Condor	1975	Sydnay Pollack	Lorenzo Semple, Jr David Rayfiel
To Be or Not to Be	1942	Ernest Lubitsch	Edwin Justus Mayer
To Kill a Mockingbird	1962	Robert Mulligan	Horton Foote
Top Gun	1986	Tony Scott	Jim Cash Jack Epps, Jr
Twelve Angry Men	1957	Sidney Lumet	Reginald Rose
Twilight's Last Gleaming	1977	Robert Aldrich	Ronald Cohen Edward Huebsh
The Ugly American	1962	George Englund	Stewart Stern
Under Fire	1983	Roger Spottiswoode	Ron Shelton Clayton Frohman
Union Pacific	1939	Cecil B. DeMille	Walter de Leon, et al.

Film	Year	Director	Scriptwriter(s)
The Vanishing American	1926	George Seitz	Ethel Doherty
The Verdict	1982	Sidney Lumet	Sidney Lumet
Viva Villa	1934	Jack Conway	Ben Hecht
Viva Zapata!	1952	Elia Kazan	John Steinbeck
War Games	1983	John Badham	Lawrence Lasker Walter Parkes
Washington Masquerade	1932	Charles Brabin	John Meehan Samuel Blythe
The Washington Merry-Go-Round	1932	James Cruze	Joe Swerling
The Washington Story	1952	Robert Pirosh	Robert Pirosh
Watch on the Rhine	1942	Herman Shumlin	Dashiell Hammett
The Way We Were	1973	Sydney Pollack	Arthur Laurents
White Nights	1985	Taylor Hackford	James Goldman Eric Hughes
Who'll Stop the Rain	1978	Karl Reisz	Judith Rascoe Robert Stone
Wild in the Streets	1968	Barry Shear	Robert Thom
Wild River	1960	Elia Kazan	Paul Osborn
Wilson	1944	Henry King	Lamar Trotti
Winter Kills	1979	William Richert	William Richert
WUSA	1970	Stuart Rosenberg	Stuart Rosenberg
Young Mr. Lincoln	1939	John Ford	Lamar Trotti
Z	1968	Costa-Gavras	Costa-Gavras Jorge Semprun
Zoot Suit	1981	Luis Valdez	Luis Valdez

Index